The Chinese State in Transition

One of the more commonly and widely held beliefs outside the People's Republic of China about the changes wrought by the reform era is that there has been no political change. The attention of the outside world focuses inevitably on Beijing and national level politics. Nonetheless, it may actually be at the more local levels that changes in politics and the state are most obviously made manifest.

The contributions to this volume clearly and convincingly demonstrate that the state and politics in China have changed considerably since the beginning of the 1980s. An international line up of experts explore the meanings of local initiatives through case studies, assessing their contribution to improving governance, questioning how they can be sustained, and revealing the political nature of normative standards. Each contribution focuses on a different policy area including cultural strategies, housing, land politics, corruption, peasants' burden and cadre reforms, women and gender, and international relations.

The Chinese State in Transition is an important read for students and scholars of Chinese politics, social and public policy, and governance.

Linda Chelan Li is Associate Professor in the Department of Public and Social Administration at the City University of Hong Kong.

Routledge Studies on China in Transition

Series Editor: David S. G. Goodman

The Chinese State in Transition

Processes and contests in local China

Edited by
Linda Chelan Li

Routledge
Taylor & Francis Group

LONDON AND NEW YORK

First published 2009
by Routledge
2 Park Square, Milton Park, Abingdon, Oxon OX14 4RN

Simultaneously published in the USA and Canada
by Routledge
270 Madison Avenue, New York, NY 10016

Routledge is an imprint of the Taylor & Francis Group, an informa business

© 2009 Editorial selection and matter, Linda Chelan Li; individual
chapters, the contributors.

Typeset in Times New Roman by
Taylor & Francis Books
Printed and bound in Great Britain by
CPI Antony Rowe, Chippenham, Wiltshire

British Library Cataloguing in Publication Data
A catalogue record for this book is available from the British Library

Library of Congress Cataloging in Publication Data
  The Chinese state in transition : processes and contests in local China /
  edited by Linda Chelan Li.
     p. cm.
  Includes bibliographical references.
  1. Local government – China. I. Li, Linda Chelan.
  JS7353.A8C454 2008
  320.80951 –
  dc22   2008003330

ISBN 978-0-415-46667-7 (hbk)
ISBN 978-0-203-89366-1 (ebk)

For all the players in the flowing waters

Contents

Tables

Contributors

Louise Edwards is Professor of China Studies at the University of Technology, Sydney, Australia, and Convener of the Australian Research Council's Asia Pacific Futures Research Network. Her most recent book is *Gender, Politics and Democracy: Women's Suffrage in China* (Stanford University Press, 2008). Other publications include *Men and Women in Qing China* (1994, 2001), *Censored by Confucius* (1996) (with Kam Louie), and three volumes jointly edited with Mina Roces: *Women in Asia: Tradition, Modernity and Globalization* (2000), *Women's Suffrage in Asia* (2004), and *The Politics of Dress in Asia and the Americas* (2007). Her current research includes an exploration of women and war in China.

Ting Gong is Professor of Political Science at City University of Hong Kong. She has done extensive research on corruption and anti-corruption reform, government ethics, post-communist transformation, and bureaucratic behavior. Publications include *The Politics of Corruption in Contemporary China: A Policy Outcome Analysis* and many journal articles and book chapters. She was a Fulbright scholar to Hong Kong and has received grants and awards from the National Endowment for the Humanities, American Political Science Association, and American Association of University Women. Her most recent work is an edited volume, *Building Clean Government in the Asia-Pacific Region.*

David S. G. Goodman is Professor of Contemporary China Studies at the University of Technology, Sydney. Recent publications include *China's Campaign to "Open Up the West"* (2004), and *The New Rich in China: Future rulers, present lives* (2008). Continuing research projects includes a study of the social, economic and political interactions between the new rich and the state in local China (with Beatriz Carrillo and Minglu Chen); and research into German adventurers in China 1870–1937 (Yixu Lu).

You-tien Hsing is Associate Professor of Geography at the University of California at Berkeley. She is the author of *Making Capitalism in China: The Taiwan Connection* (Oxford University Press, 1998). She is now completing a book on the relationships between land and territorial politics in China's late-socialist transformation.

James Lee is Associate Professor in Housing Studies at the Department of Public and Social Administration, City University of Hong Kong. He obtained his doctorate at the School for Policy Studies at the University of Bristol and is a founder of the Asian Pacific Network of Housing Research. Recent publications include *Housing and Social Change: East–West Perspectives* (Routledge, 2003) and *Housing, Home Ownership and Social Change in Hong Kong* (Ashgate, 1999).

Linda Chelan Li teaches Chinese politics and political analysis at City University of Hong Kong. Her research covers intergovernmental relations and spatial politics, politics of public finance, and institutional change. She is author of *Centre and Province: China. Power as Non-Zero-Sum* (Clarendon, 1998, 2002) and editor of *Towards Responsible Government in East Asia* (Routledge, forthcoming). Her article in *Political Studies* (1997) was awarded the Harrison Prize as the best paper published that year. She is now working on a monograph on rural tax reform and institutional change processes, and a project on inter-governmental zoning of responsibilities.

Tim Oakes teaches geography at the University of Colorado at Boulder. Recent publications include *Travels in Paradox* (2006), *Translocal China* (2006), and *The Cultural Geography Reader* (2008). He is currently completing a monograph on cultural development in rural China, and compiling an edited volume on tourism and religion in China. His research focuses on regional cultural development and China's culture industries, and, in particular, tourism development and the cultural theming of space in China.

Chengxin Pan is Lecturer in International Relations at Deakin University, Australia. He received his Ph.D. degree from the Australian National University, and has published in journals such as *Alternatives, Pacific Review,* and *Political Science,* as well as several Chinese journals, including *American Studies Quarterly* (*Meiguo yanjiu*) and *The Chinese Journal of International Politics* (*Guojizhengzhi kexue*). His research focuses mainly on Chinese foreign policy, U.S.–China relations, Taiwan, and international relations theory. He is currently working on a book manuscript examining Western representations of China in international relations.

Yapeng Zhu is Associate Professor in Public Policy at the School of Government, and Centre for Public Administration, Sun Yat-Sen University, Guangzhou, China. He completed his undergraduate and graduate education in Guangzhou and Hong Kong, with research focus on housing reform and social policy in China.

Preface

Each contribution in the volume draws from the ongoing research of the authors; pulling them together here serves the purpose of elucidating something in common, or in contradiction, about local China's political and social change rather than attempting to *manufacture*, or assert, anything in addition. This bias towards an 'inductive' approach stems from an observation of the diversity and fluidity of the Chinese state in the contemporary period, and thus a felt need to 'center-place' the individual pieces with the maximal degree, in order to capture best the ups and the downs of each flow of the moving waters.

A project of this kind – despite its 'individualistic' inclination, as noted, cannot be undertaken without the active participation of a collective. For this I need to thank the enthusiasm, and intellectual vigor, of each of the contributors, as well as their patience with my various communications and requests. This current volume is an expanded and substantially revised version of a special issue in the journal of *Pacific Review* (vol. 19, no. 1, March 2006). The idea of having a special issue on the local state of China was first suggested to me by Kevin Hewison and embedded in my long-term research on local China. The book volume would not, however, have been possible without support from Shaun Breslin, the journal co-editor, and the editors at Routledge, of Taylor & Francis Books, by their agreeing to the republication of ideas originally floated in *The Pacific Review*, and in the professionalism in seeing through the production of the book. Louise Edwards' and Chengxin Pan's contributions at the book stage have extended the scope of coverage of the original papers to gender and international relations. David Goodman's conclusion puts the '(un)finishing touch' to the discussion – and suggests more questions to probe in future research.

I am sure each of the contributors will have a long list of individuals and groups to thank; perhaps I can take the liberty here of proposing a vote of thanks to our families, whose active support and quiet tolerance has been instrumental to the successful execution of our individual research programs that constitute the solid foundation of this collective endeavor; and to Yamin Xu, whose patience and professional attention to detail were a delight to find during the meticulous preparation of the book manuscript. Finally, special thanks is extended to 'all those players in the flowing waters' of the local state(s) and segments of society in the land we call 'China'; for all their tears and sweat, joy as well as sorrow, this book is dedicated to them.

Linda Chelan Li
City University of Hong Kong
December 2007

Introduction

The state in transition

Linda Chelan Li

The state is best understood, it is said, through local "practices" and the production and reproduction of its images (Gupta 1995: 375–6). Day-to-day interactions between the multitude of petty officials, local service-providers and social groups in the community shape the popular image of the state, and the arising discourse about the state feeds the subsequent practices. The state is more than its constituent organizations, instruments in use (for example monopoly of legitimate coercion), or the actors involved. Above all it is *not* an autonomous and monolithic entity above the society but, as described in Migdal's "state-in-society" approach, is constitutive of the processes of negotiation and contestation over the rules of daily behavior, and reflected in the images as perceived among multiple actors (Migdal 2001: 11).[1] This stress on the discursive nature of the state, and the fluidity of state images and practices as product of contestation in a specific time-space, finds echoes in Bourdieu's discussion of social space and the relational (Bourdieu 1998a: 3–4) and Foucault's "state as governmentality" (Burchell *et al.* 1991: 103).

Three interrelated messages as regards research on "the state" as the "relational" and "process" consequently emerge. First, more attention needs to be paid to the lowest echelons of the state organization where the majority of the people had their first-hand experience with the state, and where decisions made "high-up" in the state hierarchy are translated into practices in society.[2] Second, research needs to adopt an approach that sees processes and actors on either side of the state–society boundary – which is essentially blurred and permeable—having similarly important, if different, roles in the shaping of "the state," and society. Finally, given the fluidity and contingency of existing state practice and image, the researcher needs to be modest in the conclusion drawn from substantive observations obtained at a specified time-space. As Hirschman (1970: 339) warned more than thirty years ago, "the immediate effect of social analysis is to convert the real into the rational or the contingent into the necessary." This may be a sin impossible to escape from, since any statement—or language—requires a degree of generalization. What is demanded is perhaps self-awareness on the part of the social analyst, and with it a difference in the *kind* of statements (and thus the level of generalization) produced, and a modesty in what we as the analyst may imply for future action.[3]

Research on the Chinese state has placed a premium on the province and the locale, not least because the continental scale of the territorial boundary adds a further dimension. Size brings, potentially, greater substantive diversity in endowments, actors, attitudes, practices, and discourse. The "Provincial China" Project spearheaded by David Goodman, which involved a good portion of those in the China field in the 1990s, for example, exemplified the need to disaggregate China into provinces and localities, and the unitary Chinese state into multiple, and often competing, local states.[4] Contributions in the current volume add to this legacy by delving into the complexity and fluidity of processes of contest amongst multiple actors in and out of "the state."

Four interrelated clusters of themes are addressed in this volume, whilst each contribution focuses on a different policy area—cultural strategies, housing, land politics, corruption, peasants' burden and cadre reforms, women and gender, and international relations. First, in light of the abundance of local entrepreneurialism noted in the literature, how have local initiatives impacted on local governance, in terms of an improvement in welfare, sense of well-being, or procedural propriety? How are we to understand the local initiatives in their contexts? Second, given the desirability of some policy outcomes, how could they be made to last—especially in well-entrenched areas of state practices historically resistant to change? How is institutional change possible? Third, with many local officials criticized as corrupt, how is corruption defined and contested? Why are some behaviors defined as corrupt and others not? What constitutes the contestation process behind the delineation of rules of propriety, desirability, and legality? How does the contestation over the normative implicate the processes over competition for desired resources? These three themes of discussion all center on "domestic" processes and actors within the Chinese state-and-society. The fourth and last extends our analysis to processes beyond the national border, and examines the role of translational actors in processes of change in the Chinese state, as well as their interaction with domestic actors in effecting changes—in the arenas of furthering women's rights, or, more specifically, against violence against women, and the articulation of a "new" foreign policy discourse. The embeddedness of the state in society is vindicated in its being *constituted* in the domestic as well as international community.

These questions follow and build on one another. Taken together they explore the meanings of the local initiatives and assess their contribution to improving local governance, and question how they may possibly sustain, reveal the political nature of normative standards, and embed all these questions in a broader context involving transnational actors and processes. Permeating the inquiry are observations of multiplicity of actors, their embeddedness and differential capacity of actors to disembed, the fluidity and specificity of the situation, and thus diversities across situations, and the pervasiveness of the discursive and the rhetoric in the contestation processes.

Making sense of, and assessing, local initiatives

It is a nice coincidence that two chapters in this volume have as their focus local initiatives in Guizhou, a poor inland province in south-west China with a relatively high ratio of national minorities. As Tim Oakes notes in his contribution on cultural strategies of development, "Guizhou was [a province] established for military reasons ... It was a frontier region with no economic base, and no dominant cultural system or coherent society". It is thus reflective of the local entrepreneurialism that, short of other more traditional endowments in the province, Guizhou officials from province to village have responded eagerly to the "cultural turn" in the central policy on economic development, and produced a multitude of local projects and a new industry of cultural tourism within a relatively short time. Noting some apparent parallels between Guizhou's cultural strategies and "entrepreneurial cities" in recent North America, namely the co-involvement of the "public" and the "private," the question arises whether the critique of the neoliberal turn in North American cities for local governance—"privatization" of public spaces and the subsequent erosion of the ground of democratic governance—applies also to cultural "theme parks" in Guizhou's towns and villages. The constitution of the Chinese state, the "public domain," the "private," and thus "state–society" relations in China is, however, significantly different from the contemporary Western situation. The specificity of the Guizhou cases is such that, the chapter notes, *Tunpu* culture is "not a public good subject to privatization because it has itself been *created* within the process of privatization" (emphasis added). The challenges of cultural strategies in Guizhou, Oakes observes, "lie not in preserving Zukin's public–private divide, but in insuring a just regime of privatization". A just regime of privatization of course still requires the participation of the public, and the appropriate designation of state authority. So the central question is: What implication does the cultural strategy of development have for local governance and the public domain?

Also drawing parallels with neoliberal developments in the developed economies, in Chapter 2 James Lee and Yapeng Zhu tell us that neoliberalism has, apparently, taken root in a major social policy in formerly, and still formally, Socialist China. Housing was traditionally provided out of state coffers in the days of central planning, though managed locally and dispersed in hundreds of thousands of state-funded work units. A program of housing commodification, set in place in the 1990s, sees housing increasingly "privatized," with market volatility and exclusion replacing the arbitrariness of state bureaucracy. Through a case study on Guiyang, provincial capital of Guizhou, the authors assess the efficacy of housing commodification in alleviating previous inadequacies in housing provision—and thus its relevance to improving urban governance. They find that, in contrast to expectations and official rhetoric, housing reforms have aggravated housing inequalities. They also observe a stark indifference, if not ignorance, on the part of Chinese officials, of the problems of neoliberal housing policy in the developed market economies.

Whilst both pieces similarly draw on the neoliberal framework in their analysis, differences over the substantive nature of the initiatives under examination contribute to differential emphases in their discussions and conclusions. To the extent that "culture" was "used" instrumentally as yet another factor of endowment to enhance local economic development—hence the emphasis on cultural tourism as the core of the strategy—the question became one of equitably distributing economic benefits and costs across the community. As the three local cases show, how benefits and costs were distributed, as well as the process leading to such, has a salient bearing on the *perceived* legitimacy of the cultural projects in the local communities. The communal sharing pattern in Jin Family Fort, where the cultural project went under a village communal organization with broad participation, is contrasted with two other cases where benefits were perceived by local villagers as being privatized—and ripped off—by either the town leader or a private company.

Improved local governance involved more than the material side—that cultural strategies of development served their intended function as an alternative route to economic well-being. A sense of ownership amongst local villagers, or lack of it—alienation—of the cultural resource was also part and parcel of the quality of governance, and this extended beyond the ownership over the "product" of cultural tourism, or the benefit from it. These two aspects, material and socio-psychological, were interrelated and often mediated by institutional arrangements and governance structures that premised participation. The question was: did the *kind* of product matter? Would the use of culture, as against other resources, in the local strategy of economic development make any difference to the processes of contestation over ownership and governance?

If the nature of local culture and cultural tourism itself may have made a difference, it could be because culture essentially requires some degree of communal participation and cooperation to thrive. Villagers may thus be prone to feel their "old" local culture—a free public resource normally available to all residents—distorted and even lost in the new, commercial cultural projects, and become more inclined to air their grievances. At the same time, the project managers may be better placed to see the benefits of enlisting the support and participation of villagers for greater commercial success—thus the company staff in Azure Dragon had talked at length about their commitment to "communal tourism." Whilst the commitment may be rhetorical, as Oakes suggests, rhetoric should not be entirely ignored—in terms of whether anything substantive would eventually result from it.[5] In this vein, contrary to the Western critique of neoliberal privatization, exploiting the public resource of local culture in Chinese villages may ironically provide a structure *conducive* to the emergence of participatory governance, and subjects demanding such.

The account of housing monetarization policy asks a direct question: whether the replacement of in-kind benefits with cash subsidies contributed to better provision of housing goods, and thus enhanced the quality of urban life. Here the parallels with neoliberal developments in the West appeared to be close. State actors were similarly preoccupied with fiscal stress and assumed that the market would fill up what the state retreated from; Chinese cities were going down a familiar path, as in the West, with commercial robustness of the housing market on the surface barely masking the increasing marginalization of the poor. It does not mean, however, that the shortfall of the market in Guiyang was the same in Liverpool; nor could a simple reversion to housing-in-kind benefits provide a remedy. The biggest problem with the commodification reforms in China, as Lee and Zhu point out, was its limited scope—the reform had as its targets only those urban residents working in the state sector, whether in the government, party organizations, or state-owned enterprises. Housing-in-kind benefits had previously been available largely to this privileged segment of the urban population only, and thus a reform that focused on monetarizing the in-kind benefits was necessarily of limited value when assessed in terms of improving urban governance on the whole.

This inherent weakness of the reform was compounded by the developing socio-economic situation in Chinese cities—the traditional state sector was on the decline, either in terms of economic robustness or the proportion of urban population working therein. Ironically this decline of the state sector had precipitated the centrality of fiscal stress in the design of the housing reform. The more the state sector was weakened, the more housing reforms were motivated, from the supply side of policy, by the need to minimize *burdens* of the state, than by considerations over how to fulfill better the state *responsibility* in the provision of housing as public good to an expanding, and increasingly heterogeneous, urban population. The assessment of housing monetarization reforms in the chapter therefore stretches beyond the story of the state actors, or the immediate recipients of the reform. The policy has failed to reduce housing inequalities, despite progress in achieving objectives intended on the part of the suppliers. Social policies, as products of state practices, are constituent of the acts and perceptions of heterogeneous actors "in" and "out" of the state—not as subjects *vis-à-vis* objects, but as co-subjects contesting the definition of the boundary of a policy: its meaning, relevance, and assessment.

How may changes last?

What impact an initiative may bring is contingent not only upon its relationship with the totality of context it is embedded in, as discussed above, but also upon its durability. A change needs to "last" in order to have sustained impact of *any* sort. This sounds such "common sense" that the temporal dimension has often been assumed and swept into the background.

The literature on institutional change tells us, however, that sustainability cannot be taken for granted, and that many emergent changes have failed to take root. Path-dependency writers have argued that the accumulation of small differences in the sequence of events tends to lock history in arrangements which though subsequently found to be suboptimal would still be resistant to change for the better (Bassanini and Dosi 2001). In this light, whether novelty will occur—breaking away from the historical path—becomes a matter of contingency and serendipity, something that "just happened" and that was not thought of before (David 1985; Arthur 1989).

Omission of the temporal is less likely when we place the emphasis squarely on the "process" when interpreting state practices, as contributions in this volume do, given that the concept of "process" implies a time dimension wherein "things take place." My discussion of rural tax and government reforms, in Chapter 3, explicitly addresses the issue of reform sustainability—which is seen as the largest challenge of rural tax reforms in China. The chapter sketches the limits of local fiscal initiatives, in Hubei Province, in sustaining the reduction in state extraction on peasants—and thus the danger of the possible collapse of the reforms—and points to the potential of an initiative in another institutional field (transforming the human agent) in sustaining the change in the fiscal arena. The emerging literature on "path creation" has suggested the mobilizing capacity of the "embedded" human agent in change (Garud and Karnoe 2001: 12–15). In this case, the capacity to mobilize includes both the ability of Xianan's local leaders in launching innovative cadre reforms, as well as the resultant agency of the returned officials—a product of the cadre reforms—in sustaining and facilitating further change in the locality.

Insofar as the agency–structure debate has pervaded social science literature for generations (e.g. Layder 1994; Archer 1988, 1995, 2000, 2003; DiMaggio 1988), specificities in the contemporary Chinese situation has brought further complications to the discussion. For one, the role of agency in Chinese politics appears to be at the same time overwhelmingly large and indeterminate. The authoritarian nature of the Chinese state and the coarseness of many laws have given rise to a conventional wisdom which assigns a dominant role to leadership and personalities in making things happen.[6] On balance, after considering all factors affecting change, it is often argued, it is still the leaders, and the top central leaders in particular, who call the tune. On the other hand, *how* agency works to effect change is somewhat unclear, as there is a simultaneous emphasis on the web-locks of constraints on the leaders, and consequent ambivalence as to the circumstances whereby leadership *can* make a difference. This in fact indicates the underdevelopment of a theory of agency in the understanding of Chinese politics, despite previous attempts to articulate the genesis of politics in terms of various models.[7]

Given the scale of change witnessed in China since late 1970s, it is surprising to find the tons of pessimism in the literature: reforms are said to be on the brink of collapse, governance problems running out of control, and the socio-political structure about to collapse (e.g. Chang 2001). It seems that as reform progresses into the "core" arenas—government and political reform, state-sector reform, rule of law, etc.—the web-locks of constraints are posing greater difficulties to change, to the point that the whole reform process would, soon, grind to a halt. It is in this context that the rural tax reform was once widely seen to be doomed almost as soon as the central government announced it (Qin 2000, 1997). At the same time, there are also analyses which see an alternative picture of dynamism, of change, and of actors *looking for* improvements.[8] These analyses tend to focus on the process, and see the making of reform and change from *within*. The differences in perceptions are analogous to what Garud and Karnoe (2001: xii, 8–9) say of the path-dependency *vis-à-vis* path-creation analyses. In the case of path dependency, change is seen from the vantage point of the "outsiders" using the "logic of consequentiality." Any departure from current accepted practices is considered a "mistake" whose survival is suspect. Mistakes that survive are seen as "accidents" of history—products of contingency—whose significance can only be known in hindsight. On the other hand, path creation sees departures from current practices as conscious, "mindful deviations" of entrepreneurial actors, who possess the intellectual capacity to "disembed," or break away, from existing practices, including the capacity to withstand the pressures arising from the dissonance of the departures with the rest of existing practices and negative feedback of other actors.

The difference is not, I shall argue, one of seeing or not seeing change, but whether the analyst sees sufficient thoroughness of the processes unfolding. It is about the *kind* of change that is perceived. The "insider" perspective of the "path-creation" strand of analysis allows the analyst to peep into changes-in-the-making, embedded in their historical context. It is thus better placed to lead the analyst to ask questions regarding how specifically the actors (and which groups of actors) make changes possible, what considerations lead them to "break away" from previous practices, against what resistance from whom, and how the resistance is gradually mitigated. Garud and Karnoe describe the challenge of these "entrepreneurs" in making change thus:

> In sum, the embeddedness of action generates several challenges for entrepreneurs. Not only do they have to disembed from embedding structures, they have to also overcome the resistance they may generate in the process. Moreover, they have to mobilize elements of the network in which they are embedded to further their efforts while preventing the process from spinning out of control. It is no surprise that path creation processes are fraught with failure!
>
> (Garud and Karnoe 2001: 12)

The "border" position and previous life experience of the Party Secretary in Xian-an—he had been a state cadre as well as a "free" man in the market in coastal cities—may have made him in favor of change. Having crossed over the state–society boundary himself he was likely to imagine the potential benefits of encouraging a similar "cross-over" of identities amongst local officials. At the same time local circumstances at that historical juncture had largely precipitated the events, or at least supplied the motivation to seek change. The county was facing harsh governance problems in late 1990s— huge debt, mounting financial crisis, and a failing economy—making change, *any* sort of change, appear mandatory. Actors, leaders or rank and file, in or out of the government, may have become more receptive to the *idea* of change under such a dire situation, though at the same time they may also feel weary of the prospect of *actual* change given the shortage of resources—as change costs. The main contribution of Secretary Song, as other "entrepreneurs" on other occasions, lies in the redefinition of costs and benefits—making reforms that would otherwise appear costly and unaffordable "profitable" and thus worth doing.

Distinguishing the "good" from the "bad," and making a profit from it

Assessment is essentially an evaluative exercise fueled by normative judgments. Assessing initiatives assumes we know what we want, that which defines "good," as against "bad," results. Such judgments are likely to vary across actors for a single subject, so that in assessing initiatives the analyst needs to be sensitive to the question: *Whose* judgments are dominant? Another question is: Why these judgments? What are the underlying considerations? Whatever the judgment and whoever holds it, the constitution of the judgment, its context and background are *not* to be taken as facts but part of the problematic—themselves requiring explanation.

Ting Gong, in Chapter 4, problematizes the phenomenon of pervasive corruption and, in particular, the relationship between corruption and decentralization. As a phenomenon and a concept, corruption carries an essentially "bad" connotation: it is something undesirable and even morally wrong, despite what the functional school says about the constructive role of corruption in specific contexts. But why are some acts corrupt and others not? How do some acts become perceived as corrupt? Are there differences across actors over the definition of corruption? Gong focuses on the linkage between decentralization and corruption when addressing these issues, given the empirical coincidence of the two in contemporary China. "What explains the proliferation of corruption at mid- and lower government levels we witness in post-reform China, when wide powers were devolved to local officials?", the chapter asks. Gong argues that decentralization *per se* is not to blame; the "incompleteness of power devolution" is. The "structural limitation" of China's decentralization process—namely the weakness or absence of downward accountability—has produced a peculiar situation since the 1980s wherein local state actors doubled as the agent of the central state as well as *de facto* principal in many areas of governance, and in economic management in particular. This Gong describes as the "double identity" phenomenon in post-reform China: local government actors being *agents* entrusted with widened yet *delegated* authority by their principals at the upper levels of the state structure, whilst being quasi-independent *principals* themselves, with their own interests and objectives at variance with those of the superiors.

This double identity has resulted in intense tension between state actors at various levels, a process You-tien Hsing describes in her discussion of intergovernmental dynamics (Chapter 5)—province, city, county, township, and village—over rural land interests. The urban-based city governments have sought to expropriate rural land use rights, and thus profits therefrom, through state regulations and administrative practices, giving themselves a legal right in some cases, and *de facto* monopoly in others, over the transfer of rural land use rights. The nature of land as a locally based resource, however, accords township leaders an added premium in the struggle for control of this valued resource, giving rise to a variety of regulatory, spatial, and organizational strategies the chapter elaborately illuminates.

These "strategies" and "brokering" tactics by township leaders in the two "in-between spaces" between the townships and the urban-based upper levels, at one end, and between townships and the quasi-autonomous villages, at the other, became forms of local "corrupt" practices in Gong's discussion of corruption and decentralization. As Hsing points out, nationally ordained rules require all rural land, which is collectively owned, to be first converted to state ownership before its land use can be transferred to outside investors. The distribution of quotas for farmland conversion across levels of government was so designed that literally township governments have been deprived of any room to convert farmland to other uses. Most decisions at the township levels regarding transfer of land use rights or changes in land use purposes are therefore pushed to the brink of illegality.

The political embeddedness of the normative is further revealed in local fiscal management practices. Local state actors are found to be invariably hoarding and developing resources in the extra- and off-budget sectors at the expense of the budget—in order to buttress local fiscal autonomy and economic well-being, in both institutional and individual terms. Whilst such practices have their roots in the broader institutional contexts—fiscal, political, and administrative—wherein local state actors are situated, and where central state actors play a major role in their constitution, the lack of downward accountability, or the "incompleteness of decentralization," has led to these practices being swept into the gray zone between the outright corrupt and illegal, and the ambiguously "inappropriate." How the line between the illegal/corrupt and the tolerable inappropriate is to be drawn is subject to all sorts of political manipulation and contestation, the configuration, and the results, of which vary from case to case.

The two chapters have different starting points: Gong seeks to explain corruption and its relations with decentralization, and Hsing elaborates on the processes and configurations of territorial politics over rural land. Yet together they display to us the political nature of the normative as well as how the politics is played out between multi-tiered state actors. They converge in calling for a more complex treatment of the decentralization processes beyond the unilateral top-down compliance approach to power. Not only that each tier of state actors is simultaneously a principal of the lower levels and an agent of the upper levels—the "double identity"—but how the principal–agent relationship plays out in any one context is far more fluid than a focus on compliance can reveal. What is at the crux of this is the relational nature of politics, and the actors therein. As Hsing notes, "the political and organizational characteristics of the local state [actors] lie in its *relationship* with [actors in] other local states" (original emphasis), and by extension with the central and societal actors. This has pushed the notion of the state as a relational process between actors one step further—*since the actors whose interactions define and constitute "the state" are in fact themselves also a product of the relations with other actors.*[9] An interesting result of these interactions is, as the chapters note, how the politically embedded normative further impacts, in a "feedback loop," on the unfolding struggle for substantive interests. The normative—what constitutes "good" and "bad"—is itself underlined by struggles over interests and also feeds the subsequent contestations.[10]

The state in transnational society

Chapters 6 and 7, by Louise Edwards and Chengxin Pan, respectively, extend this volume's discussion beyond the usual borders of the state, making the point that transnational actors and processes play a substantial part in constituting state changes. More importantly, these "extra-territorial" developments are not merely an addition to the domestic story, but often actively interact with the latter so that they become mutually constitutive and need to be understood in their totality. Notwithstanding the practical necessity of a self-selected focus of analysis, and this volume is no exception, such selection necessarily limits the analysis to part of the picture. Edwards and Pan send us the timely reminder that an investigation of the change processes of the Chinese state cannot stop at its "legal" borders.

Louise Edwards' chapter on the evolving movement for women's rights (Chapter 6) exhibits the complexity and multiplicity of interests and outlooks being negotiated. The three major domestic actors—the All China Women's Federation (ACWF), V-day activities and the Domestic Violence Network—occupy different positions in the official–unofficial, or state–society continuum. Unsurprisingly they have displayed quite diverse agendas in relation to women, have attracted and engaged with different international partners, and tend to talk to a different audience. What is interesting is that, despite these variations and the differential interests they harbor, they seemingly all contribute to an expanding social space within which social sensitivities are challenged. The rich complexities that Edwards elaborately describes display to us how, in the case of each domestic actor and their respective interactions with international actors, the originally disparate agendas of the actors come into play with one another and the impacts these have had on the unfolding discourse on women within the Chinese state and society today. Further to this, moreover, there is the issue of how one domestic actor, acting with and in the context of its transnational partners, and with the resultant impact they have produced, has impacted on the parallel processes of another domestic actor. As Edwards points out, the V-day activists' connections to an international constituency are driven entirely by (other) local Chinese actors even though the initial impetus came from outside China: "the ACWF has helped build the conditions in which more radical activities—such as those of the V-day activists and performers—are able to function". Interactions are multifaceted and all-rounded, permeating not only the domestic–transnational interface but also among the various domestic actors, and between state and society. Thus, Edwards writes, "local domestic actors are not necessarily divorced from the state but rather interact with it in multiple and diverse ways through complex webs of social and political relationships." All in all, she concludes, "the different styles of activism promote different reactions between the local actors themselves and between the local actors and the state."

While addressing transnational influences Edwards' emphasis is still placed largely on the domestic dimension. Her analysis sees transnational processes from the angle of domestic actors, including their impact on the latter, and how the latter "uses" the former. Pan's discussion of the "Peaceful Rise" strategy in Chapter 7, on the other hand, dwells explicitly on the "external" side of the story—that is, how transnational actors and processes have contributed to the emergence of the "Peaceful Rise" strategy and discourse—whilst acknowledging that there is a domestic side of the story. The differential choice of focus is perhaps attributable to the nature of the subject matter, women's matters *vis-à-vis* international relations. It is material to note, nevertheless, that *both* domestic and transnational processes count in either subject matter.

How might we interpret the "Peaceful Rise" as a new official foreign policy discourse in the context of Chinese foreign policy and domestic concerns? Is it something of genuine novelty and importance or old wine in new bottles? Pan suggests that the notion of "Peaceful Rise" be understood in the broader context whereby the Chinese party-state has sought to redefine, and reconstruct, its basis of political legitimacy within the Chinese and global society. To the extent that a new "social contract" focusing on economic development and improvement of livelihood has replaced the previous one centering on revolution and class struggles in the domestic context, the Peaceful Rise discourse is the centerpiece of an international "contract" that the Chinese party-state articulates to win goodwill and acquiescence from the international community. Of particular interest is the process whereby the discourse was formulated, as well as accepted internally within the Chinese party-state. On this Pan's chapter reveals a complex and fluid process involving actors ranging from the dominant international power (the U.S.), the major domestic player (the MOFRET), and a variety of international non-governmental organizations and institutions (for example the World Bank and the World Trade Organization). As in Edwards' exposition on the women's movement, the multiplicity of parallel processes and agendas of these diverse actors is apparent throughout the process. Implicit in the messages of both chapters, and indeed in all contributions to this volume, is the role of contingency and the somewhat dialectical nature of the course of events as diverse actors interacted, leading to developments which are often beyond the original intentions of any of those.

Let us now turn to each of these chapters in turn and see the details of the processes, before we come to the concluding observations of David Goodman (Chapter 8)—and pointers for further research and thinking on the Chinese state.

Notes

1 Philip Abrams (1988) talks about the state as a structure or system, and an idea, but often in social analyses the state is reified—made into an "entity, agent, function or relation over and above the state-system and state-idea." The diverse social actors disappear behind the veil of a reified state.

2 On this Gupta (1995: 376) complains of the scarcity of "rich ethnographic evidence" on "what lower-level officials actually do in the name of the state"; and Bourdieu (1998a: 2) asserts that "the deepest logic of the social world can be grasped only if one plunges into the particularity of an empirical reality".

3 On a related concern, James Scott (1998) talks of the impossibility of capturing in text local practical knowledge, or *metis*, which is knowledge resultant from the constant interaction of the human mind with the time-locale specific situation. Codification and description of the practice necessarily involves simplification and thus distortion. A decision contingent on a historical situation becomes a rule, which is then employed independently of the total context in which the original decision is embedded.

4 The ongoing Project has organized a series of annual/biannual conferences in China, produced several edited volumes and a series of background outlines on provinces, and gave birth to the *Provincial China* journal, just citing its major direct outputs.

5 Scott (1990: 18) talks about how the receiving end of rhetorical commitments could still extract some concessions from the other party even in the extreme case of asymmetrical power relations between slave and master.

6 See, for instance, Fewsmith (1994: 6), where the top leaders were explicitly attributed the key role behind the reform process *in general* in China.

7 See Lieberthal and Oksenberg (1988) for a discussion of the rationality, power, and bureaucratic politics models. The theoretical inadequacy of the understanding of the agency role of central government actors is discussed in Li (1997), in the context of central–provincial relations.

8 Some examples are Daniel Kelliher's story on early rural reform in the late 1970s (Kelliher 1992), my chapter on rural tax reform in this volume (Chapter 3) and two other papers on pioneering local reforms (Li 2004, 2005), the papers in

Cheung et al.'s edited collection on provincial leaders and strategies (Cheung *et al.* 1998), and the edited volumes under the *Provincial China* Project (Goodman 1997; Hendrischke and Feng 1999; Fitzgerald 2002).

9 The classic discussion of politics as relational is in Niebuhr (1963: 65)

10 This discussion on the normative is continued in another collective project investigating the processes and meanings of "Responsible Government" in the East Asian context, also published by Routledge (Li forthcoming).

1 Cultural strategies of development

Implications for village governance[1]

Tim Oakes

Since the early 1990s, culture has come to be recognized as a significant regional development resource in China. On January 10, 1990, *People's Daily* printed a speech by Minister of Culture Li Ruihuan titled "Some Questions Relevant to Enhancing the Outstanding Elements of National Culture" (*Guanyu hongyang minzu youxiu wenhua de ruogan wenti*). According to Guo Yingjie, this speech was the Party's green light for the development of national and local folk cultures, resulting in the rapid publication of many books, magazines, and encyclopedias on regional folk art, opera, dance, acrobatics, painting, and calligraphy. In his speech, Li also instructed that "cultural sites and relics," ancient texts, and manuscripts were to be preserved, protected, and restored; that new buildings, especially libraries, museums, theaters, schools, parks, and bridges, should contribute to a "physical environment that exhibits distinct national features" (Guo 2004: 31). Guo interprets Li's speech and its implications in the context of the Party's post-1989 turn to traditional culture, part of a broader effort to rekindle nationalism and shore up its legitimacy within and control over an alienated society. But the new regionalist renaissance initiated in part by Li's speech can also be interpreted as part of a broader "cultural turn" in regional development strategies, one in which cultural resources have come to be viewed as possessing equal if not greater economic potential than traditional factor endowments typically marshaled by local governments in their development planning.

In addition to the Party's efforts to rekindle national pride in the wake of widespread post-Tiananmen malaise, the cultural turn in 1990s regional development was also a direct outcome of the state's fiscal decentralization. With central government revenues in a dramatic free fall because of a dysfunctional tax system inherited from the planned economy, fiscal responsibilities were increasingly devolved to local governments (see Oksenberg and Tong 1991; Wong 1991; Wong *et al.* 1995; Lardy 1998; Wedeman 1999). This resulted in a new entrepreneurial outlook on the part of many local governments as revenue generation came to be regarded as the primary function of the local state. In this climate of entrepreneurialism, local culture is being viewed increasingly not just as a resource for pride, nationalism, and Party legitimacy, but as a viable and even dynamic economic sector capable of significant revenue generation, particularly in situations where the local state's capital investment resources were limited. As Minxin Pei (2003) has noted, however, this entrepreneurialism has not reversed the declining effectiveness of the Chinese state to fund public services at the local level. The turn to culture raises the question of whether cultural strategies of development have ameliorated or exacerbated the government's increasing inability to provide for the public's basic needs.

Examples of the cultural turn in China's regional development abound (Feng 1999a; Oakes 2000; Goodman 2002). On a provincial scale, there have been efforts to reconstruct provincial identity by mobilizing regional cultural symbols in the hope that a popular sense of regional cultural identity will somehow translate into a vibrant commercial economy, increased investments, and increased revenues. Prominent examples include the rise of Nanyue culture in Guangdong (Lary 1996), Chu culture in Hubei (Friedman 1994), merchant culture in Shanxi (Zhang Zhengming 1998) and Anhui (Zhou and Li 1998), and Gan culture in Jiangxi (Feng 1999b). Municipal, district, and county governments have also been involved in exploiting cultural resources for development purposes. Often this simply involves turning a local specialty product into a "culture" in order to laden its exchange value with symbolic capital. Thus, counties throughout China have been promoting themselves as hearths of such things as "Hunan lotus culture," "bamboo weaving culture," "paper-cut culture," "bamboo shoot culture," "liquor distilling culture," "tea culture," and so on. These examples illustrate the way that culture is often viewed in simple instrumental terms, as a mere label meant to enhance the value of an export product. Yet cultural strategies of development often mean much more than this.

While there remains a great variety of ways in which local governments approach culture as a development resource, there is consistency in the view that the culture industries represent an enormous untapped resource for many places. Thus, while local governments are increasingly interested in promoting local culture for development, they are hoping to rely on a growing commercial sector in order to develop these resources. This entrepreneurial approach to development—which could be characterized in terms of a public–private partnership in the development of cultural resources—is remarkably similar to that taken by many North American cities. The "entrepreneurial city" emerged in the context of a broader transformation in the United States political economy whereby public goods provision was transferred to the private sector. Despite being widely viewed as a withdrawal, or shrinking, of the state *vis-à-vis* the market, this "neoliberal revolution" in fact saw a growth in collaboration between government and private actors. As argued by critical geographers, the concept of the "entrepreneurial city" suggested that North American urban governance had been transformed from a system of managerialism and public oversight to one of market boosterism. Cities, it was argued, were privatizing formerly public industries and services (such as education, utilities, and public transport), and turning to the private sector to promote urban economic growth (Logan and Molotch 1987; Jonas and Wilson 1999). One particular criticism of urban entrepreneurialism argued that it ceded to the private sector the public spaces within which urban street democracy was thought to thrive.

Culture necessarily played an important role in urban entrepreneurialism because turning cities into economic growth machines meant emphasizing their unique place-based amenities and endowments. Thus, in addition to being redefined as entrepreneurial rather than managerial, city governments were seen as deliberately fostering a cultural economy. Cities sought to attract culture industries to invest in the urban labor market while at the same time helping to produce and improve the city's image. In an age of flexible accumulation, mobile capital, and geographically expanding labor markets, cities now competed with one another for exposure in a globalizing economy. Place-based attributes like local cultural distinctiveness thus became important in distinguishing one city from its competitors. Logan and Molotch (1987: 294) argued that municipal officials were "in the business of manipulating place for its exchange value." Selling places, however, was not at all a risk-free prospect. David Harvey (1989b) argued that North American cities became market players and that they assumed the financial risk of private investment. Entrepreneurialism was a risky undertaking in terms of urban governance because development projects became "such a focus of public and political attention that they divert concern and even resources from the broader problems that may beset the region or territory as a whole" (Harvey 1989b: 8).

Since the emergence of entrepreneurial cities in North America, culture has become a key focus of international development on a much broader scale. Culture is now recognized throughout much of the world as a vital partner in the generation of economic value chains. Disputes over the treatment of the "culture industries" have taken up a greater and greater share of WTO negotiations, and this was true in the case of China's WTO accession as well. And culture has become central to the development agenda promoted by UNESCO, as evidenced by its promotion of the "World Decade for Cultural Development" (1988–97). Culture is now regarded as the key to sustainable economic development. As noted by Michael Keane (2004: 82), "This kind of cultural development is based on the vision of a future in which national governments deliver basic public services such as telecommunications, health, and education, while facilitating the conditions for value-adding knowledge-based industries based upon sustainable development models" (see also Matarasso 2001; Yúdice 2003). We also see here a belief that cultural strategies of development are a vital part of a larger package of "good governance" on the part of the state.

If cultural strategies of development are indeed comparable between local governments in China and those in North American cities, then the following question presents itself: what are the implications of China's cultural strategies of regional development for local-level governance? Asking this question, of course, implies several others. What is the role of the state in China's cultural strategies of regional development? To what extent does the entrepreneurial city model match China's regional political economy? Have cultural strategies of development in China resulted in the privatization of formerly communal cultural resources? If so, has the privatization of culture had any impact on the state's provision of basic welfare? Or, have cultural strategies in fact succeeded in generating a stronger sense of local identity? Has cultural development resulted in stronger social networks and community ties, resulting in more effective local self-governance? This chapter represents a preliminary attempt to address these questions by looking at the ways cultural strategies of development in Guizhou province have influenced village governance. I examine three case studies, each revealing different ways that villages have engaged state development strategies, each with different outcomes. The chapter thus raises an additional question to those above: how do cultural strategies—which are typically thought to emerge from and predominantly benefit urban regions—relate to *rural* communities? In a situation where public money seldom flows down to the villages, do cultural strategies improve village access to welfare provision? That is, do cultural strategies contribute to the kind of governance outcomes hoped for by UNESCO, or is culture a resource that only continues the diversion of funds towards revenue generation and away from basic needs?

By examining the cases of three villages which have engaged Guizhou's incipient cultural economy in different ways, I argue that cultural strategies of development in China introduce a capital logic that greatly influences village governance. Cultural strategies create economic value where none before existed and thus initiate new struggles over ownership among villagers, state actors, and entrepreneurs. The privatization of cultural resources has presented new challenges to village governance even while it has been promoted as both an answer to the fiscal challenges faced by many rural communities and a key to the establishment of a new kind of rural citizen. As revealed in the case studies, villagers have responded to these challenges in a variety of ways. And while it is clear that cultural strategies are undoubtedly reshaping villager subjectivity in significant ways, they often do so at the cost of new kinds of social polarization.

It should be noted at the outset that this chapter does not propose a definitive analysis of China's cultural economy. Its focus is rather on the implications for governance of the local state's development strategies, in which the cultural economy figures prominently. The notion of a "cultural economy" is often associated with two broad arguments in the social sciences: first, that there has been a broad "cultural turn" in economic knowledge and, second, that the value of economic goods is increasingly dominated by symbolic or cultural properties (du Gay and Pryke 2002). Of the former argument—that culture is regarded as an increasingly important way in which we understand the economy—there is little dispute. But the latter claim remains highly debated. Thus, while Scott Lash and John Urry (1994), Allen Scott (2000), and Sharon Zukin (1995) all argue that the political economy of North American cities has undergone a cultural turn accompanied by the rise of a "symbolic economy," Daniel Miller (2002: 173) has argued that there is no convincing evidence of such a shift and that the assertion that the economy is now more cultural than before represents "a sleight of hand through which a shift in academic emphasis is presupposed to reflect a shift in the world that these academics are describing." Regardless of whether China's economy can be said to have undergone some sort of "cultural turn" in any empirical sense, I argue that the local state nevertheless *behaves* as if this is in fact the case. The cultural economy in China is thus very real in a policy sense, if not in an economic sense, and such policy has specific material outcomes on the local scale. Describing these outcomes is therefore the primary objective of this chapter.

Cultural strategies of development in China

As Jing Wang (2003) has observed, culture is now treated in China as an economic sector subject to regulation through state policies and promotion through state entrepreneurship. In 2001 the "culture industries" (*wenhua chanye*) were officially recognized among those economic sectors in which there would be a withdrawal of state capital, to be replaced by private investment. Then at the 16th Party Congress in 2002, according to Wang, a distinction was made between public cultural institutions (*wenhua shiye*), in which the state was to maintain dominance, and commercial cultural enterprises (*wenhua chanye*), from which the state would gradually withdraw. The latter included higher and professional education, sports and entertainment industries, audio-visual production, exhibitions, performance industries, and tourism. The former, non-commercializable sectors included compulsory education, institutions responsible for the preservation of national cultural artifacts, libraries, museums, and cultural work stations.

The Party's decision represents an attempt to define the boundaries of what is acceptable behavior on the part of local governments in terms of commercially developing cultural resources. After more than a decade of relatively unregulated cultural strategies, the Party was perhaps increasingly concerned about the blurring of market and public interests in the field of culture. In this light, the 2002 decision can be seen as an attempt to put the brakes on the increasing privatization of cultural resources as a result of local governments pursuing cultural strategies of development. As with many other aspects of China's reforms, the state finds itself trying to balance its ideological preference for control of public goods while recognizing the benefits of market incentives to spur regional economic growth.

China's culture industries have come to be regarded by local governments as a powerful resource for a host of objectives, from poverty alleviation to industrialization to revenue generation and attracting external investment.

Cultural development has become a buzzword of local state economic policy. "Culture," Wang (2001: 71) argues, "is a top agenda item for public policy makers, city planners, and both the central and local states." Culture is a site where political and economic capital can now be accumulated in China: "The state's rediscovery of culture as a site where new ruling technologies can be deployed and converted simultaneously into economic capital constitutes one of its most innovative strategies of statecraft since the founding of the People's Republic" (Wang 2001: 71–2).

At the local level, Wang (2001: 86) cites the so-called "Guangdong phenomenon," in which the Guangdong Provincial Institute of Cultural Development Strategies launched numerous cultural programs and festivals in 1994, "utilizing culture to promote business." Recognizing the growing power of the symbolic economy, the local state started taxing cultural industries around this time, while making donations to cultural institutions tax deductible. At the same time, there was a growing awareness "of the worth of signs (both written and visual)—logos, trademarks, design patents, and brand names (the so-called invisible assets)—and no less important, the image-capital of a city" (Wang 2001: 87).

Yet cultural strategies do not necessarily mean a straightforward instrumental approach to "culture" as an economic field, in which x investment yields y output and revenue. Cultural strategies are also viewed as a broader governance mechanism. Local states thus find themselves asking the following question: "How might cultural programs be developed to encourage populations to be more resourceful and self-regulating?" (Keane 2004: 80). The use of culture as a governance tool was, significantly, pioneered by the private sector, which for some time now has been undergoing a "cultural turn" of its own in terms of enterprise organization. Firms now emphasize their "corporate culture" as the key to success in the marketplace. The beauty of culture, argues Stuart Hall, is that,

> rather than constraining the conduct, behavior and attitudes of the employees by the imposition of an external regime of social control, [culture] endeavors to get employees subjectively to *regulate themselves*. The strategy is to get the subjects to align their own personal and subjective motivations and aspirations with the motivations of the organization, to redefine their skills and capacities in line with the personal and professional job-specifications of the firm, to internalize organizational objectives as their own subjective goals. They will use what Foucault calls the "technologies of the self" to "make themselves up," to produce themselves—in du Gay's terms—as different kinds of enterprising subjects. Regulation through the medium of "culture change"— through a shift in the "regime of meanings" and by the production of new subjectivities, within a new set of organizational disciplines—is another, powerful, mode of "governing *by* culture."
>
> (Hall 1997: 235)

Deployed by the state, therefore, cultural strategies potentially achieve more than just economic outcomes. They can be instrumental in creating new subjectivities which contribute to the state's desired governance outcomes. On the village scale, cultural strategies are meant to create enterprising subjects along the lines of the corporate employees discussed here by Hall. On the urban scale, as Wang (2001) has argued, they seek to create consuming subjects whose demand for leisure culture will draw them to the products offered by their enterprising rural counterparts.

In part, this means that cultural strategies are aimed at generating public enthusiasm and participation in development by cultivating a sense of regional identity and cultural pride that will translate into popular support for the local government and enterprises engaged in commercial development and market expansion. Thus, according to an "official's manual" on cultural development written by Zhou Shangyi and Kong Xiang (2000), popular enthusiasm for the local government's selected cultural symbols is fundamental to a locality's ability to attract and generate economic development.

Zhou and Kong cite Walter Benjamin and note that China has entered the age of industrial mass production and that because of this the culture industries have become a major sector of the economy. "Mass replication" of culture is now possible through the increasingly commercialized film, broadcast and print media, and advertising sectors. Rather than signaling the demise of local cultural distinctiveness, Zhou and Kong see the industrialization of popular culture—the rise of commercial culture industries—as an important opportunity for the promotion of a locally flavored symbolic economy. This makes it very important, they argue, to recognize and understand regionally specific culture in China, because for them culture has become *the* fundamental element of economic development. The primary role of the local state, they claim, is to create symbols around which a local cultural identity can be formed and mobilized. Producing images and cultural symbols has thus become *the* new field of local governance. If done well, the production of local cultural images and symbols can spur commerce, enrich development, and attract investment and human capital (Zhou and Kong 2000: 21). In particular, cultural development is seen to lead to new types of economic activity: the service sector, the entertainment industries, and the hi-tech sector. This is particularly important to localities whose capacities for income generation have been limited by an economy dominated by low-priced primary goods such as agricultural, forest, or mineral products. The key to this is the local government's ability to select and promote the right symbols and produce the kind of space attractive to external investment. While the state can no longer plan the economy, Zhou and Kong assert, it can develop partnerships with the private sector in which the state provides the culture, and investors provide the capital.

It is significant to note that Zhou and Kong advocate precisely the same approach to development that Sharon Zukin critiques in *The Cultures of*

Cities (1995; see also Zukin 1991). The symbolic economy of culture, she argues, produces new kinds of spaces and new kinds of symbols, and its production system is increasingly formed by public–private partnerships, such as the BIDs (business improvement districts) in New York City, which act to displace the public goods provisioning functions of a depleted municipal government. The public spaces of modernist urbanism—city squares, green parks, neighborhood playgrounds—are thus replaced by privatized spaces meant to look "public" but in fact oriented toward consumption and tightly regulated to keep non-consumptive uses to a minimum: shopping malls, festival markets, pedestrian streets.

As revealed in the title of a collection of essays on the decline of urban public space in North America, the model for these cultural strategies is Disney (Sorkin 1992; see also Wilson 1992). And it is therefore ironic that Disney World and Disneyland should idealize "public space" with their "Main Street, USA" and other versions of nostalgic simulacra. The Disney theme park model of an America that never was has become a competitive development strategy for city planners throughout the U.S.—dubbed "new urbanism"—promoting the reclaiming of cities for the people. The strategy, according to Zukin, is straightforward (and reminiscent of Zhou and Kong's advice for local officials in China): develop a visual image of the city, market it as the city's symbol, pick an area of the city to reflect this image—waterfront commercial complex, beaux-arts train station, street of red-brick shops, whatever—and turn it all over to a private company to manage. Disney World pioneered this approach as "America's urban laboratory" for festival marketplaces, shopping malls, museum displays, ski resorts, and planned residential communities. And Disney's phenomenal success makes the simulacra of the symbolic economy very real.

Zukin's argument is that the cultural economy of themes, symbols, and aesthetics is fundamental to establishing social order. Disney World is a "landscape of power" which orders space and subjectivity, reining in the unruliness of spontaneous place-making. Here, *visual* images of culture play a particularly important role, for they are easily commodified, lend themselves well to mass reproduction, and are called upon to define new spatial identities. Visual culture is a "euphemism for the city's new representation as a creative force in the emerging service economy" (Zukin 1995: 268). Similarly, Zhou and Kong stress the importance of the local state's selection of a clear and concise *visual* symbol of local culture. Visual symbols, they point out, are easily marketed and readily recalled by locals and outsiders alike; they both attract external investment and offer a sign around which new enterprising and consuming subjectivities may be given meaning.

Zukin (1995: 273) also notes the central role played by tourism, particularly in the early development of the cultural economy. Tourism naturally fits the transcience and image creation of a service economy based on mass media and telecommunications. On a local level, developing tourism works well with real estate interests and absorbs, to some degree, men and women in the workforce who have been displaced by structural and locational changes. Nevertheless, Zukin continues, these kinds of cultural strategies like tourism represent a "worst case scenario" for cities; they suggest the *absence* of new industrial strategies for growth in the hi-tech and knowledge sectors (Storper 1997; Scott 2000), but they are always available when a city has few other cards to play.

Zukin's view of cultural strategies as a "worst case scenario" stems from her belief that culture deployed by an entrepreneurial state not only leads to the erosion of the "public domain" (Drache 2001) but in fact *masks* that erosion with the popular spectacle of consumable culture, thereby serving to enlist public support in the destruction of their own public spaces. The new subjectivities of cultural development, according to Zukin, regulate themselves in the interest of capital. Cultural strategies, then, represent a Gramscian project of manufactured consent. Because of their ambiguous symbolic qualities cultural resources are freighted with ideological baggage. When public spaces are requisitioned in the name of cultural strategies of development, then, they no longer serve the interests of "the public."

Any application of this line of critique to the situation in China necessarily raises questions about whether such modernist dualisms as "public" and "private" or "state" and "market" can be translated at all. Western conceptions of an autonomous democratic civil society, upon which much of Zukin's critique is based, do not have easily identifiable equivalents in China; nor can a clear separation of state and society be delineated (Kraus 2000). China's traditional "civil" institutions, such as lineage and temple associations, merchant and trade guilds, or even social networks of *guanxi* ties, cannot be seen as serving a social function autonomous of the state. Rather, they often serve as fundamental to *building* the state from the locality upwards (see, for a related argument, Fitzgerald 1995). Whereas Zukin sees in cultural strategies the violation of a public–private divide vital to free democratic governance, the Chinese context for such strategies is significantly different. In China today, when the state turns to the development of cultural resources, it does not necessarily imply the violation of a public–private divide, but perhaps the marshaling of civic resources toward which the state has often turned for effective governance on the local scale. At the village level, as will be discussed in the case studies (see pp. 27–33), cultural strategies do not so much privatize existing "public goods" or "public spaces" but create new products and spaces which are immediately subject to struggles over ownership.

Nevertheless, the Chinese state's calculated policy approach to the development of leisure culture clearly reminds us of Zukin's point that if public space is to be ceded to private interests, then a new consumer ideology of leisure is also necessary to fill this privatized space with seemingly public activity. The consuming subject inhabits with pleasure Zukin's new spaces of public–private partnership (shopping malls, theme parks, festival markets, pedestrian streets). Similarly, in China the state has collaborated with the market to produce a new consuming subject in urban China by, for instance, shortening the work week to five days, implementing three national "golden weeks" for travel and leisure, lowering interest rates so residents can spend more, and shifting entertainment into the realm of "middle-class" consumers rather than elites (i.e. replacing the old *gongfei* banquet culture). The "cultural economy," Wang (2001: 76) comments, is now "the center of gravity of everyday life and is, therefore, the bull's-eye for public policy making."

If the cultural economy marks a new ideology of everyday life in China, then it is also important to note the harmony between such strategies and a broader neo-conservative intellectual agenda of re-evaluating traditional, pre-revolutionary models of localism and community as fundamental to promoting China's "unique" path toward modernization (see Lin and Galikowski 1999: 23–30; Wang 1998). "Culture" has become a term laden with associations of pre-revolutionary life, in which social hierarchies and polarization have become part of an organic system, a "true path" to which localities feel encouraged to gradually return. This, at any rate, is the neo-conservative message which has been picked up loud and clear by my village informants in Guizhou. One village head, for instance, had this to say as he led me through his village, pointing out the ornate architectural features of the residences of former landlords:

> Before liberation, this was a very cultured village. Over one-third of the households were landlords! ... These days, Jiang Zemin and Deng Xiaoping consider the landlords the advanced representatives of economic progress. We should understand this. To me, they weren't landlords, they weren't exploiters. They were people who worked hard, saved their money, and advanced the village along with themselves.

Cultural strategies in Guizhou

What the village head made clear in the above quotation is an important relationship between cultural strategies of development and understandings of governance in China. For him, the deployment of "culture" as a development strategy clearly meant a revision of official attitudes toward the landlord class. It was only the landlords, after all, who "had culture." And it was the landlords who bequeathed a cultural heritage to the village, in the form of an attractive built environment, and a tradition of rituals and festivals which were now the village's primary development resource. In seeing a clear connection between "culture" and "landlords," then, the village head articulated an understanding of culture as the resource which the village had somehow lost under Mao, was now working hard to regain, and which would return the village to its former prosperity as a "rich village of landlords."

The specific case of this village—Ox Market Fort—will be discussed in greater detail on pp. 30–32. But it is mentioned here to convey both the relationship between cultural strategies and village governance and the fact that "culture" is regarded first and foremost in Guizhou as a resource laden with both untapped economic potential and unmistakable connotations of a negation of the Maoist project of state socialism. It is in this respect that culture signals an enterprising subjectivity of the reform era. An understanding of culture as a whole way of life does not precede an understanding of culture as both an economic sector and an ordering of society. More importantly, this understanding is shared by local intellectuals, officials, and many villagers alike.

Like hundreds of localities throughout China, many counties and municipalities in Guizhou have been actively pursuing cultural strategies in order to jumpstart commercial, service-oriented industries capable of restructuring local economies away from primary resource dependence. As with the rest of China, many of these are merely designed to market a specific product. Many localities promote their own drinking or liquor culture, others promote batik, embroidery, or silver jewelry cultures of ethnic minorities, and still others promote a variety of tea cultures. Some localities seek to promote distinctive performance traditions, such as "exorcism drama culture" (*nuo wenhua*) in northeastern Guizhou. Other strategies are based more on ethnicity, such as the "bronze drum culture" (*tongguo wenhua*) promoted in the Miao regions of southeastern Guizhou, or the "fortress" (*tunpu wenhua*) culture of central Guizhou's Han villagers. And there are provincial examples as well, the most prominent of which is probably "Yelang culture," named after the ancient kingdom which ruled the area during the late Warring States era.

It may be surprising, then, to note that Guizhou has in fact been relatively slow to pursue cultural strategies of development at a provincial scale. In a recent collection of brief essays marking the 590th anniversary of Guizhou's founding, the problem of identifying a suitable regional culture for Guizhou was explicitly addressed (Long 2003). Guizhou was established for military reasons, rather than emerging as a distinct socioeconomic or cultural entity. It was a frontier region with no economic base, and no dominant cultural system or coherent society. Nearly six hundred years later scholars and officials still struggle with the question of how to construct a regional culture to aid Guizhou's development. Recounting a long history of outside—mostly military—influences, due to its strategic location and "crossroads" position between Sichuan, Yunnan, Guangxi, and Hunan, the book argues that if Guizhou has a regional culture, it ought to be called a "highway culture" (*tongdao wenhua*). Guizhou, then, is seen here as a province of immigrants, and its culture is a unique mixture of transplanted peoples who brought their customs along and reshaped them accordingly.

It is perhaps for this reason that *tunpu* "fortress" culture of the central region around Anshun has grown in popularity since the late 1990s. The *tunpu* people are the descendents of early Ming soldier-settlers sent to conquer Yunnan, garrison the frontier and guard the post road. Local scholars and officials have increasingly been involved in promoting *tunpu* culture as a symbol of those who came to "open the road" and create Guizhou. *Tunpu* thus marks the crucial moment in Guizhou's provincial history (Yan and Gao 2002a; Jiang 2004). *Tunpu* heritage is Guizhou's heritage. The *tunpu* people are the "pilgrims" of Guizhou; their villages—unique in architecture and ritual practice—are the Jamestowns and Williamsburgs of provincial history. *Tunpu* was thus ripe for mobilization as a cultural strategy, helping to develop a tourism-based commercial economy for the central region of the province. That *tunpu* represents Han folk culture was also important. For many local scholars, this was a significant aspect of their interest in the context of the 1980s "roots searching" movements and general post-Cultural Revolution malaise. *Tunpu* revealed how the Han had not lost touch with their cultural roots in spite of all the turmoil of the recent decades. *Tunpu* could also be valuable in the current drive toward modernization, as a reminder of Confucian Han culture and values as China becomes increasingly urban and "Westernized." It was increasingly recognized, therefore, that *tunpu* culture could be developed as a tourism resource for urban Han eager to get back in touch with their roots.

By the year 2000 interest in *tunpu* had climaxed into a kind of folk culture fever in Guizhou. In addition to the spate of research articles and monographs, dozens of popular books were published about *tunpu*, many of them very well produced, with high quality photographs (Guizhou Sheng Luyou Wenhua Yanjiu Zhuanbo Zhongxin 2001; Anshun Shi Wenhuaju 2002; Zheng 2002). Some were large-format "coffee table" books identifying *tunpu* as Guizhou's folk culture *par excellence*. In 2001 eight *tunpu* villages received state-level recognition as national heritage protection sites. And in 2002 one *tunpu* village—the case of Azure Dragon discussed on pp. 27–30—turned itself into a pay-at-the-gate heritage theme park, run by an enterprising local with the cooperation of the township and county governments. By 2003, the second-best selling book in the province was *600 Years of Tunpu*, by two well-known Guiyang journalists (Yan and Gao 2002b). The book offers a compelling narrative of folk roots for an urban population eager to think of Guizhou as culturally distinctive and worthy of cultural pride.

When a district government in Anshun sought to promote the commercialization of the rural economy, it thus invented a new festival centered on *tunpu* culture. The festival, named "Canola Flower Festival" (*youcaihuajie*), was timed to occur during the peak blooming—in early spring—of the region's chief winter cash crop to attract tourists and help villagers to understand the value of their crop in a new "cultural" way. As a district official told me, *youcaihuajie* is meant to inculcate in villagers a "culture of commerce" as well as encourage them to take a broader view of their development resources. Canola, she said, produces value twice. Farmers have no trouble understanding the market value of pressed vegetable oil, which is negligible, but it is harder for them to grasp the value of the blossoms as a commercial resource. This entails an understanding of the symbolic economy, and the goal of the festival, she said, is to introduce farmers to this economy and teach them that, ultimately, it holds far greater potential for income generation than what they will ever get from just selling canola oil. The festival thus represents an instrument not simply for income generation, but for new subject formation as well, generating in farmers an enterprising attitude toward symbolic resources.

In addition, the district government along with several counties and townships have been promoting other aspects of *tunpu* cultural tourism—such as a "mountain song festival"—as a means of introducing the symbolic economy to villagers. The state-level heritage designation status awarded in 2001, for instance, means that local leaders must convince villagers that their old houses and indeed the very space of their village itself as a "cultural landscape" hold commercial value simply by virtue of the way they look to outsiders. Farmers are encouraged to think of preserving the village environment as part of their "jobs" in the new cultural economy. *Tunpu* tourism introduces a commerce of aesthetics which is said to hold the key to poverty alleviation and future prosperity for all in the community because it promises both income generation and a new attitude on the part of villagers. Yet the case studies on pp. 27–33 reveal that such an attitude is grasped more quickly by some than others, and that this makes a huge difference in determining the distribution of benefits as well as the effectiveness of village governance within the new cultural economy.

Lily Tsai (2002) has observed that state investment in rural industrialization and other revenue-generating schemes often has the effect of diverting resources away from public welfare projects. As the case of Ox Market Fort suggests, cultural development can have the same outcome. But the issue is not simply the diversion of resources away from public welfare, but a more profound sense of alienation among villagers from the very resources around which a coherent and functional village society can be built and maintained. As the case of Jin Family Fort indicates, however, such cultural alienation is not always the outcome, but rather depends on whether village leaders act primarily on their own behalf or on behalf of the village. Thus the primary issue is less whether public goods are becoming privatized than whether villagers can collectively maintain control over the privatization of newly developed cultural resources. The case studies suggest that because of the model adopted by the local state—one which puts private entrepreneurs at the center of cultural development—the deck is stacked against the likelihood that villagers will be able to maintain such collective ownership. This, then, suggests that while cultural development may indeed be producing a new enterprising subject that is self-governing, the more common outcome is merely a regulated subject that has no independent position in village governance.

Tunpu cultural development: three case studies

As part of a broader research project on *tunpu* cultural development in Guizhou, I have been doing fieldwork in several villages in central Guizhou since 2002. Fieldwork has been in collaboration with scholars at Guizhou Nationalities Institute, with the assistance of scholars at Anshun Normal and Vocational College and Guizhou Academy of Social Sciences. Three case studies illustrate three different village governance outcomes of the local state's promotion of *tunpu* culture as a development strategy. Each of the three villages is recognized by local governments—at municipal, district, county, and township levels—as a key site of *tunpu* cultural tourism development. But each has undergone a very different process by which the commercialization of *tunpu* culture has affected village governance.

Azure Dragon: a tunpu *culture theme park*

From the local government's perspective, the village of Azure Dragon has been by far the most successful in turning culture into a commercial industry.[2] In 2001, a local entrepreneur named Jin Xiesong formed a joint-stock-holding tourism development company to promote *tunpu* cultural tourism in the village. He had been a cadre in the township government in the 1980s and then worked for the county Supply and Marketing Cooperative in the early 1990s. He was then sent to Shenzhen to open a window enterprise for the county and there he gathered information on tourism promotion and development. In 1999 he was back in Azure Dragon with a vision of the village as a theme park attraction like those he saw in and around Shenzhen. He recognized the village's natural advantages, located just off the planned route of a new Guiyang–Kunming expressway, as well as being the gateway to a provincial-level scenic area that already attracted a modest flow of tourists. He hooked up with a friend who had good relations with the Construction Bank and whose uncle owned the region's largest distillery. They rounded up a group of investors (none of whom lived in Azure Dragon itself), then turned to the county and township governments, which provided some nominal investment but, more importantly, backed the project politically. The township provided some buildings it owned in the village rent free and helped promote the project to higher levels. Jin also enlisted the support of the village elders association (*laonian xiehui*) and formed a village tourism association, which was meant to provide a forum for villager involvement in the project. By 2001 tourists were arriving in the village, where for a flat entry fee they were treated to a variety of cultural performances, displays, and activities. By 2005, some three-fourths of all foreign package tourists visiting Guizhou were being brought to Azure Dragon.

Azure Dragon is now regarded by the municipal government as the model for *tunpu* cultural development at the village level. It has emerged as a successful tourist site, attracting day tourists from the provincial capital (a mere hour away on the newly completed Guiyang–Kunming expressway) as well as tour groups from as far away as Nanjing, Hong Kong, and Taibei. But its model status derives from the innovative partnership between Jin's company and the local governments at the township and county levels. As stated in an internal document from the municipal construction bureau strategizing future *tunpu* cultural development and circulated to village leaders in the region, "The agreed-upon model is 'government + company + peasant households + peasant tourism associations.' This model is based on that developed successfully in [Azure Dragon]." The Azure Dragon model embraces the idea of local government providing the institutional and political support while the private sector provides the capital and collects the profits. For instance, government support was necessary in order to relocate the primary school out of the old Confucian School (which is now a tea-house and exhibition center) and into a new building just outside the old village. The local government is also seen as providing the "culture" since it maintains regulations on cultural preservation that benefit the company's profitability as a tourist site. While the preservation plan has been written by the company, it is enforced by the village committee and the township government, which promulgates regulations prohibiting any alteration of village houses that threatens the integrity of the village landscape as a cultural resource for tourism development.

At the same time, the government helps with the company's efforts to develop new cultural resources. For *youcaihuajie*, for example, the company staged a temple fair (*miaohui*) and with the government's help brought together a variety of cultural displays and performances from throughout the area. The fair featured many ritual activities which typically only occur during Spring Festival or during mid-summer—times less convenient for tourism. The outcome was cited by local government officials as an example of the creative blending of commerce and culture that cultural development strives for. As one company official told me in 2004:

> You could say that we [the company] have created a new temple fair, one different from a traditional fair. Ours is much larger in scale; it encompasses the whole township. Everyone comes. We have many activities: burning incense, "carrying the bodhisattvas" [*tai pusa*], "carrying the pavilion" [*tai tingzi*], "carrying the big general" [*tai dajiangjun*]. We only started "carrying the big general" last year, but it was also done in the past. But people didn't carry bodhisattvas at traditional temple fairs; we just started that last year too, along with carrying the big general. We put various cultural practices together. It's a kind of *tunpu* cultural development. We all came up with the ideas together, the business people, the government, and the people in the town.

Azure Dragon's success, as this official's final words suggest, is also attributed to the community's support for the company. Indeed, villagers consistently conveyed to me their appreciation to the company for cleaning up the village, improving the streets and bridges and canals, and making the village appear "civilized" and "cultured." This was an obvious "public good" from which all villagers benefited.

However, there is also evidence that commercial success in tourism does not directly translate into good governance for Azure Dragon, or even economic benefits for villagers, despite the generally positive attitudes with which most villagers regard tourism development. First is the fact that, while the company's commercial success has obviously benefited shareholders, villagers have expressed frustration that there is no mechanism whereby company profits are distributed to the village itself. The company has several responses to this frustration. It points out that villagers benefit from the "clean and civilized" village that the company has created, and that the company provided funds for a new primary school. And while shares have not been offered to villagers, the company argues that villagers have a short-term investment perspective that justifies their being left out of the investment pool.

From the perspective of the villagers, there is no longer any distinction between local government and the company. The company pays the salaries of all the village leadership and has in some ways substituted itself for the village committee in governing the village. While the company claims that some 400 villagers are members of the tourism association, very few villagers have any understanding of such an association or what its function might be. The few who are familiar with the association do not distinguish it from the company and, according to the actual members of the association interviewed, there had never been a meeting informing villagers of company decisions or seeking their input since the association had been founded in 2001. It is also significant to note here that the head of the association in fact earns a salary, which is paid by the company, and the association's office is located within the company headquarters.

But the loudest complaint of the villagers is not that their tourism association does not represent their interests, but that they have no control over the landscape in which they now live. The majority of villagers interviewed in Azure Dragon expressed frustration and anger over the "contradiction" between the interests of the company and the villagers concerning the maintenance of their homes. Most villagers could not afford to maintain their old homes in the old style. Instead, they watched them steadily fall apart, unable to build a cheaper and safer cement block replacement because of the village's heritage preservation rules. Most complained that the cost burden of refurbishing houses for tourism fell to them, with the company reaping the profits and the government threatening punishment if houses were rebuilt without complying with preservation guidelines. In this respect, tourism has significantly increased the cost of living by requiring a higher standard of maintenance without providing any compensation toward meeting such a standard.

Generally, villagers have been reticent to take their frustrations to the village committee for fear of being criticized for opposing tourism development and because the village committee is generally regarded as indistinguishable from the company itself. It is thus both ironic and disturbing that company officials have consistently stressed in interviews the importance of villagers sharing in the benefits of tourism development. Indeed, this rhetorical commitment to "community tourism" has earned the company accolades from no less than the president of the World Tourism Organization, who visited Azure Dragon in 2003. The company has also been featured as a model of sustainable rural tourism for the rest of the province. Yet the shadow cast by the company's success has made the needs of basic village governance nearly invisible.

Ox Market Fort: the privatization of culture

Ox Market Fort is one of a cluster of eight *tunpu* villages which received state-level status as a cultural heritage site in 2001. Since then, the village has seen a modest number of visitors, but it has not developed a commercial tourism industry of comparable scale to Azure Dragon. Instead of a joint-stockholding company, tourism in Ox Market Fort is organized and promoted solely by the village head, Wang Ji, who makes repeated trips to the township, district, and municipal government offices to cultivate ties with potential sources of development grants for the village. Wang is widely known throughout the region and his efforts to promote his village have earned him feature articles in the provincial flagship newspaper *Guizhou Ribao* as well as features broadcast on Guizhou television station. He is indeed a tireless advocate and activist for Ox Market Fort, and his ties with local government have paid off considerably. The village has received several grants for restoration work, a parking lot for tour buses, bathrooms for tourists and a reception hall, and a newly built and paved road directly to the village from the township center. In addition, several grants have enabled the village to stage numerous festivals to attract tourists.

With about one-quarter of the population of Azure Dragon, Ox Market Fort is not a large village. Its high profile in the township and district governments is well known throughout the region. Many comment that, while Azure Dragon is a "company-directed village," Ox Market Fort is called a "township [government]-directed village," referring to the number of grants that Wang has been able to collect. Nor is this surprising to many. Before the revolution the village was one of the wealthiest in the area, with a high portion of landlords and considerable influence in the local government. Its current success is regarded by many as a confirmation that China is returning to pre-revolutionary patterns of wealth distribution. Outsiders expect that the village's high profile has translated into a prosperous village overall.

Yet there is in fact widespread discontent and alienation in Ox Market Fort because Wang Ji is widely believed to be corrupt and few villagers have seen any direct benefits from government grants, tourists, or any related activities. The widespread attitude of villagers is that "*tunpu* culture" is a village resource that has been privatized by Wang Ji so that only he benefits from its production and sale. The situation is similar to those documented in hundreds of cases throughout rural China, of collective assets becoming privatized and sold for the benefit of a few enterprising locals who are typically in positions of political leadership which enable them to capitalize on the economic restructuring associated with rural reforms (see Unger and Xiong 1990; Croll 1994; Muldavin 1997). Yet in this case the collective resource is not a fish pond or a grove of trees or a coal mine, but "culture." Wang could be regarded as the new "landlord" of Ox Market Fort, but the only significant asset he owns is the village's culture.

Wang's "ownership" of village *tunpu* culture manifests itself in several ways, from the perspective of others in Ox Market Fort. Visitors who come are usually given a personal tour of the village by Wang himself—whenever he isn't currying favor in the township or city, that is—which includes a well-practiced narrative highlighting the architectural features of village houses and lanes, village history, and the history of *tunpu* people more generally. The tour is regarded as Wang's domain, even though some villagers profess that they would tell a somewhat different story were they introducing the village to outsiders. The tour also typically includes a meal at Wang's house, a large two-story cement structure at the edge of the village with a large satellite dish on top. Villagers call it "Wang Hotel," and it is the most visceral symbol and reminder of the personal enrichment Wang has enjoyed. Villagers widely suspect that the house was paid for by siphoning off funds from government grants to the village.

Another aspect of Wang's "ownership" of *tunpu* culture is his organization and staging of cultural festivals for tourists. Many in the village suspect that Wang kept much of the money the village received to stage the first *youcaihuajie* in 2003 and so most refused to participate in 2004. Yet this is not merely an issue of corruption and embezzlement for many villagers. The problem is a more general sense of alienation from *tunpu* culture, which villagers regarded as Wang's exclusive business. Like the village coalmine that Wang owns and profits from, "*tunpu* culture" is widely regarded as Wang's private business, a business he has been able to develop as a result of his strong ties to government patrons. Such an attitude comes about because the whole *idea* of *tunpu* culture is a new and vaguely understood concept for villagers. *Tunpu* represents the new economy of the outside world to them, rather than the daily life practices and rituals of the villagers themselves. From the perspective of the villagers, the government's cultural strategies of development are really no different from any other commercial development strategy in which the focus is on industrialization and revenue generation rather than basic governance. "Culture" is just another product to them, one which their village head has been able to successfully monopolize.

Wang Ji himself expresses a great deal of frustration with village suspicions of his corruption. Without his leadership, he claims, the village would be nowhere. He regards himself as an advocate for the village and believes that his fellow villagers just don't understand the way the new economy works. "Knowledge," he says, "is the key to success today. Not your skill in making things"—a remarkably prescient statement for a village head from Guizhou province! Yet the skill with which Wang has been able to turn the idea of cultural heritage and preservation into economic gain has created a sense of dispossession among fellow villagers and an attitude that culture is just another source of inequality. Several villagers, when asked, said that if they were in charge of village development they would not focus on *tunpu* culture at all, so convinced were they that it could never benefit everyone equally. Instead, they said they would emphasize village scenery to attract tourists—nearby mountains and caves. "Culture," for them, signifies a return to a pattern of governance that recognized the authority of traditional elites.

Jin Family Fort: a village association takes over

Jin Family Fort's cultural development has occurred by virtue of the fact that the village is host to the large annual festival of "Carrying Wang Gong" (*taiwanggong*), held on the 18th day of the first month in the lunar calendar. Wang Hua was a local official of Anhui who lived during the sixth and seventh centuries and whose loyalty to the Sui emperor earned him the posthumous title of Wang Gong. During the early Ming campaigns in Guizhou and Yunnan, in which a large portion of the soldiers came from Anhui, the army's successes were attributed to Wang Gong; he thus became the patron deity of many *tunpu* settlers following the campaigns. The Wang Gong cult remains popular in parts of Anhui, Jiangxi, and Zhejiang, but the *taiwanggong* festival in Jin Family Fort is said to be China's largest celebration of Wang Gong. While the village has always celebrated *taiwanggong*, it was not until the late 1980s that the government officially declared its tolerance for the festival. By the 1990s, local officials were openly attending the celebration, which not only drew thousands of neighboring villagers, but many from other regions of China as well. The festival has come to be seen as an instrumental event in the promotion of *tunpu* culture. During the three-day event, local officials seek to organize related promotional events by which they might be able to sell the region to potential investors or encourage returning natives to donate funds for the development of their home town.

The fact that the festival represents a prime opportunity for migrant workers to donate some of their earnings directly to the village has caused a shift in the local government's attitude toward the festival from reluctant tolerance to active promotion. The festival, in turn, has become the year's most significant fiscal event. The state's appropriation of the festival, however, has not led to the kind of alienation one sees in Ox Market Fort; nor has it occurred in conjunction with a partnership arrangement with a private company, as in the case of Azure Dragon. Instead, festival organization remains firmly under the control of the village itself, in the form of a seven-member "18th Association" which not only organizes the festival but is the most powerful voice representing the interests of the village to the government. The association's power is manifest in the central governance role that it plays in providing for basic village welfare, as well as weighing in on the key political decisions of the village committee. The association has become the body that local government must rely upon for the provision of basic welfare because of the financial resources it is able to muster. Ostensibly, the association collects donations (about 8,000 yuan annually) for the staging of the festival and the maintenance of the Wang Gong temple in the center of the village. But it also acts as a rural credit association by providing loans to villagers in need, and overseeing the fiscal needs of the village generally, such as infrastructure maintenance and improvement, and healthcare and education provision. During the festival, a portion of the association's collections is also distributed to each household in the village in "red bags." This gives the association considerable collective authority; all important decisions involving village expenditures must, for instance, first meet its approval.

It is because of the fact that village governance is organized around the "superstitious" cult of Wang Gong that the state has until only very recently kept its distance. This has seemingly been to the advantage of the village, which despite the disruptions of the Great Leap Forward and Cultural Revolution has managed to maintain the authority of the association for generations. And while villagers are happy to promote their festival for tourism—with increasing numbers of foreign and Chinese tourists participating each year—there is agreement among village leaders that future tourism development will be managed by a company initiated, financed, and run by villagers themselves, in order to avoid the discontent that is increasingly apparent in Azure Dragon. Indeed, other villages in the region have made similar moves, collaborating with local scholars to formulate development plans that explicitly seek to *avoid* the Azure Dragon model while still *appearing* to follow the basic formula of having a private development company run the village's tourism business. Because Jin Family Fort's festival is such a spectacular cultural event, it has long attracted the attention of local scholars, and they play a significant role in advising the village on its development strategies. Indeed, without any assistance from the local government, the village held a conference several years ago to plumb the advice of local scholars.

Cultural strategies and the struggle for ownership

What is clear from the above cases is that the governance outcomes of cultural strategies at the village level depend greatly on the local contexts within which those strategies are played out. It should also be clear, however, that culture is not itself the key to the sustainable development and "good governance" outcomes that organizations like UNESCO hope for. When viewed from the distanced perspective of academics, officials, and development practitioners, culture appears to have the potential to produce a new kind of self-governing, and even enterprising, citizen because—the argument goes—cultural strategies inject new empowering meanings into the practices of people's daily lives. *Tunpu* cultural development has indeed sought to transform villagers into enterprising subjects of heritage promotion and self-regulation, by promoting an entrepreneurial model at the village level. It is this approach which has, for instance, caught the eye of the World Tourism Organization, as a potentially sustainable model of rural tourism for developing countries. And clearly, as the case of Jin Family Fort indicates, cultural strategies have in many ways empowered villagers to govern themselves effectively and justly.

Yet Jin Family Fort's experience appears to be more the exception than the rule in central Guizhou. This is because—as revealed in the cases of Azure Dragon and Ox Market Fort—cultural strategies have produced not new empowering meanings for the formation of new subjectivities, but new *products*. It is the ownership of these cultural products that becomes the key issue in whether or not cultural strategies can improve village-level governance in China.

From this perspective, the argument—as advanced by Zukin—that a turn toward cultural strategies of development has resulted in the privatization of a formerly public domain tends to miss the key issues at stake in rural China. *Tunpu* culture is not a public good subject to privatization because it has itself been created within the process of privatization that continues to sweep across post-reform China (Qin 2003). Cultural strategies are producing new products rather than privatizing public goods. The challenges of cultural strategies lie not in preserving Zukin's public–private divide, but in insuring a just regime of privatization. Cultural development in Azure Dragon and Ox Market Fort has generated an entirely new logic of capital accumulation. The link between culture and sustainable development or "good governance" proceeds on the assumption that culture is somehow different from other products. The case studies here suggest, however, that cultural production invites the same struggles over ownership as other forms of production. Thus, while cultural strategies are indeed shown here to be lucrative in terms of income generation, they only intensify the conflicts over privatization that have eroded village-level governance in China's reform era.

Even in the relatively successful case of Jin Family Fort, where *tunpu* cultural development has strengthened the ability of a local social institution—the 18th Festival Association—to substitute for the state in the provision of basic village welfare and public goods, cultural strategies have only made it easier for the state to withdraw from its fiscal responsibilities. The 18th Association now substitutes for the state at the village level, and one wonders if this is really the kind of governance model that should be promoted throughout China. Lily Tsai (2002: 26) has argued that community social institutions such as lineages and temple associations play an increasingly important role in village governance. The reliance on such institutions by village leadership can prove very effective in mobilizing resources for public projects that otherwise would not get addressed. However, Tsai also points out that this very reliance on community institutions can replace rather than complement formal governance. "Fundraising," she argues, "does not produce the same outcomes as governmental responsibility for public welfare." Along these lines, one could argue that cultural strategies contribute to rural China's simmering governance crisis by encouraging the local state to redefine its role in terms of cultural production rather than welfare provision. Such an outcome can be seen in each of the three case study villages, where governance has come to be defined in terms of state investment in cultural development and little else.

Finally, it should be made clear that cultural strategies themselves are not to be condemned because of the challenges Guizhou villagers face in making them work. Culture remains the most significant development resource in rural Guizhou. But it needs to be viewed by the local state and other institutions as more than a product. We should not forget that culture is "the means through which people create meaningful worlds in which to live" (Negus 1997: 101). Treating culture in these broader terms, rather than the instrumentalism so often seen in the actual practices of cultural development, may begin to resolve the kinds of conflicts that have developed in places like Azure Dragon and Ox Market Fort.

Notes

1 The author gratefully acknowledges the support of the National Science Foundation, award no. BCS-20243045. This chapter is the result of collaborative research conducted with Wu Xiaoping, of Guizhou Nationalities Institute. Additional assistance was provided by Du Wei, Luo Yu, and Yang Zhu. They are not responsible for the content of the present essay.
2 All names of places and people in the case studies are pseudonyms.

2 Neoliberalizing Chinese cities

Housing reform and urbanization

James Lee and Yapeng Zhu

Although housing reforms since 1979 have substantially improved the living conditions of urban residents in China, many major cities are still plagued by poor housing standards and acute housing shortages. Even after two decades of reform efforts, many urban residents continue to rely on work units for housing because they cannot afford to buy or rent in the private market. Urban governance is now more chaotic than in the late 1990s since the process of rural–urban migration has reached a new level of complexity, closely associated with the issue of political instability arising from a national policy of uneven development between the rural and the urban sector. To alleviate the housing problem and to improve urban governance, the government introduced the housing monetarization policy (HMP) in 1998 to replace the old in-kind welfare housing system. The housing function of the work units (*danwei*) is to be gradually taken over by the market, or what Davis (2003) termed "the recommodification of urban housing." Unfortunately, this policy is premised on a problematic assumption—the belief in the capacity of the market to solve the housing problem. Although the government is well aware of the all too familiar perils of such a precarious project—one that possibly leads to a chain of events involving first a property bubble, to be followed by an economic crisis caused by rapid asset devaluation, dwindling wealth, and then squeezing homeowners to foreclosure as they lack the means to repay bank loans.

Nonetheless, the neoliberal turn in housing development in China is still being heralded as a one-size-fits-all method in urbanization and economic development. Using a neoliberal perspective and data from a case study of HMP implementation in Guiyang, this chapter argues that housing reform in a neoliberal direction is likely to create more housing inequalities than HMP originally sought to reduce. Moreover, with more private housing investment, China has set herself on a familiar course of urban change which currently besieges many governments in the West—the marginalization of the urban poor as a result of rapid urbanization. Such new socio-spatial segregations will give rise to a new set of urban problems and conflict situations which may be more serious than those which the housing reform set out to resolve (Wang 2004). In this chapter, we shall first discuss the early process of housing privatization and also the background leading to the HMP in 1998. There then follows a discussion of the neoliberal turn in China's urbanization and its resonance with what is happening in the West. We then focus on Guiyang as a case study, highlighting HMP's theoretical roots and why it is considered essentially part of the neoliberal turn. Finally, we conclude by discussing the limitations of the model on eradicating housing inequalities and its broader implications for urban poverty and social segregation.

Failure in governance: housing shortages, inequalities, and early reform

Before 1980, China adopted a socialist, work-unit-dominated welfare system. This system involved a mixture of three components: socialist ideology, welfare philosophy, and clan tradition (Zhao and Bourassa 2003). The main goal of the socialist tradition was to eliminate social inequities and class exploitations. Thus most of China's private housing came into public ownership in the 1950s (Wang and Murie 1996; Zhou and Logan 1996). China then established its own urban welfare system fully tied to the workplace, leading to a massive post-war construction of workers' housing distributed on need-based criteria and distributed through work units and the city housing bureaus. Unfortunately most of this housing was of poor built quality and rent levels were kept so low that they failed to generate enough resources to sustain even basic maintenance. Public ownership of urban housing by the work units also discouraged private investment and hence resulted in severe housing shortages. For example, in 1989, nine years after initial reform, China recorded 5,388,403 households (about 10 percent of the urban population) in need of housing, of which 469,481 had a per capita living space of less than 2 m (Chen 1998). Housing shortages have aggravated the inequitable housing allocation amongst not only different types of enterprises, but also individuals. First, the allocation of investment funds favored housing of state-owned enterprises more than housing under city bureaus and collective enterprises (Lee 1988). As a result, 74.4 percent of collective enterprises, compared to 32.8 percent of state-owned enterprises, were unable to house their employees (Yang and Wang 1992). Welfare housing and its related administrative allocation system also led to widespread corruption, where some cadres gained more than their fair share of housing through *guanxi* (personal relationships). The quasi-clan system caused significant inequity amongst different work units and in the late 1970s the problem became so serious that the government was forced to act through reform. Moreover, the labor force had become greatly immobilized under the old welfare housing system as jobs were tied to housing. Employees were inclined to stay put, while enterprises were reluctant to lay off redundant workers. Some economists have suggested that such labor immobility accounted for much of the low productivity in the 1960s and 1970s (Chen 1998).

From the outset, the goal of housing reforms was to abolish the old system and achieve housing privatization, commercialization, and socialization. Privatization involves the sale of publicly owned dwellings to sitting tenants, thus reducing the state's burden. Enterprises could then put scarce resources to more profitable use. Also, housing reform is considered useful in freeing enterprise managers from nonproductive decision-making so that they can concentrate on improving productivity (Chen 1998). Commercialization involves the establishment of a housing market where housing can be commodified and exchanged, while socialization involves the transfer of housing management from the control of the work units or local housing bureaus to professional housing management firms (Zhao and Bourassa 2003). Reform of the urban housing system started in 1980 and during the course of the reform private home ownership became a popular choice. The source of housing construction funds has also become privatized and as a result the central government's share of housing investment fell from 90 percent in 1979 to 16 percent in 1988 (Chen 1998). By 1990, the average per capita living space was nearly double that of 1978, and the number of households with less than 4 m per person had fallen by 2 million, to 5.38 million (Bian and Logan 1997).

Indeed, the housing reforms of the 1990s did produce significant changes in several dimensions. By 1995, 46 percent of urban households lived in dwellings built during the 1980s, while 20 percent lived in homes built since 1990. The percentage of families living in self-contained apartments rose to 50 percent in 1992. In 1995, the State Council announced steps to regularize housing provident funds (HPF) throughout the country as a primary means to promote home ownership. In addition, reforms were made to the banking system, enabling individuals to take out a mortgage for home purchase. At the end of 1994, 30 percent of urban households held some form of ownership right in their home. In 1999, a study by the Sinomonitor and the British Market Research Bureau revealed that the percentage of homeowners in urban areas of China has risen to 59 percent. Xie Jiajin, Chief Economist at the Ministry of Construction, reported at the 2006 International Conference on Housing Finance that an estimated 80 percent of all public housing had been sold to the people. Owner-occupation, a much cherished form of tenure in Western industrial societies, has reached 72.8 percent, while the ratio of private home sales to public housing was 97:3 (Xie 2006).

However, taking China as a whole, such progress must be understood with some caution. Housing reform since 1980 is fraught with two major problems. The first concerns tenure preference. From cadres to workers, many still consider housing provision a core responsibility of the state, not the individual. Housing is regarded as having a distinct welfare nature as many work units refuse to implement housing reforms thoroughly. Second, under the old welfare housing system, wide disparities existed amongst work units due to their different profit levels. Workers doing similar jobs in comparable positions but in different work units found themselves with widely different housing conditions. Housing inequalities were thus prevalent and deeply embedded. During the housing reform era, such inequalities have continued because work units remain dominant providers of housing goods. In addition, horizontal inequity across different work units has worsened. Khan *et al.* (1999) documented a sharp increase in income inequality between 1988 and 1995. During the same period, housing subsidies became less equally distributed, with 41 percent of subsidies in 1995 received by households in the top 10 percent of income distribution (Bian and Logan 1997). Housing policy accounted for 37 percent of overall inequality in the distribution of urban incomes in 1995.

Housing as the new growth focus: the genesis of the HMP

In 1998, when Zhu Rongji became China's premier, the new administration faced many thorny economic issues as a result of the Asian financial crisis. Amongst them, China's exports decreased considerably and millions of workers were laid off from state enterprises. As a means to offset the impact of the unfavorable economic environment, stimulation of domestic demand became an inevitable alternative (Guo 1999: 68–78). Rapid economic growth was crucial to ease unemployment and to maintain social stability. Within this context, the housing industry was positioned as "a new growth focus" (Guo 2005). It was expected that the growth of real estate and housing investment would help channel individual consumption to the property market and consequently stimulate economic development of related sectors such as construction, home furnishing, electricity, and home appliances. HPM, as a new policy initiative under this context, provided direct cash subsidies to urban residents in lieu of in-kind housing subsidies. With this cash allowance, urban residents were expected to meet their housing needs in the open market, in conjunction with financial resources from family savings, housing provident funds, and private mortgage loans.

HMP was implemented in successive stages. First, the provision of rental housing through work units was terminated from 1998. Work units were prohibited from building or buying housing from the market for rental purposes. Second, the housing fund formerly provided to the work units for buying or building housing has been transformed into cash subsidies for workers. Meanwhile rent reform continued, while the sale of public housing became the priority (State Council 1998). Third, a multilayered housing provision system was established, providing housing to people according to their labor positions: high-income earners to buy private housing; medium- to low-income households to buy low-cost housing; and finally low-rent social housing to be reserved for the poorest (State Council 1998). The whole idea behind HMP is thus reminiscent of the concept of a housing ladder commonly found in Western industrial societies (State Council 1998).

Housing and urbanization in China: the neoliberal turn

That China should be the focus of an inquiry into the extent of neoliberalism's possible impact is remarkable, given its history and its continuing status as a nominal "communist" state. Indeed, it is only as a consequence of major geopolitical turning points like China's rapprochement with the U.S. in 1972, or the end of the Cold War in 1989, that a discussion of the possible impact of neoliberalism on China makes any sense at all. One curiously neglected area to date is the impact of neoliberalization on China's urbanization. Since the commencement of economic reforms in the late 1970s, China has quietly undergone one of the world's most dramatic urbanization processes in modern times. While in 1978 only 18 percent of its population were classified as urban residents, the 2000 census revealed an increase to 456 million—some 36 percent of the country's total population. If the urbanization rate of 1995 continues, China will have a 50 percent urban population by 2010 and 64 percent by 2020. Supra-rapid urbanization is also evidenced by the increase in the number of cities. In 1978, there were only 193 cities in China. By the end of 2000, the number was 663, a more than threefold increase in two decades (Wang 2004). Successive rural reforms in the 1980s meant a huge supply of surplus rural labor. Coupled with the concentration of capital and development policies in the new cities or new urban centers, China has managed to create the all too familiar scenario in what David Harvey described as capital and space amalgam (Harvey 1989a). Multiple circuits of capital succeed in revaluating the urban landscape, transforming formerly worthless city land into plots worth billions.

The intellectual roots of neoliberalism can be traced to the post-war writings of Hayek and Friedman (Bourdieu 1998b). It gained widespread prominence during the late 1970s and early 1980s as a political strategy to deal with the sustained global recession of the preceding decade. Faced with the decline of traditional mass industrial production as well as the crisis of Keynesian welfare policies, the old industrial West began to dismantle the basic institutional components of post-war politics and create a series of new institutional arrangements and policies to justify the deregulation of state control over major industries, assaults on organized labor, and the shrinking of the welfare state. Translated into global public policies, neoliberal politics comes in all sizes and shapes. However, amongst activists and academics alike, all have come to agree on the following principal elements concerning neoliberalism: (1) a mixture of neoclassical economic fundamentalism; (2) market regulation in the place of state intervention; (3) economic distribution in favor of capital; (4) moral authoritarianism with family as the core social value; (5) international free trade principles; and (6) intolerance of trade unionism (Moddy 1997: 119–20).

The impact of the neoliberal turn on the urbanization process is apparent when major economic activities are taking place in cities. Neoliberalism has come to transcend, not simply the physical structure, but also the social relationship between people, work, and place, notably the value of the "home." Housing inequalities seen in this light are thus much more complex than a deprivation of space and basic needs. Liberalization of China's new political economy is now closely intertwined with the country's latest process of socio-spatial division (Wang 2004). This then brings us to the most important observation of China's new urban question. The linchpin of China's economic reform policy is the belief that the market, properly regulated and liberated from all forms of unnecessary interventions, represents the optimal mechanism for economic development. The HMP to a great extent follows this logic, in anticipation that ultimately all housing needs could be met by the market.

What follows immediately from the above observations on China's urbanization are the striking similarities with what has been keenly observed in many Western urban industrial economies and what many anti-liberalist academics are hotly contesting (Peck and Tickell 1995; Bourdieu and Nice 1998; Harloe 2001; Brenner and Theodore 2002). The central idea is that the 1990s was a decade in which the term "neoliberalism" became a major rallying point for a wide range of anti-capitalist popular struggles. The key contention is that there is a stark disjuncture between the ideology of neoliberalism and its everyday operation in capitalist societies. On the one hand, while neoliberalism aspires to create a utopia of the free market, it has in practice entailed a dramatic intensification of coercive, disciplinary forms of state intervention in order to impose market rules upon all aspects of social life. On the other hand, whereas neoliberal ideology implies that a self-regulating market will generate an optimal allocation of investment and resources, neoliberal political practice has generated massive market failures, new forms of social polarization, and a dramatic intensification of uneven development in all spatial dimensions, particularly in terms of housing-related social divisions (Forrest *et al.* 1990). In short, the neoliberal shift in government policies in many Western industrial economies tends to subject the majority of the population to the power of market forces while preserving the protection for the strongest (Brenner and Theodore 2002: 15–16).

On a more practical level, neoliberalization does affect urban development in at least three distinct ways. First, capitalist urban development is always characterized by a pattern of *uneven development*. It is a key expression of capital's relentless drive to mobilize particular territories and places as forces of production. Each stage of capitalist development is associated with a distinctive, historically specific geographical landscape in which some places, territories, and scales are systematically privileged over others as sites for capital accumulation (Harvey 1982; Massey 1995). Second, since the social relations of capitalism are permeated by tensions and conflicts which undermine or destabilize the accumulation process, the state is seen as a vital institution in which successive *institutional fixes* evolve to regulate these uneven developments. Neoliberalism thus represents a complex, multifaceted project of socio-spatial transformation by the state to maintain and restore disequilibrium arising from the system's inherent instability. It contains not simply a utopian vision of a fully commodified form of social life, but also a concrete program of institutional modifications through which the unfettered rule of capital is to be upheld. Third, all neoliberal urban projects involve "the creative destruction" of existing institutional arrangements and political compromises through market-oriented reform initiatives, and the creation of a new infrastructure for market-oriented economic growth, commodification, and the rule of capital (Brenner and Theodore 2002). In Table 2.1, we can observe the likely effects of the destruction and creation on these three dimensions: (1) the restructuring of the welfare state; (2) the restructuring of the housing market; and (3) the transformation of the built environment. For example, low-rent social housing will be reduced or eliminated, to be replaced by private home ownership for every household. The UK is a typical example, where this process began in the early 1980s, and by 1998 most rented social housing had been turned into privately owned homes through deliberate neoliberal housing policies (Forrest *et al.* 1990; Jones and Ward 2002; Malpass 2004; Raco 2005).

It can be observed from these three linked, familiar urban processes that neoliberalization has indeed brought instability and change to the social system through various institutional changes. The market has assumed many former state responsibilities in terms of forging a new housing, social welfare, and neighborhood configuration, one which constantly emphasizes

Table 2.1 Neoliberal urbanization and its impact on institutional change in Western industrial economies

Site of regulation	Destruction of existing institution	Creation of new institution
1 Restructuring urban housing markets	Elimination of public housing and other forms of low-rent accommodation; elimination of rent control	Creation of new opportunities for speculative investment in the real estate markets; introduction of market rents and more owner-occupation housing
2 Transformation of the built environment	Destruction of traditional working-class neighborhoods to make way for speculative redevelopment of real estate projects	Creation of new privatized spaces of elite/corporate consumption; reconfiguration of local land-use patterns; creation of gated communities and other purified space of social reproduction; intensification of socio-spatial polarization; competitive pricing for urban land
3 Restructuring the welfare state	Local relays of national welfare services are retrenched	Expansion of community-based sectors and private approaches to social-service provision; imposition of work on welfare recipients

competition and privatized consumption. New urban spaces with much clearer boundaries (e.g. a gated community or a self-enclosed housing estate) are created to replace existing communities. This spatial process is both inclusive and exclusive, with an ultimate aim that cities will become increasingly central to the reproduction, mutation, and continual reconstitution of neoliberalism itself.

China's housing reform in the context of neoliberal urbanization

Superimposing the above discussions onto the current context of major Chinese cities *vis-à-vis* their urbanization process and housing reforms, we discover a striking resonance with what has been happening in major Chinese cities in recent decades.

Uneven housing development and the transformation of the built environment

After two decades of housing privatization and commercialization, many Chinese cities are now not simply spatially transformed, but segregated, with pockets of poverty permeating the urban arena. From Chongqing to Shanghai, no one who visits China today can fail to witness the enormous transformation of its built environment. The introduction of massive new capital and a general breakdown of planning have resulted in a situation of "chaos" or acute uneven urban development in many Chinese cities (Wang 2004: 25–50). New urban "enclaves" are constantly created in the form of luxurious new condominium apartments, often advertised as an "oasis in the city," marking a distinction from the surrounding poor old *danwei* housing. David Fraser's study of Shanghai real estate advertisements suggested that the home is being constructed as the central site of social interaction and consumption. People acquire not merely a domicile like in the old communist days, but a personal and private terrain that repudiates the severe constraints on personal life imposed in earlier decades by the Maoist work units (Fraser 2000: 27). In a recent study of uneven housing conditions in Chongqing and Shenyang, Wang (2004:103–5) suggested that housing itself should also be considered as a cause of poverty, since poor housing conditions inherited from the previous economic system and the associated weak financial position of families could also cause poverty. On the one hand, the creation of the HMP and the push for private home ownership could well be seen as the destruction of the old neighborhood to make way for new private housing projects which could not be afforded by the old neighbors. On the other hand, the replacement of the old welfare housing system by the HMP means the *creative destruction* of an existing institutional arrangement by market-oriented reform initiatives and the creation of a new infrastructure for growth. After 25 years of urbanization, much of the transformation of the central part of big cities in China has been completed, leaving only small patches of traditional housing areas in bad locations. In contrast with the traditional old housing areas which one can still find in cities like Shanghai, the new urban landscape consists of many new zones and districts, such as central business districts, high-tech development areas, special economic zones, and new residential districts for professional foreign workers. The Ministry of Construction reported in 2003 that the main housing problems were no longer to do with overcrowding, but much more to do with urban poverty. The 2000 National Population Census revealed that 71 percent of urban housing was made up of purpose-built housing units, while on average residents in urban areas can only enjoy 0.75 of a room per person. In addition, there were still 15 million urban households with less than 8 m of floor space per person and only 72 percent of urban families have electricity or gas as the main fuels (Liu 2003). Neoliberal urbanization has succeeded in carving out a new urban China fragmented by the continual destruction of old neighborhoods and communities, resulting in the creation of new poverty and social exclusion.

Restructuring of the welfare system

One policy that has played a significant role in China's economic reform is the successful shedding of most welfare functions from the central government to the local government, and from work units to local communities. Social welfare services are either gradually "socialized" to the municipal level or are completely privatized. Socialization of welfare services is considered essential in solving financial problems of bankrupt enterprises and is considered a form of "institutional fix" seeking to balance emerging social conflicts. Neoliberalization in the form of welfare state restructuring is sometimes phrased as *welfare pluralism*, or *mixed economy of care*, or, more recently, the creation of a *social care market*. In a recent study of the evolution of the Western welfare state, Gilbert (2002) argues that the new millennium will be marked by a steady global convergence of the way in which social welfare is governed by world cities, irrespective of their ideological origins, or the way their welfare systems are organized. This will involve the emergence of what Gilbert (2002) calls *the enabling state*, in which government will have little or involvement in direct social welfare provision. Social welfare arrangements are now increasingly designed to facilitate people working as well as to enable the markets and the nongovernmental organizations to assume an expanded role in providing social protection. Given this global trend of welfare state restructuring, it is interesting to note that China's welfare restructuring is following similar routes. Wong (2001) argues that socialization is the most fundamental change in terms of social policy development in China since 1949. Since the economic reform in the late 1970s, three important welfare financing methods have been detected in the social welfare sector. First, there has been a substantial degree of devolution from central to local government, and also to communities. Second, funding sources have been much diversified. Third, the proliferation of fee-charging has transformed a hitherto closed welfare system into one which takes on a competitive edge. All these changes could not be viewed as simply part of the process of transition from a socialist to capitalist state. They represent a new configuration of social relationships and community identity: one which is characterized by breaking down the dependency of workers in the *danwei* through the creation of a new bondage and new relationship between home ownership and the people. A new set of social relationships is now built around the "home" and how it is related to other homes in a new "gated community." Davis (2003) argued that as a result of such an enthusiastic embrace of market transactions, the commercialization of welfare goods and housing, the post-Mao leadership has fundamentally realigned the long-existing paradigm of the state–society relationship. This makes the housing question in China particularly intriguing as it is no longer simply about housing. It now has much to do with a new element of social division and an urban environment actively realigning its internal order.

Evidence from Guiyang

To better appreciate the micro-effects of neoliberalization in the housing sector, we will examine the case of HMP implementation in Guiyang—the provincial capital of Guizhou. The reasons behind the choice of Guiyang are twofold: first, Guiyang has adopted a rather unique approach in terms of improving housing inequalities, which has been used as a demonstration model for other provinces since 1999. As one of the chief architects of the HMP policy in the central government, Mr. Guo Shuqing (2005) (the CEO of China Reconstruction Bank and a leading economist) was appointed Deputy Provincial Governor of the Guizhou Province, overseeing HMP implementation during the period 1997–2001. As such, Guiyang was deliberately chosen by China as the experimental city for HMP implementation. Second, despite being located in a poor province of Western China, Guiyang had strong leadership and a track record of effective governance in the past. This thus significantly reduces the usual effects of policy implementation variables in our study and thus enables us to focus more easily on the direct impact of the model.

Guiyang has an area of 2,403 km and a population of 3.48 million in 2003. GDP in 2005 was 52.5 billion yuan, while per capita income was US $1,700 (Guiyang Business Bureau 2006). Consumption expenditure per capita was 5,036 yuan, which was 14.3 percent lower than the national average of 5,874.87 yuan in 2003. Living space per capita was only 2.7 m, while most dwellings were of poor build quality. From 1950 to 1978, only 226,443 million yuan were invested in housing and a mere 3.31 million m of dwellings were completed, providing housing for just 60,000 households (Guiyang Municipal Housing Reform Office 1992:101). Housing construction was speeded up as a result of the economic reforms. During the 12 years from 1978 to 1990, total investment on housing was increased to 1.74 billion yuan, seven times the total investment for the period 1949–78 and more than 6.35 million m of public housing was completed. In spite of these achievements, there was still an acute housing shortage since some 260,000 m of old and dilapidated buildings have to be demolished annually. Although the government spent 101 billion yuan in fixed capital investment on housing construction in 2005 ("Province View" 2006), it was not sufficient to satisfy housing needs. Throughout the country, the biggest stumbling block for HMP implementation is the difficulty encountered by the provincial government in garnering sufficient finance for the provision of a cash allowance. Many provinces failed to implement HMP according to schedule because the provincial governments could not find additional housing resources under the old welfare system. Thus only a small number of strong enterprises were able to implement the policy in the initial phase.

The solution adopted in Guiyang is by way of a complete revaluation of the existing housing stock occupied by public servants, taking into account, for the first time since the housing reform, the location and physical conditions of the property. This is an improvement from the previous welfare housing system, under which all housing units were assumed to be of identical locational value, with differences only in size and layout. Revaluation is then followed by an assessment of housing entitlements of individual workers according to their labor position, which includes salary level and seniority. Workers are assigned an individual housing allowance account into which a notional sum is deposited, showing the housing entitlements accumulated over their entire working life until 1998. They are then informed of the differential between their current asset value and their accumulated entitlement according to a formula. In practice, if a cadre occupies a flat above and beyond his or her entitlement, under the Guiyang system, s/he has to make up the monetary difference between the assessed market value of the current home and his or her entitlement by means of reimbursing the housing bureau. Conversely, those who are underprovided are compensated with a grant. They may choose to purchase either their existing homes or other private housing in the market. All public tenants are then given full property rights so that they can exchange their flats in the market once they settle such differences. New workers, who have never been provided with public housing, are given a lump sum allowance plus an additional monthly allowance to assist them to purchase a flat in the market.

This model marks a significant departure from the former in-kind welfare housing distribution where flats were distributed according to the individual work unit's own set of criteria and resource situation (Zhu and Lee 2004). Many people in Guiyang were skeptical about the model at the beginning. However, from local governance, the model has been implemented with considerable success. Its initial success can be attributed to several causes. First, as a poor provincial capital, Guiyang could not afford to adopt generous subsidy schemes as in other wealthier cities such as Shenzhen,

Guangzhou, and Nanjing. It must therefore seek more innovative ways to implement HMP (Guo 2000: 521–4). Second, strong and professional leadership played an extremely important role in planning and implementing the reform.

Theory and practice: from use value to exchange value

Guo's (2005) model of housing reform is premised on three guiding principles:

1 The idea of housing recommodification is deeply influenced by what Western housing economists now widely use—a two-sector housing model comprising the rental and the home ownership market. Housing demand is considered essentially rooted in rent-level changes. The demand for home ownership is thus considered to be affected both by the *demand for space* and by the *demand for investment assets*. The historic low rent level under the old welfare housing system is considered a stumbling block in the formation of a market-oriented housing sector and must therefore be changed. In order to transcend to full market operation, rents and wages must be increased simultaneously in order to make home ownership affordable.
2 *Differential land rent* should be considered an essential component of housing costs and benefits. In Guo's view, one of the main reasons why housing inequalities exist widely throughout China is that housing costs do not reflect locational qualities (Guo 2005: 534–55). As a result, all housing units are assumed to have a uniform land cost. Thus a flat in central Shanghai costs the same as one in the suburban area. But in any mature housing market housing and land are always expensive in better locations and cheaper at less advantageous sites, thus reflecting differential land rent (Guo 2005: 36–9). If the HMP disregards this factor and merely distributes housing subsidies according to entitlement, it will inevitably entail a great deal of housing inequalities once the houses are exchanged. Those workers who happen to live in a good area will stand to gain a lot more than those who live on the fringe of the city.
3 Housing affordability must be linked to the income level of target users or buyers. The early experience of housing reforms in many coastal industrial cities such as Shanghai and Nanjing was that house prices rose much faster than wages. In the Guiyang model, it is stipulated that once the price–income ratio (or what is generally termed the affordability ratio) has gone beyond 4, work units will need to provide a cash allowance for workers, in order to maintain housing affordability (Guo 2005: 534–55).

The Guiyang model is also built on two important operational subsidy concepts: (1) the existing housing stock subsidy (EHSS) and (2) the supplementary housing subsidy (SHS). Existing subsidy principally refers to the lump sum housing subsidy which is provided to public servants under the new policy in recognition of their services to the government before 1998. The following formula roughly describes how this subsidy is calculated:

EHSS =
stipulated subsidies according to rank and work years × 1998 wage level

Table 2.2 illustrates the various entitlements under the EHSS scheme. For instance, the director of a mid-size government department who worked for 20 years gets 1,093 yuan × 20 years = 21,860 yuan, while a junior staff member gets 624 yuan × 20 years = 12,480 yuan. Theoretically, the money generated from this formula is the growth engine behind the Guiyang model. The idea is that when respective households receive EHSS, together with money from the Housing Provident Fund, bank mortgage, and their own savings, they will be able to afford to buy a private in the market. In some way, the EHSS will act as their first down payment, as in many Western housing markets.

Guo (2005) considers national housing reform to be both "complex" and "simple." The complex part refers to the multiplicity of housing inequalities deeply entrenched within a highly inefficient allocation system. The simple part refers to the huge amount of underutilized real estate assets trapped within the welfare housing system. According to Guo (2005), China had approximately 3 billion m of public housing stock in 1997, with an estimated redevelopment value of 4,500 billion yuan (Guo 2005: 534–55). What many Chinese officials considered a national finance burden, he saw as a strong financial asset that could be turned into private consumption and investment. The problem is: In what ways could these assets be transferred and distributed fairly amongst the people? The answer, he suggests, lies in the creation of the EHSS, which, when properly administered, would be able to generate demand for private home ownership, hence transforming China's housing system, which used to be based entirely on use value, to one which is based on exchange value.

SHS refers to the new housing component in the wage package and is considered the second part of the HMP. When the values of the existing housing stock are distributed, the next step is to incorporate housing

Table 2.2 Standard of EHSS in Guiyang

Position	Space entitlement (m²)	EHSS entitlement (yuan)
Junior staff and workers	20	624
Head	25	780
Vice-Director	30	936
Director	35	1,093
Vice-Secretary	45	1,405
Secretary	50	1,561

subsidies into the wage package in the form of a monthly cash subsidy given to employees. However, as the financial situation of different enterprises varies tremendously and many enterprises in Guiyang cannot afford to provide the SHS initially, the provincial government has used the HPF as a transitional substitute for SHS. Accordingly, employers and employees each contribute 5 percent of the workers' salary into the HPF. From an economic viewpoint, these two types of subsidy represent different levels of supply-led housing consumption, leading towards more investment and growth (Guo 2005: 439–46). In Table 2.3, it is shown that just prior to HMP implementation in 1997 the Housing Reform Office estimated that a total of 292.86 million yuan had to be mobilized by the provincial government for the implementation of SHS. This represented a major pointer of housing investment compared to any normal year prior to HMP. The Guiyang government simply could not afford this level of investment in 1997 without making use of the HPF provisions.

Housing inequality in Guiyang

Like in other parts of China, there had always been serious housing inequality problems before the HMP reform in Guiyang. According to a 1998 study, housing inequalities between different work units in Guiyang were quite substantial (see Table 2.4). The housing situation was better in government departments than in collective enterprises. Generally speaking, provincial-level government departments had better housing than their counterparts at the municipal and district levels. Major state enterprises fared better than medium-sized and small state enterprises or collective enterprises. Per capita space was 14 m for provincial government departments and 11 m for municipal government departments, while employees in state enterprises and collective enterprises had only 10 m and 6 m, respectively. Housing inequalities amongst different work units and employees were

Table 2.3 Estimated Housing Provident Fund contribution, 1997

Work units	No. of employees	Per capita annual salary (yuan)	(A) Employee contribution to HPF5% salary (million yuan)	(B) Employer contribution to HPF5% salary (million yuan)	(A) + (B) (million yuan)
Government departments	22,526	5,668	6.38	6.38	12.76
Municipal enterprises	306,411	5,864	89.84	89.84	179.68
Provincial enterprises	171,250	5,864	50.21	50.21	100.42
Total	500,187	–	146.43	146.63	292.86

also aggravated by shifting reform strategies. One example is the shifting price structure of the sales of public housing to sitting tenants over time. The pricing strategy of public housing sales also varies tremendously across cities and provinces. Broadly, there are two levels of pricing: *biaozhun* (standard) price and *chengben* (cost) price. The *biaozhun* price of public housing carries comparatively a higher subsidy component than the *chengben* price (Table 2.5). However, the sale of public flats at the *biaozhun* prices was terminated in 1998. All remaining flats have since then been sold at the *chengben* prices. This created an equity issue since those who opted for home purchase before 1998 benefited much more from the standard pricing. There were also a large number of employees who had no access to public housing and hence no benefit from the welfare housing system.

Housing inequality is also affected by ignoring the differential land value of public flats in different locations. Prior to the 1998 reform, uniform rent and housing price increases were applied to all public housing without taking into account land value. This created inherent inequalities once public housing units were sold and exchanged. In Guiyang, land values doubled from 1992 to 2000 (Table 2.6). Land values in the best locations (Grade 1) are worth four times those in the poorest locations (Grade 6). Although these prices were set administratively, unlike in the pre-1998 reform, they now reflect the market price to a greater extent. One major criticism of the HMP in Guiyang is that old workers' interests are heavily protected under the new policy. Originally conceived as a play-safe political tool to pacify

Table 2.4 Housing entitlements in Guiyang, 1998

	Per capita space provision (m^2)
Provincial-level government departments and institutions	14
Municipal-level and district-level government departments and institutions	11
State-owned enterprises	10
Collectively owned enterprises	6

Table 2.5 Evolution of rent and price of public housing in Guiyang, 1992–8

Year	Average rent for new housing (monthly yuan/m^2)	Average rent for old housing (monthly yuan/m^2)	Biaozhun (standard price) (yuan/m^2)	Chengben (cost price) (yuan/m^2)
1992	0.4	0.4	230	348
1995	0.9	0.7	515	700
1997	1.2	1.0	515	700
1998	1.7	1.5	–	850

Table 2.6 Land values in Guiyang

Land grades	Land values in 1992 (yuan/ m²)	Land values in 2000 (yuan/m²)
Grade 1	600	1,190
Grade 2	450	1,190
Grade 3	350	970
Grade 4	250	640
Grade 5	200	410
Grade 6	150	280

those who feared that their housing interests would be hampered under the new policy, it gradually develops into built-in inequity since the preferential sales policy provides "the old workers" with the opportunity of gaining extra income from heavily discounted public flats (10–20 percent of market prices) (Zhang 1998).

Neoliberalization, urban poverty, and social segregation

In spite of the theoretical and practical soundness of the model, what we have found in Guiyang's experience is troubling. First, by means of pushing the EHSS, the government falls neatly into what we have earlier suggested— the relentless pursuit of marketization as well as a dramatic intensification of coercive, disciplinary forms of state intervention in order to impose market rules upon all aspects of housing. Meeting housing needs is not the primary objective. Economic development is. The following quotation from Guo makes it clear:

> The core purpose of housing reform, put simply, is about shifting in-kind housing allocation to cash subsidy, to eliminate wastage, to normalize pricing, to improve housing quality, to prevent corruption, to achieve a fairer income distribution amongst workers. More important, housing reform is about enabling the housing sector to become one of the leading economic sectors of the country.
>
> (Guo 2000: 9–10)

Although the new allocation formula in Guiyang redresses some of the long-existing inequalities, the many changes of subsidy policies since the late 1980s meant that housing inequalities were already so deeply embedded that they could hardly be redressed by any single policy. More important, the HMP is largely applicable to government employees and state enterprise workers while leaving collective enterprise and private-sector workers untouched, not to mention the migrant workers, who are not entitled to any housing welfare. What we are witnessing in Guiyang is increasing house prices, uneven development, and worsening social polarization. Second, what we see from the model thus far is that the government is only interested in how full marketization of housing is possible, without considering the likely consequences of what happens to many mature housing markets in the West—that is, frequent market failures as a result of over-concentration of players and over-investment. The single-mindedness of the desire to pursue housing commodification by the government easily falls prey to a new culture of "home" wealth creation. Speculative activities in the private housing market by corporate investors from state and collective enterprises disguised as "regular investments" have already fueled prices well beyond the affordability ratio laid down by the government in the last few years. More alarming is the fact that property speculation now coexists with urban poverty. In a recent study, Wang (2004) has confirmed that while the income of the rich in the city is increasing steadily, the income of the poor is actually in decline. In 2002, the annual income of the first decile reached 2,635 yuan and it then began to fall. In fact it was suggested that, taking inflation into consideration, income levels of the poor are in constant decline in the city (Wang 2004: 53). In the next two years, the gap between the rich and the poor increased again as the Gini coefficient rose from 0.4 in 2000 to 0.5 in 2003.[1] The restructuring of China's industrial organization in recent years is perhaps one of the two most powerful social processes that led to urban poverty. The other process is about rural migrants flooding into major industrial cities for low-paid jobs. These two prime factors, as Wang (2004) suggested, fundamentally restructure China's urban space. Pockets of poor housing areas have been formed in poor state enterprise's housing estates as well as in *chengchuncun* (urban villages), which were the original settlements located in suburban areas. Due to urban expansion, the village's agricultural land has been gradually taken over for infrastructure and property development, leaving those undeveloped areas as "sandwiches" within the new urban jungle. From a neoliberal perspective, full marketization of housing according to the logic of capitalism eventually leads to a wide disparity of urban income and wealth, as well as a growing urban poverty sector. Few people take seriously the government's pledge to eradicate poverty by 2011 (Wang 2004: 143).

At the beginning of the housing reform, Guiyang homeowners were prevented from selling their public flats in the first five years. However, the restriction was soon slackened in the face of a more aggressive national drive to boost the housing market. In 2003, the Chinese government officially encouraged urban residents to trade their flats in the secondary housing market in order to move up the "housing ladder" (Qi 2003). At the same time, provincial governments were required to loosen all restrictions on the exchange of sold public flats, while sellers were allowed to retain all gains from the sales after taxes. Given the big gap in houses prices between the public and private sectors, the housing privatization scheme indeed translates itself into immense wealth disparities, resulting in a more and more polarized urban society. The successful development of Chinese cities is to a certain extent sustained by the large number of urban poor. Large-scale real estate and infrastructure development could not happen without the exploitation of low-paid labor, particularly rural migrants. During this stage of capital accumulation, the rich rely on the poor to build their wealth. Inequality and poverty, according to the neoliberal perspective, are key features of a market economy. HMP, seen in this light, is therefore primarily a tool of neoliberal development rather than a policy to improve housing conditions and to address issues of equity.

Conclusion

This chapter demonstrates how housing inequalities embedded in the old welfare housing system could to some extent be remedied under a local policy variant. However, since the HMP is based primarily on one's labor position, it excludes many who are outside the work system. Even given the special policy instruments of Guiyang (through the EHSS and SHS), it could only eradicate some of the inequalities, but not the many embedded inequities from the old welfare housing system. Perhaps this was never the intention of the HMP! Since the late 1990s, and also in the most recent effort to regulate the housing sector, the government has been largely concerned with building quality, price speculations, and, most important of all, the perceived overheating of the housing market and thus the need "to cool off" the property sector. Little effort has been spent on containing inequalities and displacement as a result of neoliberal urbanization (Ministry of Construction 2006).[2] This chapter shows that housing reform has had both a positive and a negative impact. One negative effect is its divisive segregation of the old from the new workers. Given the shifting pricing policies for public flat sales during the evolution of HMP, this segregation has created further inequalities during the reform process. Moreover, there is always a degree of arbitrariness in the setting of location prices, and EHSS also, as a rule, does not consider differential land rent in a fully competitive manner. These issues imply that the potential for inequities in housing allocation has been considerable. In cities and provinces without the kind of innovation and leadership in Guiyang, inequities arising from the HMP are likely to be even greater. This chapter suggests that to fully appreciate the implications of China's housing reform process one should not simply focus on the adequacy of developing institutions of housing governance but also needs to contextualize the Chinese situation in a broader neoliberal urbanization framework. In particular, one needs to move beyond national and local governance in order to see better the interaction amongst different scales of operation (Gough 2002; Tickell and Peck 2003). On this score, this chapter compares the neoliberal development in the West with what has been happening in Chinese cities, in particular Guiyang city in Guizhou province, and suggests that there are striking similarities between the two in terms of uneven development, social polarization, and the restructuring of the welfare system.

Although our evidence is rudimentary, it would be worthwhile to reorient housing reform research along these lines for a number of reasons. First, it should be recognized that housing reform cannot be narrowly construed from a purely economic viewpoint without adequately addressing the impact and the context of China's urbanization process. Second, the dominance of global neoliberalization amongst major world cities since the late 1990s has triggered widespread international concern about its hegemonic influence. Contemporary experiences in governance have demonstrated that urban policy, like housing, is becoming more reflective of the interests of globalized capital as democratic decision-making is seen by public officials as messy, inefficient, and less likely to produce public policies that attract and retain capital in an increasingly competitive global economy. Given China's new-found housing market and its lack of effective regulations, a full-scale mobilization of national housing assets in terms of the EHSS in Guiyang is highly risky, and could be seen as providing the fuel for an accelerated development of neoliberal urbanization—one in which the rights and interests of the ordinary urban citizens are eroded and transferred to corporations and government officials. As we suggested earlier, one important implication of the HMP is the marginalization of city residents outside of the state system, as government housing policy moved too far in the direction of unbridled neoliberalism. To maintain a sustainable housing system, China badly needs to reinvent its social housing sector, instead of passively shunning it in the name of market development.

Notes

1 An estimate by a Nankai University research team led by Professor Chen, Zongsheng.
2 The latest policy (June 2006) to regulate the housing sector is to ask developers to ensure that the actual flat size must reach at least 70 percent of the proposed construction size of the flat, in order to ward off unscrupulous developers cheating on flat size.

3 Embedded institutionalization

Sustaining rural tax reform

Linda Chelan Li

The very definitive features of institutions—permanence and path dependence (David 1985, 1986; Arthur 1989)—make institutional change contingent upon the emergence of *alternative* institutionalization processes. Apart from executing changes to a pre-existing, durable pattern, the changed, new order also needs to be sustained.[1] Without this new process of institutionalization, the newfound changes would require continuous interventions to sustain them and can become unstable, including a possible relapse to a variant of the previous situation.[2] In other words, actions *alone* will not suffice to sustain the changes originally resulting from the actions.

Then what more is required? What constitutes the institutionalization process that serves to sustain change? Making changes last has been a major preoccupation amongst observers of the Chinese rural tax reforms unfolding since the late 1990s. The reform targeted the heavy extractions imposed on the rural populations and demanded a substantial reduction in the range and level of fees and taxes. Many were skeptical of its chances of success. One popular theme of discourse maintained that the heavy tax burden was historically and institutionally embedded, that previous attempts to relieve peasants' burden, dating back to dynastic times, had all failed, and that this latest intervention was, consequently, unlikely to make any genuine, and lasting, impact (Qin 1997, 2000).[3] Ironically, the reform had in fact had considerable successes, including the "disappearance" of the Agriculture Tax nationwide in 2006.[4] Such reform achievements worked to *aggravate*, rather than ameliorate, the worry over sustainability. The bigger the difference the reform initiatives produced *initially*, it seemed, the larger was the probability that these actions could cause counteracting responses from within the status quo, to the effect that the initial impacts could be neutralized and outweighed, further actions for change made difficult, and the reform made to grind to a halt and eventually backtrack.[5] Such a scenario fits perfectly with path-dependence arguments: actions and initiatives—in the form of "reforms"— are insufficient to change the course of deep-rooted, institutionally entrenched behavioral patterns.

But why is it so? What makes existing practices so resilient and attempted reforms to change them so difficult to sustain? If, according to the theoretical literature, institutional change requires the institutionalization of the new changes for it to be complete, then what makes this institutionalization process possible? In the case of the Chinese rural tax reform, there was the perception that the objective of the reform—a reduction of peasants' burden—would undercut the interests of local officials (Wedeman 1997; Bernstein and Lu 2003; Yep 2004).[6] These interests would need to be compensated, so follows the argument, if the reform was to succeed, and peasants' burden not to rebound. The central government had, to further this aim, formulated two measures, namely local administrative restructuring and downsizing, and the provision of fiscal subsidies through central transfer payments. The intended objective of downsizing was explicitly to reduce total local government expenditures and thus the need for excessive extractions from peasants, with central fiscal subsidy as an incentive or facilitation device.[7]

This dual approach—injecting more fiscal resources from above into local coffers and making downsizing mandatory for local governments—had obvious limits, however. First, the new monies made available were necessarily limited and thus insufficient relative to the scale of the reduction in the tax burden required.[8] In the words of a central official, "the appetite in the localities for central transfers is insatiable. Central coffers simply cannot fill up a bottomless pit" (author's interviews, Beijing, 2002). Central injection of monies would have, therefore, at most a partial effect in terms of compensation. Second, it was questionable whether the sustainability problem could be met sufficiently by reducing the size of local government at the township level. The idea behind downsizing was to eliminate altogether the source of overspending, namely the township officials, or the "excess" of them. If burdens may rebound because township officials lived on extractions, then downsizing would remove, it was thought, a major source of pressure for burdens to go up. Such logic had, in part, contributed to a heated debate recently in China over the status of townships as an independent level of government.[9] This logic was deceptively simple, however. Past practice has seen governments expand regardless of previous downsizing, and official establishment figures had at best a disjointed relevance with actual strength of staff (author's interviews, Beijing, 2002; Yang 2001: 19–45; Brodsgaard 2002). Empirical studies had also raised doubts as to whether downsizing, if achieved, could produce any saving, at least in the short to medium term (Li 2004). As Li (2006a) and others had pointed out, there were inherent structural limits to the degree of local government downsizing in poorer regions.[10]

Li (2006a) observes that the central government's approach to the sustainability issue was embedded in a dualistic framework of analysis, and burden reduction was defined largely as a matter of agency control. Further to this, the current chapter offers an alternative perspective emanating from local experience. In an aggressive program of cadre reforms in a central China county, Xian-an District in Hubei Province, the chapter sees the potential that rural tax reforms—and their goal of reducing peasants' burden—may be sustained not through cost-saving exclusively but through a variety of avenues. The chapter observes that cadre reform had enabled the county to attract additional fiscal resources from senior government levels. The reform also produced some cost-saving. More importantly, the chapter contends, the cadre reform had had a positive impact on the capacity of and propensity for local officials to adjust to the new requirements demanded of governments in the broader context of transitions to a market economy. Through transforming the "structure of interests" of local officials, the cadre reform could subsequently work its way towards helping sustain the rural tax reform.

Reducing peasants' burden in Xian-an

Xian-an District had a modest economy and a rural household income level of about the national, and provincial, average.[11] Similar to many local governments, it was dependent on net fiscal inflows from upper levels to finance its rising expenditure bills.[12] The county-district commenced the rural tax reform in the second half of 2002, as part of a provincial-led development. Here two features are noted of the reform in Xian-an: (1) there was a quite handsome reduction in peasants' burden, attracting praise from provincial authorities; (2) the county secured a high level of compensation in terms of incoming transfer payments.

High burden reduction

The county registered almost instant success in achieving the reform objective in 2002, cutting peasants' burden by 56.7 percent when compared to 2001, and 66.9 percent relative to 1999.[13] In 2003, peasants' burden dropped by a further 9 percent over the 2002 level. Table 3.1 shows the details.

A few explanations of the concept, and coverage, of peasants' burden are in order here. First, the scope of peasants' burden, as used in official statistics, did not cover all revenues collected from peasants. Excluded from Table 3.1 are various taxes, fees, and charges that did not "target specifically the rural population," but were imposed on economic activities and public services generally— and thus were also paid by peasants both before and after the rural tax reform. Examples were school-related fees (books and stationery, boarding and meals, etc.), the road maintenance fee, the motor-cycle license fee, and value-added taxes. In the case of the last item, for instance, peasants needed to pay value-added taxes, as urban dwellers did, when they bought and sold agricultural and consumer products (State Council 1991; author's interviews, Wuhan, 2004).[14]

Second, the scope of peasants' burden, apart from the exclusions above, constituted three concentric circles—central, provincial, and sub-provincial— reflecting the different sources authorizing the extraction.[15] On the first circle, the centrally endorsed peasants' burden, pre-reform, included six categories: (1) Agriculture Taxes and surtaxes, (2) the three village levies, (3) the five township levies, (4) Slaughter Tax, (5) education surcharges, and (6) education fundraising.[16] Before the reform provincial government could also

Table 3.1 Peasants' burden in Xian-an (million yuan)

	1999 (pre-reform)	2001 (pre-reform)	2002 (post-reform)	2003 (post-reform)
A Centrally endorsed burden	44.7	37.1	22.9	20.8
B Provincially endorsed add-ons	4.8	0.2	0	0
C Local add-ons (*luan shou-fei*)	19.6	15.6	0	0
A + B + C Total peasants' burden	69.1	52.9	22.9	20.8
Reduction rate (%) (A + B + C)	n/a	n/a	66.9 (over 1999) 56.7 (over 2001)	70 (over 1999) 60.7 (over 2001) 9 (over 2002)

promulgate fees for peasants (for example the rural flood-control water charges in Hubei) and these constituted the second tier.[17] A third tier of peasants' burden comprised fees imposed by sub-provincial authorities, which were, in theory, illegitimate. These were described as the "local add-ons," as shown in Table 3.1. These figures were normally not reported, thus would not have been available if it hadn't been for a local survey conducted on the eve of the tax reform in 2002 (author's interviews, 2004). Furthermore, the first-—and second-tier revenues reported in Table 3.1 would need to be adjusted downwards by approximately 20 percent to as high as one-third to take into account the failure in tax collection, as part of the "abandoned land syndrome" and outgoing migrant labor.[18] The impact was that the actual burden reduction, based on revenues actually collected before and after the reform, would be smaller than the official rate.

Bearing in mind these complications, the official burden reduction rate of some 60 percent (as in Table 3.1) was still three times as high as the national requirement.[19] The local leadership also closely followed the reform-related performance indicators the provincial government imposed, and won the "distinguished performance" provincial award (*shuigai xianjin danwei*).[20] However, as I have already noted, the considerable success in burden reduction also brought the issue of sustainability to the forefront. If Xian-an could, and did, cut rural extractions by more than one-half in a single year, what other things had it also done, or did it need to do, if such initial achievement was to last?

High compensation

This question is partly answered by the remarkably high compensation rate, measured in terms of the proportion of transfer payments to the lost revenue from *legitimate* burdens, that Xian-an had obtained subsequent to the tax reform. Table 3.2 gives the details. Two observations flow from Table 3.2. First, the loss in revenue in terms of "legitimate burdens" was more than compensated by inflows from central and provincial coffers, at 120 percent in 2003, and 113 percent in 2002. These were extraordinarily high levels of compensation, bearing in mind that Guangdong Province, whose provincial budget was three times as large as Hubei's—and which was thus in a much better position to give more compensation to localities—in 2003 reported a compensation rate of *just* 70–95 percent (author's interviews, Guangzhou 2004).

Second, despite the high compensation rate, there was still a considerable shortfall of some 40 percent if local add-ons were included in the calculation. Available information indicates that *total* reduction of burdens, which would include the "illegitimate" local add-ons, amounted to some 30 percent of pre-reform local expenditure, almost doubling the share of "legitimate burdens."[21] It was plainly clear that the rural tax reform put substantial pressure on local government finances, given the historical existence of local add-ons, and the exclusion of these in the calculation of compensation through transfer payments. Table 3.3 shows the three categories of transfer payments the county received under the rural tax reform. First is a fixed amount of "regular" transfer payments coming largely out of central coffers. Its intended purpose was to make up for the *structural* shortfall of local revenue resulting from reform, since the reform mandated the slashing of fees formerly authorized by central authorities. Its calculation followed a standard, nationally devised, formula taking into account the gap between "regular" revenues and budgeted expenditures at the township and village levels, and covered basically the loss of revenue from those "legitimate" burdens.[22] "Nonregular" revenues—those illegitimately imposed local fees and charges—were not included in the calculation and would go uncompensated.

A second, smaller category is "transitional" payments aimed at facilitating the process of downsizing in local governments. As mentioned previously, the rural tax reform package required local governments, as a collateral measure, to reduce staff numbers and cut administrative costs. In practice, downsizing incurred *more* cost, as departing staff were generally paid in full (salaries plus allowances) during the first three years of absence, if not even more.[23] A survey of records found that the central government had provided for special subsidies to sweeten the process as early as 2001. Central documents

Table 3.2 Transfer payments under rural tax-for-fee reform in Xian-an (million yuan)

	2002	2003
Reduction of total burdens R (A + B + C) (over 2001)	30.0	32.1
Reduction of legitimate burdens R (A + B) (over 2001)	14.4	16.3
Transfer payments (TP)	16.3	19.5
TP as % of R (A + B + C)	54.3%	60.7%
TP as % of R (A + B)	113.0%	119.6%

Table 3.3 Rural tax-for-fee transfer payments, Xian-an (million yuan)

	2002	2002 (%)	2003	2003 (%)
'Regular' payments	11.3	70	11.3	58
'Transitional' payments	2.2	13	2.2	12
One-off payments	3.2	20	6.0	30
Total	16.7	103	19.5	100

issued in late 2001 prescribed that central coffers would subsidize, for three years, the payroll expenses for "streamlining" (*fenliu*) staff who were formerly employed within the official establishment (*bianzhinei*), whilst provinces were to shoulder the costs of those staff employed extra-establishment (*bianzhiwai*).[24] Implementation was apparently slow, however. Ministry of Finance officials still expressed reluctance to commit central funds to that effect as of 2002/3. "It was up to the localities," one senior national finance official had said, "to cut costs to cater for the loss of income previously obtained by problematic means" (author's interviews, Beijing, 2002). At the provincial level, the mentioning of central transitional payments had to wait until 2003 in a provincial report on the reform (Wang 2003a: 9–10).[25]

The third category, the "one-off payment," was solely financed within the province. In Xian-an, as Table 3.3 shows, this was an even larger sum than the transitional payments. It was also the only variable category out of the three, with the amount in 2003 double that in 2002.[26] Its share of the total transfer payments soared from 20 percent in 2002 to 30 percent in 2003. Despite its rising importance, this third category was not mentioned in provincial official documents until late 2003.[27] There were also no clear guidelines to govern its allocation. Local officials explained that the 6 million yuan sum in 2003, attributable to several sources, was generally a result of lobbying and bargaining with provincial officials.[28]

Provincial officials did not tell us how they came to this figure (the 6 million yuan). There was no pre-set, and transparent, formula to do the calculation. If there had been one, all localities would have tailored their work according to the criteria in order to secure the monies. The province could not, then, honor the commitments. It simply did not have sufficient monies to give to all those who met the required standards. Indeed this "one-off" payment is very much an uncertainty:

> We don't know for sure whether it will still exist this year, much less how much we can secure.
>
> (Author's interviews, 2004)

The rule of the game was, therefore, particularistic lobbying through achieved results. Superior levels were persuaded that good work in policy implementation merited additional rewards, though they retained the liberty to change the criteria. As it turned out, Hubei Provincial Government announced a separate category of "merit-based" payment applicable to *all* counties from 2004.[29] The criteria of award remained opaque, but the payments were now universally applied to all localities, or at least the existence of the payments itself was made known to all. To this extent Xian-an's successful implementation of government reforms, and lobbying for fiscal support in return, has had an impact on higher-level policy.[30]

Cadre reforms: building capacity or cutting costs?

What kind of government reforms had brought such substantial fiscal reward to Xian-an? Commencing in 1999, Xian-an's government reforms quickly attracted national and provincial attention. In three years the number of state-salaried personnel fell by 25 percent, and bold moves were initiated to adjust the role and structure of township governments.[31] These reforms formed the backbone of the latest local government reform at the township level across Hubei Province from 2004.[32] However, as the following discussion points out, the important implication of these government reforms did not reside in the direct savings in personnel expenses they might bring, but in their perceived potential, as reflected in the discourse on the reform, to transform local officials from being "targets" to *agents* of change.

Downsizing had, traditionally, been held to hold the key of the success of rural tax reform, and government reforms in general. The reason behind this almost sole focus on downsizing was the perception that overstaffing was *the* problem in government, so that downsizing became a natural response. Along these lines, *the* question for the sustainability of rural tax reform became this: could local government be made slimmer, so that peasants' burden would not rebound? But, as noted previously, to the extent that downsizing had aimed at cutting bills, this had more often than not failed. The 1998 State Council downsizing was an utter failure in this respect—central expenditure on staff-related items *increased* in the few years after downsizing, rather than decreasing.[33] Studies on local government also discovered a similar phenomenon: reform cost (Li 2004). A senior central official in charge of the policy admitted to the author that, despite official rhetoric, downsizing exercises nationwide had, by and large, failed to produce genuine savings:

> The reality is, we have found out, after the three-year transitional period, the state coffers still have to pay the streamlined [*fenliu*] staff, though the original plan was to have zero staff costs by then. It is thus unrealistic to expect direct saving from reducing the number of serving staff. Saving may be achieved only when there is a high level of political mobilization—under such circumstances people may feel obliged to leave without compensation. But this is quite out of the question given the socio-political climate of the present day.
>
> (Author's interviews, Beijing, 2004)

Reflecting the focus on payroll was the discourse on "subsistence finance" (*chifan caizheng*). Since the 1990s it has been commonplace to find reports complaining of the large portions of local government budgets being "eaten up" by payroll bills and staff-related costs, leaving too little monies for investment (e.g. Wang 1998; Liu 2000; Gao *et al.* 2003; Wang 2004). These reports invariably focus on the dwindling share of "productive" expenditures (*sheng chan xing zhi chu*) in the local budget, as against administrative and policy expenditures (*xing zheng shi ye xing zhi chu*).[34] However, it is misleading to take the ratio between these two broad categories as an indication of the number of state-salaried personnel, and of the efficiency of government. A close look at the statistics reveals that staff costs formed part of the "administrative and policy" expenditures only. For instance, of the total local education expenditure in 2001, payroll costs for teaching and administrative staff at schools accounted for 62.7 percent, with the rest being housekeeping (*gongwu fei*) costs (8.8 percent), operational (*yewu fei*) costs (6.5 percent), purchase of equipment (7.1 percent), minor renovation (8.7 percent), reception and entertainment (0.4 percent), and other costs (5.7 percent).[35] On the whole, payroll accounted for around 55–60 percent of the total provincial budgetary expenditures.[36] Nationally, state payroll costs as a share of gross domestic product (GDP), at 8.5 percent as of 2002, were on a par with a sample of OECD (Organization for Economic Cooperation and Development) and developing countries.[37] Ultimately, the concern in question thus appeared to be one not of overstaffing, but of the non-performance of existing government personnel. This observation was confirmed in the author's discussions in China:

> The issues are more complex than mere downsizing. There are too many and too few [people] in the government at the same time—too many at the time of distributing benefits, but too few when assigning tasks. Motivated and capable staff are in short supply.
>
> (Author's interviews, Beijing, 2002)

If downsizing cannot possibly cut costs, what benefits, in terms of improving government efficiency and performance, may it bring? On this point, Xianan's former Party Secretary, Song Yaping, had this to say, shortly after he was promoted to the provincial government:[38]

> Lack of economic development is often not due to the relative lack of resources—natural resources, capital, etc., but to an out-of-date government system wherein the government is used to perform many [unnecessary] tasks. We are stuck with a large fleet of state-salaried personnel ill-adapted to the needs of a market economy. But the crux of the matter lies less in having "too many" cadres than in what they should do. After months of investigation in my early days in office [in Xian-an], I concluded that to achieve development we had to first

reform ourselves: our government system, our job as government, and our cadres.

(Author's interviews, 2004)

Government reforms in Xian-an thus focused firmly on reforming—not just reducing—the cadres. Some headcounts were slashed through downsizing and administrative restructuring, as elsewhere nationwide, but a lot of emphasis was placed on changing the "outlook and mindsets" of cadres. This they did through an innovative scheme of "selective exposure inculcation."

Sending off cadres to coastal cities

Between 2001 and 2004, over 800 cadres were sent to various coastal cities to work for two years.[39] The scheme of sending cadres to "stand on their own feet" in coastal cities attracted the attention of the national media a few months after the first batch of cadres left home. Unlike previous cadre training programs, the "sending-off" program did not arrange "postings" for cadres. Instead, participating cadres were expected to join the fleet of migrant workers in the cities they went to, securing jobs on their own. Two amongst the first batch of 187 sent-off cadres talked about their experience in a popular program of Central Television in June 2001. One cadre, a town-ship Party Secretary before he left for Shenzhen, described his experience as commensurate with a "cultural shock":

> How I eventually secured a job there [in Shenzhen] taught me an important lesson: that we have to work our way to success. Success does not come easily. But when it does, after much frustration and numerous reattempts, you understand that it is really *yours*, and you deserve it. One can't feel more satisfied. I was quite confident when I first arrived there. I thought of landing a job at a senior management level in an enterprise, possibly as the assistant to the General Manager, or as Deputy General Manager. I applied for four jobs at that level at Shenzhen's labor center on my first visit. I waited for several days and there was no reply. My friends then told me that employers were looking for a helping hand, not a boss. I gathered, not without some struggle, that I needed to reposition myself. I then deleted my record as the Township Party Secretary from my resume and adjusted downwards my expectations in the job applications. I revised down for several rounds more before I successfully secured my present job of administrative manager.[40]

Another cadre, also a township official, elaborated on what he perceived as the major difference between work at home and in Shenzhen:

> In Shenzhen, we realize what our limitations are. The gap in standards between home and there is stark and clear. Back home, we used to have

a lot of meetings. When we had to get something done, we called together a bunch of cadres and formulated a plan. We then assigned various
tasks to others. The next step was to convene another meeting after
some time to hear reports and examine the progress of implementation,
and if necessary to revise the work plans. We spent a lot of time talking
and reviewing. Work in Shenzhen is quite different. There we not only
plan, but also execute the tasks ourselves. We have to think carefully and
in great detail during all stages of market research, operational planning, implementation, and evaluation. It is a lot tougher compared to
what we were used to. The lesson is: if you cannot deliver, others will
quickly take over your job!

(Xian-an District Party Committee Secretariat 2003: 152)

The sent-off cadres thus learned from their "near-real-life" experience of
being a "free-floating" individual, unprotected by their units, looking for
jobs in competitive labor markets in the more developed regions of China.
To ensure maximal effect of the "training," the scheme had four major
parameters.[41] First was the self-help principle in finding a job. There was no
prearranged posting or secondment between units. Second, the scheme cast a
wide net and was intended for all cadres on the state payroll, with the
exception of school teachers and medical personnel who were under 40 years
of age and had a post-high-school qualification.[42] Third was the voluntary
principle. Cadres joined the scheme through voluntary application, with each
unit distributed a quota of available places in accordance with their pool of
eligible cadres. Fourth, cadres were expected to return to the original units
after two years of "training." To symbolize this continuous relationship and
to cushion the harshness of the new environment, a basic monthly living
allowance of 150 yuan was paid to participating cadres throughout the
"training" period.

Xian-an's leaders admitted that many cadres found the scheme harsh and
difficult to live with. Internal investigations discovered that about 5 percent,
or 34, of the 646 participating cadres between 2001 and 2003 did not leave
home. Some started small businesses in the vicinity; others simply stayed
idle. On the other hand, some successfully "transformed" cadres opted not
to return after the two-year "training." As of 2003, 47 had extended their
"training" for more than a year, after the original two-year term had
expired. Table 3.4 gives more details.

Whilst some former cadres chose to stay in their new position in the coastal
cities—they had apparently adapted to their new roles—the majority did
return to Xian-an after two years. Table 3.4 shows that 165, or 72 percent, of
the first two batches of 227 sent-off cadres returned. A considerable share of
these, especially those of the first batch, were subsequently placed in strategic
positions at district and township levels.[43] Those extending their stay also
outnumbered those opting to stay home, suggesting that the scheme had so
far attracted more motivated cadres than unwilling participants.

Table 3.4 Sent-off cadres, 2001–4

Joining the scheme		Due to return (as of February 2, 2004)	Returned	Extended "training"	Staying home
2001	187	Yes	165	47	
2002(1)	40	Yes	Being	18	
2002(2)	203	Yes	arranged		
2003	216	No			34
2004	200	No			
Total	846	430	165	65	34

After five batches in a row, the scheme was tightened up in early 2004. First, to raise the quality of participants, the voluntary principle was to be more strictly applied. Units would face a severe penalty should they use the scheme to penalize "unpopular" cadres. Second, to motivate quality cadres to join the scheme, returning cadres would be given priority, where applicable, in job assignments to positions of leadership. In view of the dwindling pool of eligible cadres, those who had participated would be eligible for a second round.[44] Third, overstayers would not be paid the monthly stipend three years after the original training term ended. These cadres would remain in the official establishment and they could, theoretically, return to retire. Fourth, to improve communications with the sent-off cadres, a website was launched and individual electronic mailboxes installed.

The scheme contributed to some direct savings. The sent-off cadres, during their "training" period, were temporarily taken off the strength of their units. Each participating cadre was entitled to an annual stipend of 1,800 yuan, against an average annual payroll of 10,000 yuan had they not joined the scheme. The average balance of having 400 cadres "sent off" (an average of 200 participating cadres every year, for two years) meant an average annual saving of 3.4 million yuan, or 1.7 percent of total fiscal expenditure in 2003.[45]

There were also indirect economic gains. Returned cadres brought home extended social networks and investors. In 2003, investment projects directly attributable to returnees brought in capital of 75 million yuan. More indirectly, but no less unimportant, was the publicity generated by media attention to the scheme, through nationally televised programs and press reports. The following reflects the sentiment:

> The Central Television has followed our scheme for a full three years since 2001. It released recently [in early February 2004] a four-part documentary totaling 80 minutes. This was great publicity for us. If one minute of advertisement time on a national television program costs 60,000 yuan, we have earned a great deal.
>
> (Author's interviews, 2004)

Cutting costs or recruiting new investors *per se* was welcome, and these achievements were readily employed in official publicity on the reforms. Notwithstanding such material benefits, senior leaders stressed in interviews that the intended objective of the scheme was more about enhancing cadres' capacity to command the changes required for the new market economy and new tasks of government. The sentiment against a pedantic calculation of costs and gains was apparent in Party Secretary Song's remarks made in the context of social insurance reform, another major measure in the local reform program:

> We know the government needs to pay its share of contributions to the social insurance scheme, as the employer of state-salaried personnel. Doing so has cost us additional expenditures. But one should not see this as something negative. When assessing reform we should not focus merely on flows of monies, and on annual budgetary balances. We need to embrace a broader vision, and *there are different ways to do the calculations.* For instance, what if we do not establish social insurance, and thus avoid the additional budgetary expenditures now? The government would still have to pay for pensions when cadres retire in the future. With the insurance scheme in place, all of us start contributing to retirement funds from now on. More importantly, because we have erected a safety net in advance through social insurance, it is easier to conduct other reforms, like downsizing, thus making it possible to gain many other benefits.
>
> (Author's interviews, 2004; emphasis added)

Mr. Song was explicit that the major objective of sending cadres away was *not* about downsizing, though the program also contributed to that effect. It was meant, in his words, "to inculcate a new mindset, and change the attitudes, or orientations towards work and perception of risks amongst the cadres":

> We need to prepare our people if our reforms [fiscal, government, etc.] are to succeed. The big context is the development of a market economy. Our government institutions, and people, must change to cope with, and fit into, the needs of a market economy. Downsizing is part of the change but a narrow and sole focus on the size of government and downsizing can mislead us. What is critical is what the government does; whether it is delivering the "right" services or adding nuisances/stumbling blocks. Sending our cadres to work in the coastal cities—where the market economy was the most developed in China—will help to achieve the transformation of government, make sure the government does the right thing, through changing the mindsets of our people.
>
> (Author's interviews, 2005)

Did the scheme achieve its desired objectives? It may be premature to attempt an assessment given the recency of the reform. The elusive nature of the objective—changing the mindset and attitudes of cadres—also makes assessment difficult and vulnerable to criticism. The following remarks by a first-batch returnee, who had been promoted, give some indication as to how at least some participants, or the more successful ones, perceived the results, and the challenge, of the reform:

> Our [government] reform is not, ultimately, about downsizing, or how many cadres were sent off to work in the coastal cities. It is about enhancing change in how people think. I can observe some differences between returnees and those who do not have similar experience—just in the way they chat with others. The returnees are less interested in knowing your rank, but more in what you have done—like what kind of development you have helped to bring to the locality under your jurisdiction, this sort of thing. ... The world "out there" is large. My two-year experience as a sent-out cadre has left a deep imprint on me. Those were the days when I felt the most free and "light-hearted" in all my life—I finished my duties and there was no excessive supervision, eyes looking from behind my shoulders. After work I could do whatever I wanted, without fear or apprehension. This has a great impact on how we returnees, or at least myself, see work and life. Before when we received an instruction we tended to implement it hierarchically. If you didn't oblige you'd have trouble keeping your job. Now we place more emphasis on communication and feedback. First we'll ask what resources and from whom we can have help with this work, and what are the consequences if it fails to work out well. We are more ready to listen and enquire into the details of a situation—in other words, more "humanized" and less "crude." I can see this new attitude in work has already contributed a lot to the relatively smooth progress in our downsizing and restructuring reforms. We are not a well-off county and cannot afford generous sweeteners. Last year in the middle of a restructuring exercise I stayed up till the early hours talking to a few colleagues who had yet to agree to the plan. When one colleague eventually agreed to sign the papers he asked why I hadn't left and had some sleep. It was hard for an individual to say "goodbye" to a unit where he has worked for decades, and naturally people needed time to give consideration to it. We should have a lot more patience.
>
> (Author's interview, 2005)

Conclusion

Much in the explanation of institutional change involves accounting for sustainability, and the lack of it (or, more precisely, the discontinuation of a previously sustained pattern). Friedland and Alford (1991: 256–9) premise such processes on the contradictions between institutions. As institutions operate on different logics, the conflicts that arise when institutions interact often propel political struggles between groups and organizations that lead to further changes within each of the institutions. The interaction between the market and the family, in different institutional fields, is one example: "Capitalist markets may depend upon families in order to minimize the cost of supplying a labor force, but at the same time, the labor market may undercut the capacity of families to support reproduction" (Friedland and Alford 1991: 256). Interactions between the institutions of family and the market serve to produce, sustain, or cause further changes in each of them. In interactions between segments of the same field—fiscal institution, for example—reform initiatives by Chinese county-level leaders to rationalize sub-county segments of the fiscal system may undercut the county's fiscal autonomy efforts targeting higher levels of the system (Li 2005: 101–2). Institutional change is endogenously embedded in the interaction between parallel institutionalization processes, mediated by conflicts of interest therein.

The story told in this chapter suggests that the sustainability of rural tax reform in a central China county is likely to be contingent, if partially, upon some specific developments in the arena of government reform. Burden reduction could not be sufficiently sustained through changes within the fiscal field alone, and increasing transfer payments in particular, because of the limited capacity of the central state coffers and the "insatiable" demands for local expenses under the current interest configuration. Neither would downsizing be a solution if that downsizing cost more than was saved. Pilot cadre reforms in Hubei pointed to a possible opening to sustaining changes in the rural fiscal arena from developments *outside* the fiscal institution. The "sending-off cadres" program cherished an ambitious if also elusive agenda: to change "targets" of reform, as local officials often so described them-selves, into *agents* of reform. There were initial indications that the scheme had had some impact in this respect. Returning cadres came to perceive their roles somewhat differently, and were more efficient in delivering their duties. If behavioral change requires more time to mature, changes as reflected in discursive communications are easier to note. The scheme had injected new *expectations* into, as well as self-perceptions of, the returned cadres and increasingly into the entire fleet of cadres—and pressure to meet them. Nationwide the focus of reform had moved to reforming the government itself, as pressure to sustain early achievements in the rural tax reform was mounting. The Xian-an reform had, having secured endorsement from the provincial leadership, contributed to deepening government reforms in the province, as well as attracting national publicity. The task was daunting and the stakes were high. The wider application of local experience was often slippery, as what worked for a locality, given the multiplicity of contingency factors, might not work for the rest. That said, this chapter shows the processes in a locality, unfolding over two institutional fields, whereby the challenge of sustaining change in an entrenched state practice could *possibly* be met.

Acknowledgment

Research for this chapter was supported by a grant from the Research Grant Council, Hong Kong (RGC reference: CityU 1064/02H), and forms part of a multi-year project on the implementation of rural tax-for-fee reform and associated institutional change issues in China. Field interviews cited in the chapter were mostly done with officials in Hubei Province, either at the provincial capital of Wuhan or Xian-an District, during 2003–5, and with national officials in Beijing during 2002–4, out of a total of 69 interviews. The references to "author's interviews" in the chapter, except where the location of interviews is specified, refer to interviews conducted in Xian-an District. An early version of the chapter was presented at the 2004 conference of the Hong Kong Political Science Association, at City University of Hong Kong, May 8, 2004, and benefited from comments by John Burns, Hsin-chi Kuan, and other participants, and from Jonathan Unger and Paul Wilding amongst others outside the conference. Kin-on Li provided valuable research assistance to the work leading to this chapter, and much of what is reported here benefited from discussions with scholars in China, in particular Wang Jingyao and Wu Licai.

Notes

1 In all three major types of institutional change (institutional formation, development, and reinsitutionalization) the institutionalization of new additions is key to the process of institutional change. Reinstitutionalization sees those changes to the original institutions being institutionalized again, whilst adopting a different logic and structure from the previous institutions. It is an "exit from one institutionalization, and entry into another institutional form." In institutional development, the original institutionalization process extends to incorporate new elements and contents. It is a continuation, and elaboration, of the same institutionalization process, "a change within an institutional form." Institutional formation refers to the process of exiting "from social entropy," or "from nonreproductive behaviourial patterns" or "from reproductive patterns based upon 'action'" (Jepperson 1991: 152).

2 Indeed the power of path dependence in an institutionalized state is observed to be so strong that in the case of deinstitutionalization there is a tendency for the changes to undergo a parallel process of reinstitutionalization simply to keep the momentum of exit from the original institutionalization process. An example is the deinstitutionalization of gender and family in Western societies, accompanied by the (partial) reinstitutionalization of single parenthood.

3 A reference to the recurrence of the problem of the peasants' burden is the so-called "Huang Zhongxi rule," first coined by Tsinghua University scholar Qin Hui (1997). A scholar-official during the late Ming/early Qing period, Huang Zhongxi had commented on the futility of previous taxation reforms. He maintained that the combination of multiple fees into one tax had only created room for further fees to be added to the new, and enlarged, tax after some time, resulting in a *deepening* of the peasants' burden. Qin wrote a second article on this theme (Qin 2000), which reportedly caught the attention of Premier Wen Jiabao. See a report in *Liaoning Daily*, March 21, 2003, accessed on May 3, 2004, at http://libwisesearch.wisers.net/print.php. The concern over the sustainability of the

reform was explicit in early central policy documents on the reform, including Central Document No. 7 (2000), "A Decision on Launching Pilot Reforms to Rural Fee and Tax System," March 2, 2000, and State Council Notice No. 5 (2001), "On Furthering the Work of Rural Tax-for-Fee Pilot Reform," March 24, 2001.

4 In 2002, some twenty provinces implemented the reform on a province-wide basis. All provinces adopted reform by the second half of 2003, with an average burden reduction rate of 30 percent, surpassing the national requirement of 20 percent. See http://www.mos.gov.cn/template/article/display0.jsp?mid=2004322001794, accessed on April 15, 2004. Guangdong topped the country at 84 percent; see http://gzdaily.dayoo.com/gb/node/2004-02/09/node282.htm, accessed on April 8, 2004. In 2004 the central government, *vide* Premier Wen Jiabao's government report at the second session of the 10th National People's Congress, March 5, 2004, announced new plans to phase out Agriculture Tax in five years. By 2005, twenty-six provinces had abolished the tax, with the rest to do likewise in 2006 (http://www/mof.gov.cn/news/2005030218624745.htm, accessed on May 10, 2005).

5 Li (2006a) discusses the high risk of the reform from an agency control framework. The concern over sustainability also featured prominently in central government inspection of Guangdong's implementation of rural tax-for-fee reform in February 2004 (http://www.gdczt.gov.cn/cz news nr.jsp?newsid=2070, accessed on April 14, 2004).

6 The literature has noted two parallel dimensions in the constitution of interests of the local officials. First local officials are seen as predatory and corrupt. The second sees local officials' reliance on fees as embedded in an ill-developed national fiscal system, which overburdens local governments and leaves many mandates unfunded. Both dimensions have similarly made local officials resistant to cuts in the fees they could charge peasants, though for different reasons and demanding different solutions.

7 Central Committee Secretariat Notice No. 30 (2000), "On Reducing the Staff Establishment at City, County and Township Levels," issued in December 2000, followed by a similar reference in State Council Notice No. 5 (2001).

8 The total amount of transfer payments from central coffers for the purpose of rural tax-for-fee reform was 3.3 billion yuan (2001), 24.5 billion yuan (2002), 30.5 billion yuan (2003), and 52 billion yuan (2004) (Budget Speeches of the Finance Minister at National People's Congress annual sessions, various years). The lion's share of 3.3 billion yuan in 2001 was given to Anhui (1.7 billion yuan), the only province implementing the reform on a province-wide basis in 2001. In 2002 twenty provinces were conducting reform on a province-wide basis, and by 2003 all provinces were involved. Monies were limited as each province would have a notional average subsidy of 1 billion yuan, just over half of what Anhui secured in 2001 (author's interviews, Beijing, 2002, 2004).

9 This theme was subject of a high-profile conference, Conference on the Reform of the Township/Town Level of Government, held at the Center for Chinese Rural Studies, Central China Normal University, Wuhan, February 27–29, 2004.

10 The limits to downsizing included the difficulty of finding alternative employment opportunities, in areas where economic development was still lackluster, for the government officials leaving in downsizing exercises. There was also the observation that the major bottleneck in relieving the peasants' burden rested on rural land reform and increasing agricultural, and rural, productivity; that is, on increasing the supply of revenue, rather than focusing on reducing expenses through cutting government staff. See discussion in http://ah.anhuinews.com/system/2005/01/26/001117840.shtml.

11 Xian-an District was Xianning City (county level) until 1999, when it was renamed Xian-an and made a district of the new and enlarged Xianning City

(prefecture level). It has a population of about 0.5 million, of which 77 percent are rural. The district is accessible by main national highways and rail routes, and is one hour's drive from Wuhan, the provincial capital.

12 Local budgetary expenditures surged 56 percent, from 118 million yuan in 2001 to 184 million yuan a year after, whilst local budgetary revenue (based on the tax-sharing system formula) shrank 30 percent, from 104 million to 71 million yuan, excluding transfers (author's interviews, 2004). The significant drop in local revenue in 2002 was attributable to a revision in 2002 by the provincial government to centralize more revenues to provincial coffers. See State Council Notice No. 37 (2001), "On Reforming the Tax-sharing Scheme for Enterprise Income Tax," December 31, 2001, and Hubei Provincial Government Notice No. 29 (2002), "A Decision to Further Adjust and Improve the Tax-sharing Fiscal System," July 24, 2002.

13 The years 1999 and 2001 were the years of reference Hubei's authorities adopted in assessing reform implementation. The peasant burden for all households after reform was required to be no higher than that in the year before reform, which is 2001 for most counties in Hubei, and at least 20 percent lower than that in 1999 (http://www.cnhubei.com/aa/cal45760.htm, accessed on January 6, 2004; and http://www.cnhubei.com/aa/cal45718.htm, accessed on July 19, 2003).

14 As part of a package of additional measures intended to reduce further tax/fee extractions on peasants and to raise rural incomes, introduced by the central government in January 2004, value-added tax was waived for peasants selling agricultural products worth less than 5,000 yuan per month or 200 yuan per transaction (http://www.china.org.cn/chinese/2004/Jan/484675.htm, accessed on May 11, 2005).

15 According to Central Document No. 16 (1990), "A Decision to Prohibit Firmly Abuses in Fees, Charges and *Tanpai*," September 16, only central government may approve government funds, whilst central and provincial governments share the approval authority of "administrative" fees (*xinzhengshiyexing shoufei*).

16 State Council No. 92 (1991), "Regulation on the Management of Fees and Corvee Services Shouldered by Peasants," December 7, 1991.

17 Only the central government had, officially, the authority to impose *new* fees/charges that specifically targeted peasants after the rural tax-for-fee reform (author's interviews, Wuhan, 2004).

18 Whilst largely a nationwide phenomenon, abandoned land syndrome was rather serious in Xian-an. About one-third of the rural population in Xian-an had left home to work in cities, leaving as many as 40 percent of total agricultural land uncultivated as a result. Abandoned land was often reallocated to remaining households or migrant rural workers for cultivation, and they were taxed at a reduced rate, if at all (author's interviews, 2004).

19 See "Chinese Peasants' Burden Will Be Reduced by 20 Per Cent," *Wen Hui Pao* (Hong Kong), June 13, 2002, p. A2.

20 There were a total of twenty-one performance indicators but the four most important ones were: (1) calculation of taxable land area in accordance with policy; (2) a cap on Agriculture Tax (and surtaxes, including Agriculture Special Products Tax) at 100 yuan per *mu*; (3) burdens per *mu* (about 670 m) not exceeding the level in 2001, the year before reform; and (4) full rebates of excess burdens collected before reform to peasants. The other lesser indicators include, for instance, adequate publicity work on the reform, implementation of the individual burdens' cards scheme, delivery of Agriculture Tax notices to every rural household, abolition of all other kinds of local extractions, etc. (author's interviews, 2004).

21 Computed from information in Table 3.1 and local budget expenditure figures.

22 Ministry of Finance Document No. 468 (2002), "Temporary Methods of Central Transfer Payments under Rural Tax-for-Fee Reform," July 26, 2002; "Operational

Details of Sub-provincial Transfer Payments in Rural Tax-for-Fee Reform in Hubei Province," in Hubei Provincial Government Secretariat Notice No. 39 (2002); "A Notice on Promulgating the Documents on Reforms Related to the Rural Tax-for-Fee Reform," August 8, 2002.

23 In many cases enhanced and early retirement arrangements were offered (author's interviews, Beijing, 2002). The former Party Secretary of Xianan noted that a neighboring county (Jian-li) had a bill of over 100 million yuan for its downsizing exercise (http://ah.anhuinews.com/system/2005/01/26/001117840.shtml, accessed on March 21, 2005).

24 Ministry of Finance (MoF) and the State Commission Office for Public Sector Reform No. 75 (2001), "The Method of the Central Coffers Providing Subsidy for Payroll of *Bianzhine* Personnel during the Period of *Fenliu*," November 2, 2001.

25 The provincial report stated that central transfer payments under the rural tax reform comprised two parts: regular and transitional. But a few months back, a provincial document issued in August 2002 ("Operational Details of Subprovincial Transfer Payments in Rural Tax-for-Fee Reform in Hubei Province") still stated that transitional payments were a provincial and municipal responsibility, with no mention of any central role.

26 There was no breakdown of the proportion of rural tax reform transfer payments coming from the central *vis-à-vis* provincial/municipal coffers which Xian-an received. Province-wide, in 2003 the central government supplied a sum in the range of 1.3 or 1.7 billion yuan to Hubei, whilst provincial government supplied another 700 million yuan to the counties (author's interviews, Wuhan, 2004).

27 In late 2003 it was announced that merit-based transfer payments were to become part of a revised and more elaborate province-wide mechanism in 2004. Hubei Provincial Bureau of Finance Notice No. 14 (2003), "Temporary Mmethods to Mmanage Pprovincial Ttransfer Ppayments," printed in *Finance and Development* (internal journal edited by Hubei Provincial Fiscal Research Institute), 1 (2004), 50–3.

28 These are, for 2003: (1) achievements in downsizing (4 million yuan); (2) overall performance in government reforms (0.5 million yuan); (3) compensation for the non-collection of Agricultural Special Products Tax in 2002 (0.4 million yuan); (4) award of a "progressive unit" in rural tax reform (0.1 million yuan); and (5) others (1 million yuan) (author's interviews, 2004).

29 See note 27.

30 Another example of this kind of "implementation-led" approach to policy-making was discussed in Li (1998: ch. 7), regarding Guangdong's influence on national policy on infrastructural investment.

31 The main changes introduced include: ownership reforms to state-owned enter-prises, a social insurance system for all state-salaried personnel, administrative restructuring and downsizing, job assignment reform, coastal experience exposure for cadres, education restructuring, streamlining fee-administration for enterprises, and township government reforms (Xian-an District Party Committee Secretariat 2003).

32 Xian-an's government reforms were making a wider impact with the promotion of its Party Secretary Song Yaping to the Provincial Policy Research Office in November 2003. Hubei's provincial leadership in November 2003 promulgated a decree to promote reform experiments in Xian-an throughout localities in the province, with trial implementation in seven counties in 2004, and full imple-mentation intended for all counties province-wide by end of 2005 (http://news.sina.com.cn/c/2004-11-04/15534814599.shtml, accessed on March 21, 2005; author's interviews, Wuhan, 2005).

33 One source reported a cost of 70 billion yuan for the central government down-sizing initiative of 1998 (author's interviews, Beijing, 2002; Hong Kong, 2003).

34 The county-level budget sees the largest imbalance between these two categories of expenditure, with productive expenditures accounting for a mere 6–7 percent of the total on average. Nationally productive expenditure amounted to about 40 percent of the total. See Ministry of Finance (ed.) *Fiscal Statistical Information of Prefectural and County Levels,* various years (Beijing: Zhongguo caizheng jingji chubanshe); *Zhongguo Caizheng Nianjian,* various years.

35 Computed from Ministry of Finance (2002: 296–7).

36 The shares in the years from 1998 to 2001 are, respectively, 54, 58, 61, and 60 percent (Ministry of Finance 2002, and various years).

37 The figure for China was computed from *China Statistical Yearbook, 2003,* pp. 123, 158. The share in Germany and Hungary was around 8 percent; Portugal, Denmark, and Finland around 14 percent; Luxembourg around 5 percent; Spain around 10 percent; and the Netherlands 3 percent (Public Governance and Territorial Development Directorate Public Management Committee 2002).

38 Song Yaping, a doctorate in Economics of the Central China Normal University before he joined the Hubei Provincial Government in the mid-1980s, resigned from the government after a few years and worked in enterprises in Guangdong—Guangzhou and Shenzhen, and Hainan—as well as in Hong Kong as visiting scholar during 1988–9, before he rejoined the rank of cadres in 1998. As District Party Secretary of Xian-an from 1999 to 2003, Song was instrumental in the initiation of government reforms there. He left Xian-an after a full five-year term and joined the Policy Research Office of Hubei Provincial Government as Vice-Director in November 2003.

39 For those sent off between 2001 and 2003, 646 cadres in total, 20 percent went to the southern Guangdong cities of Shenzhen, Guangzhou, and Dongguan, 12 percent to Wuhan, 11 percent to three the Zhejiang cities of Wenzhou, Taizhou, and Hangzhou, with the rest in dispersed cities, and a small minority of 10 went overseas, including 2 to the UK, and 4 each to Hong Kong and Singapore. Most worked in enterprises, with most earning a monthly pay ranging from 800 to 8,000 yuan. Another 200 left in late February 2004 (author's interviews, Xian-an, February 2004). Song Yaping confirmed with the author in spring 2005 that this program continued to operate with a new batch of cadres sent off in 2005 (author's interviews, Wuhan, 2005).

40 Extracted transcripts of "I Am Doing Quite Fine in the South," Central Television program, *Shihua Shishuo* (*Talking the Truth*), June 10, 2001, in Xian-an District Party Committee Secretariat (2003: 148–63).

41 Xian-an District Party Committee Notice No. 3 (2001), "Selecting and Sending off Cadres to Economically Developed Areas for Enhancement," in Xian-an District Party Committee Secretariat (2003: 37–40).

42 The benchmark was subsequently lowered after the first batch to under 45 years of age and high-school qualification (author's interviews, 2004).

43 About 30 percent of the first batch of returnees secured leadership positions in the government, or were promoted (Xian-an District Government 2003).

44 Eligible cadres were estimated to number about 2,000, out of about 3,000 cadres in the administrative establishments (author's interviews, 2004).

45 Total fiscal expenditure in 2003 was 200 million yuan, including a net fiscal inflow of 35 million yuan (author's interviews, 2004).

4 Corruption and governance

The double identities of local governments in market reform

Ting Gong

The relationship between decentralization and corruption is controversial. Some scholars treat decentralization as an effective means to improve governance, as it provides a better match of government policies with local interests. Corruption may therefore decrease as a result of diffusing spending power and revenue control across different government levels with clearly defined responsibilities (e.g. Fisman and Gatti 2002; Arikan 2004). Others believe that power fragmentation, or cellularization of polity, increases the proximity between local officials and private corporations/individuals and may in fact create more opportunities for corruption, since it multiplies the risks of local capture of political power by vested interests (e.g. Prud'homme 1994; Tanzi 1998; Brueckner 2000). What explains the proliferation of corruption at mid- and lower government levels we witness in post-reform China, when wide powers were devolved to local officials? Was power decentralization to blame for rampant corruption among local officials? If the answer is affirmative—diffusion of power led to corruption—how and why did this happen?

This chapter addresses these questions by examining China's corruption in the context of its changing central–local relations. It argues that it is not so much decentralization as the incompleteness of power devolution that has contributed to the spreading of corruption in China in recent years. The incompleteness in decentralizing public authority is most clearly reflected in the development of the double identity of local government as both a *state political agent* and a *local economic principal*. As state agents, local governments have received from the central government increased discretionary power to make and implement public policies since the advent of reform. At the same time, they have also assumed the role of local economic principals, taking responsibility for protecting, promoting, and even directly managing local economies. This dual identity places both broad discretionary power and immediate economic benefits within the reach of local officials. Corruption results therefore from expanding discretionary power over economic interests of local governments.

This chapter draws on the principal–agent approach to corruption, known to students of corruption through the writings of Susan Rose-Ackerman and

Robert Klitgaard. It is built upon the analysis of an "agency relationship," which includes a principal or supervisor who embodies public interests, an agent acting on the principal's behalf, and a client or private person with whom the agent interacts (Rose-Ackerman 1978: 6). Corruption occurs when an agent betrays the interests of the principal in pursuit of his own. Despite the principal's desire that his agents fulfill the set objectives faithfully, agents generally have some freedom to put their individual interests ahead of their principal's and will do so if perceived benefits outweigh possible costs.

The question, however, is under what circumstances an agent would be prone to do so. Klitgaard points out the danger of an agent being corrupted by his client, who "seeks to influence the agent's decision by offering him a monetary payment" (Klitgaard 1988: 23). When this happens, the agency relationship breaks up, with the agent virtually working for the client instead of his principal. The agent may also betray the principal when he develops his own independent interests *vis-à-vis* his supervisor's and uses the discretionary power granted by the latter for his own benefit. This leads to a new set of agency relationships where the former agent becomes a principal embodying certain interests and recruiting his own agents to work for him.

Such evolution of "agency relationships" has taken place between the center and localities in China during the reform period. As the state retreats from socialist paternalism, local authorities have undertaken many new social and economic responsibilities and acquired unprecedented power in various areas. Thus, having long worked as mere agents of the paternalistic state, local governments now act like principals themselves, especially in handling local social and economic affairs, where they become the ultimate representatives and advocates of local interests. Local authorities may find parity between their two identities as political agents representing the state and as local economic principals defending local interests, as long as there is no conflict between national and local interests. However, tensions may arise when the two contradict each other. A common dilemma facing many local governments in China's reform process arises when strictly following the center's order as a state agent may damage local interests, while acting solely on behalf of the locality may be deemed disloyal to the center. The dilemma pinpoints a structural limitation of China's decentralization process; that is, it has not led to a downward accountability system and has therefore failed to create democratic governance. What we have seen, consequently, is a surge of corruption accompanying the development of the double identity of local governments. Those who have a vested interest in the locality spare no effort to influence local decision-makers by all possible means as the latter's scope for power rapidly expands, while local officials with personal interests at stake seek to exploit the duality of their government roles for their own benefit.

This chapter looks at the dual role of local governments as both state agents and local economic principals, and the opportunities and incentives the two roles provide for corruption. In doing so, it focuses on two particularly prevalent forms of corruption in China today—illegal land transfers and "little money lockers" (*xiaojinku*). As the chapter will show, both forms of corruption are closely associated with the unbridled expansion of discretionary power at subnational levels and the increasingly deep involvement of public officials in local economic affairs.

Local governments as state agents: opportunities for corruption

The central–local relationship in China's pre-reform era is an outstanding magnification of the agency relationship based upon uniform compliance. The role of local governments then was simply to disseminate the center's policy directives and to guarantee the implementation of state plans. Local deviation from the center was strictly forbidden and subject to severe punishment if discovered. Even during the policy oscillation and organizational breakdown of the Great Leap Forward and the Cultural Revolution, the administrative *modus operandi*, to a large extent, was still focused on strengthening central control at the expense of local discretion. Local compliance was maintained through the vertical norm control along the official ideological line, accompanied by the system of party-sanctioned appointments of the majority of key government officials at local levels, or the *nomenclatura* system. Thus, even if local governments had some special local interests to defend, they were generally unwilling to risk their personal political career to do so for fear of being accused of "localism" (*difang zhuyi*) (Chung 2000: 3).

The status of local governments in the pre-reform period as mere state agents was reinforced by a highly hierarchical administrative structure based upon so-called "vertical leadership" (*chuizhi lingdao*), where decisions were made by the center and channeled down through ministerial branches (*tiaotiao*). The local government was a weak link in this vertical chain of leadership, with national ministries assuming major administrative and economic responsibilities and sending instructions and directives downward and outward to localities. At certain times, the central leadership relied more on regional governments (*kuaikuai*) to implement its policies, such as in the early 1950s and during the Great Leap Forward of the late 1950s. Nevertheless, this did not fundamentally change the hierarchical nature of China's administrative structure: decisions were always made at the center; resources were distributed in a top-down order; and information continued to flow downwards through vertical channels.

The economic reforms and administrative reorganization since 1978 have resulted in a diffusion of state power to local governments as reformers have taken important steps to structurally and functionally differentiate government authority. The party gradually abolished within its organization those departments that duplicated the administrative institutions to loosen its control over local affairs. A wide range of decision-making powers were devolved from the central government to lower levels to promote local incentives and effective governance. Local governments acquired greater managerial power over state enterprises, more flexibility in local budgetary processes, increased freedom to approve foreign investment and to engage in international trade, and expanded jurisdiction over resource distribution and taxation.

The market-driven decentralization, aimed at releasing initiatives and incentives for growth, has no doubt reshuffled power relations among different levels of government and diffused institutional responsibilities. However, it has not fundamentally altered the logic of China's state governance—the government continues to play an important and irreplaceable role in the economy. What differentiates governance in today's China from its past is the central government's need to rely heavily on its local "agents" to rule in an increasingly cellularized power structure. With power being transferred downwards, local authorities enjoy extensive administrative and economic discretion in carrying out government policies as state agents. With the central authority gradually retreating from local administrative and economic affairs, local governments, acting as representatives of the state, not only continue to possess extra-market authority, but they have also obtained additional economic powers. They now control, among other affairs, business licensing, resource distribution, administrative budgeting, local taxation, and trade and investment in their own localities.

According to Klitgaard (1988), three structural dimensions of a government institution are most critical in creating opportunities for corruption: the monopoly power of officials; the degree of discretion that officials are permitted to exercise; and the lack of accountability and transparency in an institution. What has taken place in China's decentralization process is an increase in all three; that is, while the degree of discretion of local officials has increased to the extent of forming monopolized powers, accountability and transparency in exercising these powers have not been established. Such a structure of governance provides enough room for local officials to render favorable treatment to special interests in exchange for personal gain. This is most evident in land-related corruption activities in recent years.

Land is one of the most important state assets in China. In the late 1980s, the government abandoned the traditional practice of administrative allocation of land and began to yield land-use rights to individuals and collectives. To strengthen the role of the market in the economy, the transfer of such land-use rights has also been allowed. This has resulted in a new land-management structure consisting of three major markets: the primary market, where the government owns and leases out land; the second-level market, where developers compete and develop real properties on the leased land; and the third-level market, where the completed real properties are traded. The marketization of land-use rights has provided strong momentum for the growth of the land-developing and real estate industries.[1] Land-use rights have become one of the hottest commodities in the market, and their prices are often driven up many times higher in just a few transactions.

Market allocation of land resources through public leasing and transfer of use rights has increased the efficiency of land use. By including private businesses in public finance, it has also helped alleviate the government's financial burdens. The new land policy, however, has had particularly important implications for local governance, since land management in China is actually handled by local governments on behalf of the state. Local governments represent the state, acting as the *de facto* landowners, responsible for managing and distributing land assets (Deng 2003). The new land policy has not only enhanced the role of local governments as state agents but also reoriented their interest and behavior.

Public land leasing has without doubt served as an important source of revenue for local governments. Since the 1980s, lower-level governments have taken in hundreds of billions of *renminbi* as profit from the taxation and sale of land leases.[2] The Ministry of Land and Resources reported that in some government jurisdictions taxes on land conversion and leaseholds accounted for as much as 60 percent of local revenues.[3]

However, these massive land-leasing activities have provided opportunities for corruption as well as a property boom, as private interests find opportunities to capture public power in land transactions and work together to chip away at state assets. As a result, local officials who possess the *de facto* power to decide whether, how, to whom, and at what price to lease land often succumb to bribery, while many of them also engage in aggressive "rent-seeking" activities. A recent case reveals that Xu Youlai, former head of land administration in Zhoushan city, accepted over Y896,000 in bribes between 1995 and 2001. In addition, he appropriated nearly Y2 million of land reclamation fees from a special treasury account to help a private firm in 2000, which caused heavy economic losses to the state.[4] According to the estimate of some experts, over 20 percent of the money in property development in some localities has gone into bribery and other dishonest practices (Chen 2002).

Corruption becomes possible because land leasing in China is often subject to price negotiations, or so-called "*xieyi zhuanrang*" (negotiated transfers), despite the central government's frequent call for "public bidding" in land transfers.[5] The "negotiated transfers" often take place in an opaque rather than transparent process; nor are they subject to effective regulation. Negotiated transfers, therefore, provide good opportunities for exchanges between public power and private interests. Government officials, for instance, may arbitrarily lower the price of land leasing or utilize their net of *guanxi* (connections) to help relatives or friends obtain favorable bank loans to complete a land deal. Liu Jinbao, Vice-Chairman and Chief Executive of the Bank of China in Hong Kong, was removed from his post for violating regulations to approve over Y1.5 billion in loans to Shanghai land tycoon Zhou Zhengyi, who was not a qualified borrower but had close connections with some high-level officials like Liu.[6] It was reported that in 2002 the average cost of land leasing in Guangdong was only Y107 per m, while the price of real property developed on the leased land reached as high as Y4,000 per m.[7] Even when bidding is conducted, corruption may still take place. Local officials may disclose critical information to the party in their favor or set preferential conditions for that party in the bidding process.

Land corruption has indeed become a prevalent form of corruption in China. In the two-year period from 2003 to 2004, a total of 200,000 cases concerning illegal land deals were investigated.[8] Cheng Kejie, former Chairman of the Guangxi Autonomous Regional Government, is thus far the highest-ranking government official to be convicted for corruption involving illegal land transfers. To please his mistress, Cheng provided a close friend of hers with a land lease of 85 *mu* (0.1647 acres) at Y550,000 per *mu*, Y30 million short of the normal price. He also made arrangements for this friend to obtain loans totaling Y188 million plus some other profitable construction deals. In return, Cheng and his mistress received Y17.3 million and HK$8.04 million in bribes from this friend (Ling 2004). Another example is the Deputy Governor of Anhui Province, Wang Huaizhong. His interference with land transfers after accepting bribes caused a loss of over Y100 million in state revenue.[9] In addition to Cheng and Wang, recent fallen high-ranking officials (at the provincial and ministerial levels) from land corruption include Governor of Yunan Province Li Jiating, Governor of Guizou Province Liu Fangren, Party Secretary of Hebei Province Cheng Weigao, and Chief Justice of Liaoning Province Tian Fengqi. Even the Minister of Land and Resources Tian Fengshan was removed from his post on corruption charges. These cases provide effective footnotes on the rampancy of land-related corruption.

Rent-seeking activities in land transfers lead to huge losses of state assets. According to estimates of the Ministry of Land and Resources, illegal land transfers incur an annual loss of at least several million *renminbi* in state revenue in small cities, while the revenue loss could be billions a year in big cities (Chen 1998: 48). The total loss incurred nationwide in illegal land-leasing activities is reportedly as high as Y20 billion a year.[10]

Land corruption is also responsible for the suffering of farmers, because corrupt officials always try to get as much land as possible from farmers at the lowest possible price. The statistics of the Ministry of Land and Resources revealed that the amount farmland requisitioned for non-agricultural purposes has been on the rise since 1999, with the area of land lost in 2002 double the figure for 2001.[11] Large-scale land enclosure, coupled with avaricious profiteering activities, has had a detrimental impact on farmers. As a report in the *People's Daily* pointed out, "on one side of a land deal, local authorities reap hefty assignment charges, and developers profit amid the current property boom. On the other side, however, farmers whose land is acquired usually get meager compensation."[12] Land corruption, forced relocations, and under-compensation have fueled a surge of protests by villagers against land requisitioning in recent years.[13]

Local governments as economic principals: incentives for corruption

China's reform and especially its decentralization efforts have not only enhanced the local governments' status as state agents by devolving more power to them, but also inspired their interest in entrepreneurial development and reoriented the behavior of local governance. Gone are the days when local governments were simply waiting for and relying on instructions from the central authorities on local economic affairs. On the contrary, local governments are now doing everything possible to pull themselves up by their own bootstraps. While representing the interests of the central government as state agents, they simultaneously assume the role of advocate of local interests in competition with other localities and sometimes even with the interests of the center.

The expanded local discretion in decision-making has been accompanied by the transition of local governments from state apparatus to market-oriented players and, inevitably, the rapid development of local interests. In the pre-reform period, local governments were not responsible for their expenditures and had no strong incentives to boost revenues, because all the localities were financed through national revenue redistributions. Local governments consequently had little financial self-interest to defend. When fiscal decentralization became a critical component of reform, the central–local financial relationship experienced significant changes in two distinct periods. The first period, from the later 1970s to 1993, was characterized by a "fiscal contracting system," also known as "eating in separate kitchens" (*fenzao chifan*), where each level of government was supposed to balance its own expenditure while tapping different revenue bases. Local governments acquired independent sources of income with reduced responsibility for the national budget. As an unintended outcome, the share of the central government in budgetary revenues declined dramatically (Wong 1997). The concern over "losing control" prompted the reformers to replace the revenue-sharing with a tax-sharing system (*fensguizhi*) beginning with the 1994 financial reform. Under the new system, exclusive central and local government tax bases as well as those for shared taxes were established with a view to recentralizing fiscal management while maintaining local autonomy; this was done to provide local governments with enough incentives to develop regional economies and augment revenues (Wong 2000).

The consequences of fiscal reform are complex, as is its impact on the behavior of local officials. First of all, intermittent attempts at recentralization by the center have stimulated a strong desire in local governments to expand financial resources. This is not simply because local governments fear losing what they have obtained. The need for extra-financial resources is also a result of dramatically increased local expenditures.

While the 1994 reform significantly raised the amount of revenue that local governments must submit to the center, local governments have also been asked to shoulder more financial responsibility for social services, price subsidies, and infrastructural construction. On the other hand, unlike the central government, local governments are not allowed to run deficits because they cannot borrow or issue bonds to finance deficits unless this is approved by the center.

In addition to shrinking budgetary allocations from the center and ever-increasing local administrative expenditures, pressure to augment local financial resources has come from strong financial competition with other localities. It is well noted that China's reform in the past decades intensified regional inequality and created geographic winners and losers. As the center openly encourages local governments to pursue their individual comparative advantage, fierce battles for financial resources have broken out at subnational levels. Interregional relationships become increasingly tense as wealthier coastal areas work hard to defend their advanced economic status and the backward inland provinces vow to catch up. Local governments often feel obligated to defend local interests and maximize their own revenues. This explains why many localities have adopted protectionist measures against one another. Some regions have imposed high fees to prevent competitive goods of other regions from entering into their market; others have given preferential policy treatments to local enterprises so as to strengthen local competitiveness; and still others have ferociously fought "price wars" with other localities over similar products and encouraged local residents to buy local products only. But the pressure is also political. As the performance of local officials is now assessed less by their compliance with the center and more by local economic output, revenue growth, and improvements in living standards, they have become much more eager to improve their jurisdiction's financial well-being (Zhang 2002).

Financial decentralization has forced local governments to look for alternative revenue resources and, at the same time, triggered the development of local self-interest and bred corrupt behavior among local officials. This is most evident in the spread of local "little money lockers" where extra- and off-budgetary funds have been stored. With constraints on in-budget revenues, the only avenue open to local governments for financial expansion is to obtain irregular and sometimes illegal extra- and off-budgetary resources. Extra-budgetary revenues consist mainly of retained earnings and depreciation of state-owned enterprises at local levels. These funds emerged from the profit-retention and profit-contracting schemes implemented in the early 1980s that allowed state enterprises and their supervisory bureaus to retain a portion of their after-tax profits to create extra-budgetary funds. Extra-budgetary funds also include various public utility charges and user fees collected by agencies in the administration of state-owned enterprises. Although these funds and fees sometimes remain with enterprises or the levying agencies, local officials generally have no difficulty encroaching on them as long as the enterprises and agencies are within their jurisdictions (Wang 1994). Extra-budgetary funds are technically legal but not well regulated. While the central government regards extra-budgetary funds as a supplement to the consolidated state budget, these funds are largely beyond its control and have been growing without its knowledge, as they are usually underreported in the official records (Zhang 1999).

In addition to the irregular income that local governments obtain from extra-budgetary funds there are off-budget revenues. Off-budgetary funds are not only irregular but also illegal, as they are collected without the approval of the central government and, in many cases, against the state's policies. The main sources of off-budgetary funds include extra fees and surcharges on public goods and services, profits extracted from private enterprises, apportionments, expropriations and fines collected from local businesses or individuals, and kickbacks and bribes paid to local government agencies. While the central government may not have completely lost its supervision over local extra-budgetary revenues, it is virtually impossible for it to exert effective control over off-budgetary revenues (Sun 2001). In the late 1990s, the central government made efforts to improve the management of public monies by introducing the Budget Law and implementing new budgeting techniques. It also intensified the crackdown on off-budgetary funds. These measures brought about further fiscal stress on local governments but failed to stop irregular and illegal budgetary activities.

The rapid expansion of extra- and off-budgetary revenues indicates the divergence of local economic interests from those of the center. It also demonstrates that, with local economic interests at stake, officials at subnational levels are no longer behaving simply as state agents within the official budgetary boundaries. Under economic and political pressures, they must assume the role of local economic principals and seek every possible means to defend and expand local interests.

However, the efforts to increase extra- and off-budgetary revenues often become intertwined with corruption. The relationship between them may be seen in two areas: the way the funds in the "little money lockers" are collected and the way they are spent.

Driven by strong financial incentives and with greater political and economic interests at stake, local officials have sought to collect extra- and off-budgetary funds by expedient instead of socially subscribed means. They sometimes simply divert budgetary funds into extra- or off-budgetary revenues without the approval of the central government. This can be done by making special arrangements with enterprises, such as preferential contracts, tax breaks, and the lax enforcement of tax evasion, so that the latter pay less in state taxes and, in return, give the local government certain benefits. In these kinds of "transactions," the loss incurred in the state budgetary revenue becomes the gain in the local off-budget revenue. The local officials handling the matter may also receive kickbacks from offering tax breaks or other preferential treatments. The state treasury takes the loss, while the gain goes to either the local government or individual officials, or both.

Another, more sophisticated, debudgeting technique is to use budgetary funds to create off-budgetary enterprises. The latter pay taxes like all other enterprises, but, unlike their in-budget counterparts, their finance is not reported and therefore not subject to the state's accounting procedures; thus, their after-tax profits can be easily credited to "little money lockers" as off-budgetary funds. The most effective way to transfer budgetary money into non-budgetary assets is to strip off the productive and profitable segments of an existing in-budget enterprise and turn them into new, off-budget and sometimes private companies. Such practices become possible because, since the late 1980s, the central government has encouraged local governments and other state institutions to pursue "creative earnings" (*chuangshou*) by establishing sideline companies to help ease the center's financial burden. This policy has led to a proliferation of subsidiary companies (*zigongsi*), auxiliary enterprises (*fuzhuqiye*), and service companies (*sanchan*), since it allows all earnings to remain at the institution's disposal. Profits generated by these affiliates go directly into off-budget funds and are beyond external oversight. But, in the process, corruption tends to arise, leading to unsanctioned transfers of state revenues and assets into private hands, or "hidden privatization" (Oi and Walder 1999).

Corruption can certainly occur through loopholes in accounting or embezzlement in any institution. However, the special debudgeting techniques developed in expanding local revenues make corrupt transfers of state assets and revenues much easier and have given rise to "a massive-scale diversion of state assets and profits into the private hands of the officials in charge of them" since the 1990s (Ding 2000).

Corruption occurs when those extra- or off-budgetary enterprises and affiliates created with budgetary funds are made quasi-public or public only on paper. In fact, they are managed by individual government officials or the offspring of officials as private business entities. Consequently, a good percentage of an enterprise's profit goes into private pockets after contractual payments are submitted to the government. The case of the Anhui Mobile Company illustrates how this can be done. Anhui Mobile, a state-owned enterprise, established a communication company with Y2 million of assets in 1999, with 20 percent of its shares controlled by Anhui Mobile and the rest divided among its managers and employees. This new business made a net profit of Y35 million within just two years, and provided each of the four top officials of Anhui Mobile with Y86,500 and all the mid-level officials with Y58,000 each in its dividend distributions. A major reason that this start-up was able to make such a quick and huge profit was that Anhui Mobile gave it the two most profitable projects and also allowed it to use the existing client network. The Yuehai Railway Corporation provides another case in point. Over a period of three years from 1998 to 2000, this state enterprise appropriated Y2.62 million of construction funds from the state budget to finance seven new subsidiary companies. The leading posts in the new companies were concurrently held by the major officials of Yuehai, but they were only expected to hand in to the Yuehai Corporation a fixed amount of profit each year. All the earnings above this fixed amount were controlled by the officials themselves.[14]

These cases exhibit how "hidden privatization" takes place. It is a process where private companies, having originated from public budgetary resources, siphon off and launder state assets as they grow. These private companies have privileged access to profitable projects and production orders from the government due to their connections with the latter. They compete with other private enterprises in the market but are never short of valuable inputs and convenient outlets for their products with the help of government officials. This explains why Chen Xiaotong, the son of former Beijing mayor Chen Xitong, was able to win a highly profitable construction deal to build a compound of luxury apartments near downtown Beijing and why he was offered a 5 percent share in the project, worth Y7.5 million, from a company that was eager to build the compound (Xian 1997).

In addition to the above covert entrepreneurial means, local officials have also used overtly predatory means to expand extra- or off-budgetary funds. When this happens, the local government's helping hand that has assisted local economic growth is replaced by a hand that grabs (Chen *et al.* 2002). For instance, some local governments imposed upon enterprises (state owned or private) and individuals numerous surtaxes, fees, and fines in a capricious manner. This has been referred to as the "three arbitraries" (*san luan*) (Lin 2002): (1) arbitrary fees (*luan shoufei*), referring to ad hoc fees collected on public goods and services such as the public security fee, garbage disposal fee, road maintenance fee, sanitation supervision and inspection fee, and environmental fee; (2) arbitrary fines (*luan fakuan*), which include penalties imposed on businesses or individuals for violating national or local rules such as road occupation charges, pollution fines, and penalties for defying family planning policy and disturbing public order; and (3) arbitrary apportionments or expropriations (*luan tanpai*), comprising compulsory deposits or contributions to various funds such as public security, environmental protection, and retirement funds.

What is startling is not just the preposterous nature of these ad hoc fees, but also their magnitude. It was estimated that, during the early and mid-1990s, the total sum of irregular taxes, fees, and other income collected by various governments and agencies exceeded Y100 billion each year (Wedeman 2000). In Hunan Province, private enterprises were subject to more than 140 types of taxes and fees, while there were nearly 400 kinds of ad hoc fees in Wuxi city in Zhejiang Province (Jia 1999). When it was difficult to impose extra charges, local government agencies might arbitrarily raise state mandatory fees such as those for certificates, registrations, and permits.[15]

The irregular and arbitrary nature of revenue amassment at subnational levels dictates that the consumption of these funds cannot be made immune to abuse and misuse, especially those "off-budgetary funds" that are subject to virtually no oversight of any sort. Once financial resources abound at an official's disposal, incentives as well as opportunities for corruption will increase. In today's China, no less alarming than the illegal and predatory means used to collect extra- and off-budgetary funds is the corruption in spending these funds. To be sure, some off-budgetary funds were used to satisfy institutional needs such as staff bonuses and extra benefits, office buildings, inter-institutional relations, and speculative investments. Some localities had to use their self-collected monies to improve public services such as education, local roads, and public hygiene, since local needs far exceeded budgetary resources distributed from the center. However, off-budgetary funds or "little money lockers" are notoriously associated with the corruption of local officials. The unaccountable nature of these funds as well as the significantly expanded financial power of local officials make corruption possible. Thus, it is not surprising to see the money in the "lockers" being taken by local officials for their own benefit. The terminal decline of Hengshan Ferroalloy Factory in Jiangsu Province is illustrative. Once a medium- to large-scale state-owned enterprise whose products sold well in both international and domestic markets, the Hengshan Ferroalloy Factory was declared bankrupt in 2003 and more than a dozen of its managerial officials were arrested on corruption charges. It was discovered that the plant's 15 departments, 13 subsidiaries, and 8 provincial offices all had their own "little money lockers." Money in these "lockers" had been spent on bribery, entertainment, and bonuses, or, in many cases, consumed or taken into possession by the leaders of these units themselves. The manager of an auxiliary company, for example, used up all the Y2.6 million in his company's "money locker" in just one year simply for personal pleasure (Xie 2005).

The hidden nature of off-budgetary monies allows local officials to engage in formally proscribed activities and to pursue extravagant lifestyles. Slush funds, for example, have been used to pay for lavish banquets. As the National Statistical Bureau estimated, about two-thirds of the revenues of large and medium-sized restaurants in the country came from lavish banquets paid for with public funds each year. The annual total could be as much as Y100 billion, an amount three times the state's spending on education (Huang 1998). A popular saying, "eating bravely and taking carefully" (*dadandechi, xiaoxindena*), well describes today's reality in some localities in China: taking into one's own pocket several hundreds of thousands of *renminbi* may cause trouble, but consuming an equal amount may not be a major problem.[16] In addition to sumptuous repasts, off-budgetary revenues have also been spent on various kinds of entertainment, including dancing, bowling, sauna bathing, and vacationing in health spas. It was reported that 68 percent of the revenues of the nation's big sauna bathing services relied on the spending of public funds. Sightseeing activities were often paid for out of these funds in the name of business trips and study tours abroad, while luxurious vehicles, fancy office furniture, and sometimes housing were purchased as perks for individual officials. Some Chinese scholars estimated that as much as 80 percent of the money in self-raised funds was used for treating guests, purchasing presents, or paying bribes, instead of being spent on institutional advancement. Sometimes money in "little money lockers" was even secretly transferred into personal bank accounts to become private assets (Lin 2002).

This can be seen in the case of Chu Shijian, former Chairman of the board of the Hongta Group. The case brought to light a "little money locker" including more than Y1 billion and $25 million directly controlled by Chu. Without his signature, no one could have access to the money. He used the money for personal matters as well as "rewards" for those who collaborated with him in corrupt activities (Huang and Qiu 1997). It is clear from the above that the local self-interest developed in the course of fiscal decentralization and interregional competition has dramatically increased incentives for local governments to expand financial resources, leading to the proliferation of extra- and off-budgetary funds. Though the original intention in creating these funds may have been to encourage greater productivity and efficiency within the locality, the easy availability of these unaccountable funds has nevertheless contributed to the surge in corruption among local government officials.

Conclusion

The central problem examined in the principal–agent approach to corruption is how the principal loses control over the preferences and actions of the agent due to supervising difficulties, while the agent develops his interests independent of the principal's. The principal's failure in supervision is caused by resource constraints, but it may also occur because defection of the subordinate takes a variety of forms and varies across policies (Brehm and Gates 2000). The evolution of the principal–agent relationship as such has been demonstrated in our analysis of China's changing central–local relations in the reform period. In the two cases examined on pp. 77–9 and 83–5, land corruption and "hidden privatization" in extra- and off-budgetary activities, we see the center's control over resources being weakened while local interests grow to the extent that power over land and financial resources is misused and abused, leading to a prevalence of corruption. However, the so-called "local defection" in the context of China is more complicated than a matter of resource redistribution or a failure in the center's oversight. Since the reform, weakening supervision from above has undoubtedly nurtured the deviation of local interests from those of the center, but deviation of interests alone may not necessarily lead to a surge in local corruption. This chapter offers some important findings on the relationship between decentralization and corruption. First, the decentralization process has made local governments in China powerful state agents with significantly expanded scope for power. Reform changes power relations, but does not alter the nature of political power exercised by local officials. As authority devolves from upper levels, local officials have more opportunities and fewer constraints in using, and abusing, their power. In many areas of resource allocation, they have become the ultimate authorities in determining who gets what, and how and when. Furthermore, the surge of local self-interest and the need to protect these interests have transformed local officials from mere state agents into local economic principals or market-driven players with entrepreneurial and sometimes predatory behavior. The fact that many economic interests are now within easy reach provides a strong incentive for corruption.

As a result of decentralization, the relationship between local governments and enterprises under their jurisdictions has become increasingly intimate. Walder is correct in pointing out that local governments have developed organizational characteristics in many ways like those of industrial firms (Walder 1995). Many localities in China experienced local government-led economic growth based on what Oi terms "local state corporatism," where local officials acted as the equivalent of a board of directors, or sometimes more directly as chief executive officers, in a corporation (Oi 1992). Many government officials or former officials have been directly involved in business activities and gained a new identity as "cadre entrepreneurs" (Gong 1996) or "red-hat businessmen" (Yang 2004). In the early stages of transition to a market economy, the helping hand of the government may be necessary, and the government is expected to gradually withdraw from direct involvement in the economy in order for the transition to be completed. In China, however, this has yet to happen. Rather, the development of local governments' double identity as both state agents and local economic principals has allowed government officials to remain at the center of economic activities and placed economic interests within reach of local officials. Public power and private economic interests have become so intimately connected that government officials can easily shove their oar into money-making opportunities to enrich themselves.

That said, the point here is not that there is anything wrong with decentralization, but that China's decentralization is incomplete and has not yet addressed the structural causes of abuse of power at various government levels. Decentralization is more than just a process of devolution of power; it is where intergovernmental devolution of authority gets institutionalized with downward accountability and its overall goal is to facilitate greater representation of public interests. A decentralization process, thus, has three major components (World Bank 2005): power deconcentration, official accountability, and public representation. A decentralization process without increased accountability and representation becomes mere reallocation of power. On the other hand, when powers are transferred to lower-level officials who are still held accountable to their superiors, such power reshuffles fall short of meaningful decentralization. Finally, decentralization without increasing the participation of those most affected by the exercise of power defeats its ultimate purpose—democratic governance. The ongoing decentralization process in China lacks two of the structural essentials: downward accountability and public representation. What has happened instead in the course of decentralization is that, with differentiated power relations, the scope of power in the hands of individual officials has actually expanded. While power has changed hands (from upper to lower levels), it continues to serve as an effective means for acquiring personal gain, thereby leading to corruption. Decentralization without accountability and representation thus brings about the localization of corruption. This is where the danger of incomplete decentralization lies.

Notes

1 Shanghai alone, for example, built more than 1,000 skyscrapers in the 1990s and expected to add some 500 more in the following decade (Ramo 1998: 64).
2 For example, Guangdong province earned Y9.4 billion, or 42 percent of its revenue, from land leasing in 2002 (*Beijing wanbao* (*Beijing Evening News*), January 3, 2003).
3 Ministry of Land and Resources (2003), *Guotu ziyuan diaoyan* (*An Investigation of National Land Assets*), Beijing: Zhongguo Dadi Chubanshe.
4 For details, see "Corrupt PRC Land Official Receives Life Sentence", *FBIS-China*, February 10, 2002.
5 It was reported that by 2003 only about 5 percent of the land leasing nationwide had gone through a bidding process, with the rest all being done through negotiations (*Nanfang ribao* (*Nanfang Daily*), March 12, 2005).
6 The case attracted a lot of public attention domestically and abroad. See "Shanghai Land Tycoon Zhou Zhengyi Detained on Loan Irregularities", *FBIS-China*, June 2, 2003.
7 See note 2.
8 The data were disclosed in an interview by CCTV's anchorman Bai Yansong with the Deputy Director of the Land Management and Utilization Bureau of the Ministry of Land and Resources (www.xinhuanet.com, July 4, 2005).
9 The case was well publicized in the Chinese media. See, for example, *Ta Kung Pao* (Hong Kong), February 23, 2004.
10 See note 1.
11 See note 2. This was further confirmed by the World Bank's country brief showing that arable land in China shrank by 4.3 percent in 2003 alone (www.worldbank.org.cn/English/content/China04-04.pdf, accessed on May 30, 2005).
12 *Renmin ribao* (*People's Daily*), August 7, 2004.
13 A study conducted by the Institute of Rural Development at the Chinese Academy of Social Sciences gathered 130 cases of rural protests in the early part of 2004 and found that 87 of them were related to land disputes (Zhao 2004).
14 The cases are cited in Zhang Shan's (2005) article, which discusses various ways to encroach upon state assets.
15 In Hebei Province, for example, the fee for a birth certificate was more than twenty times the amount stipulated by the state. *Renmin ribao* (*People's Daily*), June 21, 1999.
16 In 1998 a deputy bureau chief in Tainjin was sentenced to death with a two-year reprieve for spending Y530,000 of public funds on eating and entertaining during a fourteen-month period. This is believed to be only the first case of harsh punishment for extravagance (*Mingpao*, November 1, 1998).

5   Land and power brokering in China's townships

You-tien Hsing

This chapter concerns the process of power at the periphery of state bureaucracy, with a focus on township governments and their land development projects since the late 1980s. There have been debates over the relationship between the central and local state in post-reform China. That debate is mainly focused on whether the central state has waned, and the local state been empowered by decentralization; and whether the local state has turned developmental or predatory as the result of decentralization.[1] While the debate offers great insights into the *outcome* of decentralization, less attention is paid to the actual *processes* of territorial power under the grand scheme of decentralization. I will explore the latter issue in this chapter, and will treat decentralization as a contentious process of power reconfiguration instead of a top-down policy package. The concept of "process of power" is framed in the Foucaultian sense that power is not a fixed, cardboard-like entity and enclosed regime, but an open, endless strategic game (Foucault 1982).

In order to understand the working of decentralization in specific historical moments and places, we need to unpack the general category of the "local state" and identify the specificity of each level of the local state. Examples of such efforts abound.[2] I follow the footsteps of these writers, and choose to focus on the township government.[3] I will examine the workings of the township government not just as an atomized actor, but also in its *relationships* with other state actors. The political and organizational characteristics of the local state lie in its *relationship* with other local states, especially those immediately above and below it in the territorial hierarchy.[4] The power process of township governments can be better understood in their interaction with the governments above them, and the village collectives below them. The theoretical assumption is that the state itself is a set of multilayered territorial processes rather than a consolidated outcome and unitary actor (Crzymala-Busse and Luong 2002; Corrigan and Sayer 1985).

The relationship built around the township government is particularly interesting because of townships' power position between the state and the peasantry. Lying at the lowest level of the state hierarchy, the township government has limited formal authority. Yet it is also the most authoritative representative of the state in the villages. Located in this in-between space, township government officials' political power bears two main characteristics.

One is the high level of *uncertainty* in their delegated power. The general principle of hierarchical supervision in China's bureaucratic system leaves the boundary of authority between levels of governments under-defined. Thus, the scale, the scope, and the sustainability of township governments' formal authority depend on the will of their superior governments. The latter can extend or withdraw township governments' authority over resource allocation, and add or reduce township governments' responsibilities in policy tasks. To cope with such uncertainty, township government officials' strategies would be to bypass the scrutiny of the superior government while increasing the control over immediately attainable political and economic resources before they are taken away by the superior government.

The second feature of township governments' power is their under-defined authority over the villages. As ambiguity produces uncertainty in township governments' relationship with the superior government, such ambiguity proves to be an advantage for township governments in stretching their authority downwards over the villages below them. Theoretically the villages are "autonomous organizations," not a part of the state system. In practice, however, the Chinese Communist Party (CCP) state has become a strong presence in villagers' lives through various organizations. The party branch secretary, appointed by the township party branch, is generally recognized as the "*yibashou*" (the number-one boss), while the elected villagers' committee chair serves as the "*erbashou*" (the second man in charge) of the village.[5] As a result, the commanding hierarchy of the CCP has made the villages an extension of the party-state, and village leaders subordinate to township governments.

The ambiguity of the administrative status of villages gives township governments an under-defined authority over them. Taking advantage of such ambiguity, township governments would try to stretch their influence and consolidate their control of village resources, including village land. With the uncertain and under-defined power, township officials operate as power brokers between the state and the peasantry.[6] In this chapter, I will use the case of land rights transfer and farmland conversion to illustrate township governments' power brokerage between the superior urban government, at one end, and villages, at the other. I argue that the property relation is a power relation, and the township officials' property brokerage conditions and is conditioned by their power brokering between the state and the villagers.[7] The main source of information comes from my fieldwork in towns and villages in Hebei, Sichuan, Shanghai, and Guangzhou between 2001 and 2004.

Urban dominance in rural land development

The rapid expansion of Chinese cities and the conversion of rural land for non-farm uses since the 1980s, especially in the eastern coastal regions, have been well documented (Lin 2005).[8] Urban expansion into rural areas has been led primarily by the urban government on the bases of two legal and administrative institutions.[9] One is the state's ultimate claim over rural land under the persistent state land tenure system. The other is the shift from a rural- to an urban-centered territorial governing system. Township governments' land development strategies are conditioned by these two institutions.

The state's claim of rural land is a general legal stipulation. The Constitution of the People's Republic of China (PRC) stipulates that urban land belongs to the state and rural land to the collectives. Yet it also says that the state has the ultimate claim over "all land in China," including both urban and rural collective land. The Land Management Law further stipulates that the state can requisition any land for "public interests."[10] Under this general yet powerful principle of the state's ultimate claim over all land in China, those who represent, or claim to represent, the state are able to requisition rural land that is constitutionally designated as collective owned. Although collective land requisitions have to be based on "public interests," the lack of definition of "public interests" has made this condition not a constraint, but a legitimizing factor in collective land requisition.

Parallel with the legal regime of state land tenure are the administrative devices for reinforcement and implementation. The first device is the *shift from rural- to urban-centered territorial governance* in the 1980s. During the Maoist era, China's urban and rural areas were governed by two separate systems. Within each province, there were urban governments administering small urbanized and suburban areas, leaving the majority of the provinces ruled by rural-based administrative units like prefectures and counties (Chung and Lam 2004: 949–50). Since the majority of the Chinese population and land were rural at the time, prefectures and counties commanded greater influence than cities over rural resources, including rural land.

Territorial administration underwent a major shift from a rural- to an urban-centered system in the early 1980s. Since 1982, based on the principles of comprehensive regional planning and rural–urban integration, provincial governments started to turn rural counties and prefectures into cities, and/or merge them with existing cities.[11] When a prefecture is merged with a city, rural counties (and townships below the counties) that were previously under prefecture administration will be ruled by the newly created prefecture-level city. These new prefecture-level cities are in fact city-regions that include urban centers and the rural hinterland within their jurisdiction. The key element of such jurisdictional restructuring is to put the rural hinterland under the administrative authority of the government of prefecture-level cities, called "*shi guan xian*" (city governing counties) or "*shi dai xian*" (city leading counties).[12]

The principle of hierarchical supervision in China's territorial and bureaucratic system gives the leading city government an increased personnel and budgetary autonomy from the supervising provincial government, and the commanding authority over its rural hinterland and rural governments. This new regime of territorial governance has reversed the previous system of county-centered rural governance and placed rural counties and townships under the administrative authority of the newly created or expanded urban government. Urban governments are now designated leaders of city-regions that include both the urban centers and rural hinterland. The principle of "regional integration of rural and urban areas" turned out to be an attempt to shift the control of rural areas and resources from rural to urban governments.

Another device is the territorially oriented *new land management regime* that emerged in the mid-1980s and was symbolized by the establishment of the new Ministry of Land Management in 1986. Local bureaus of land management were established in the ensuing years. The bureaus at the municipal and district/county levels are formally recognized as the exclusive representatives of the state (Wu 1998).They were granted authority to prepare annual land-use plans, allocate quotas, and issue licenses for farmland conversion, requisition collective land and transfer it from collective to state ownership, and monitor land-lease sales.[13] The stated mission of land bureaus is farmland conservation. Yet under the growth-minded urban government leaders, local land management bureaus have become an important channel for the urban government to control rural land inventories, and oversee farmland conversion and land-lease sales.

One of the key tools of urban government's land control is *urban development plans*. Urban development plans are drawn on the basis of population and economic growth projections, which are often inflated. The inflated growth projection in turn helps justify the incorporation of large areas of village farmland into the "planned" urban areas, limit the use of the land in the planned area by rural townships and villages, and legitimize urban governments' expansion into rural areas. Another effective tool is the *quota system of farmland conversion* for non-farm uses. The Ministry of Land and Resources draws national annual land-use plans and allocates a quota of farmland conversion to individual provinces. Provincial bureaus of land management then allocate the quota down the territorial hierarchy to subprovincial local governments. While the urban governments bargain with their supervising government agencies for a larger share of the farmland conversion quota, towns and townships at the bottom of the hierarchy are often left with few quotas of farmland conversion. This system in turn made the townships' farmland conversion automatically illegal in most cases. Yet another decisive advantage of the urban government over rural land is the urban government's *monopoly of the land lease market*. In 1988, China's land leasehold market was formally established. It makes a clear distinction between ownership and user rights, and gives the latter a price tag with a fixed period of leasing time. But the newly established land-lease market is open to state-owned land only. Villages as owners of the rural collective land are not allowed to lease out their land to outside investors.[14] Rural land can be leased out only after being converted to state ownership. This means that urban governments have the exclusive authority to expropriate rural collective land through the procedure of land requisition (*zhengdi*).With their self-defined "public interests," they use their own development companies or team up with developers to build commercial housing complexes, industrial parks, development zones, markets, golf courses, resorts, and amusement parks.[15]

Equipped with legal rights and administrative authority over rural land, and armed with the policy tools of urban development plans, farmland conversion quotas, and a land-lease sales system, urban governments seem to have a decisive dominance over rural land. Compared with the urban government, rural-based townships have limited legal rights and administrative authority in land rights and land use. But townships have become increasingly active and important in rural land development since the mid-1990s. As higher-level urban governments seem to have monopolized the administrative resources and legitimacy to control the rural land, how do low-level townships manage to carve out their land interests? What are their strategies for bypassing the scrutiny of urban governments to assert their own control over village land? The following section will address these questions.

Brokering property rights

Township governments' strategies for controlling the rural land are conditioned by their peripheral power position within the state, and their financial and political crises since the mid-1990s. At the bottom of the bureaucratic hierarchy, township governments not only have limited formal authority, but also bear the heavy tasks of collecting both state and local taxes from the peasants, and carrying out highly unpopular public policies like family planning and cremation. In addition, the townships' financial condition started to deteriorate in the mid-1990s. Under the scheme of fiscal decentralization, with stagnated provincial transfers and increasing local expenditures, townships have been heavily dependent upon extra-budgetary revenues that are generated locally, especially profits from township and village enterprises (TVEs). But many of the TVEs started to fail in the mid-1990s, due to the lack of economies of scale and increasingly competitive markets for low-end products. Many township governments fell deeply into debt crises, and could barely pay government overheads and staff salaries.

In the early 2000s, with the emergence of the discourse of "*san-nong wenti*" ("three-agricultural problems," namely, problems of peasants, villages, and agriculture) and "reducing peasant burden," township cadres are seen as the major cause of local corruption and peasant burden by the public and the media. Worse still, agricultural taxes, which were the bases of local government finance in agricultural regions, were abolished in 2004; and there have been more talks about downsizing local governments, especially township level governments.[16] Already the weakest link in the state bureaucracy, the township's political legitimacy is further threatened and the uncertainty of its power position within the state system increased. In the formal process of urban governments' requisition of collective land, township officials are responsible for negotiating with village leaders for compensation and relocation. But township officials have limited incentives to carry out the thankless tasks. One disincentive comes from the intra-state profit-sharing scheme. The Land Management Law stipulates that of the total conveyance fees 30 percent should be submitted to the central government, and 70 percent can be retained by local governments.[17] However, township governments at the bottom of the state hierarchy often receive little. Among the local governments, provinces and prefecture-level cities get 20 percent each. The remaining 30 percent of the total is kept by county-level governments. Townships' share is usually not fixed, decided by county-level governments above them, and can be as low as 5 to 10 percent.[18] From the township leaders' perspective, the reward does not match their demanding tasks of negotiating with and relocating villagers in the process of *zhengdi*. It takes a lot of persuasion, mobilization meetings, and frequent home visits, often in the after-dinner hours, when villagers are back from the fields. Because development projects are financed by bank loans, township officials are often under great pressure to remove the peasants and clear the sites for the construction to start as fast as possible. They also have to be skillful enough not to trigger conflicts that will lead to villagers' *shangfang* (personal visits to lodge complaints to higher-level governments) or *xinfang* (letter visits). *Shangfang* and *xinfang* can not only seriously delay development projects, but also have negative effects on cadres' performance evaluation.[19]

Township leaders are also keenly aware of the huge profit that urban governments make from leasing expropriated land to outside developers, usually ten to twenty times higher than the compensation paid to the peasants.[20] Under financial pressure and political uncertainty, and tempted by profits from land, underappreciated township leaders start to launch their own land development projects. In some cases the projects are totally legal, like renting collective land designated as construction land to investors to build factories. This arrangement does not involve the highly sensitive issue of farmland conversion, nor does it require the formal procedure of leasing and land rights transfer from the collective to the state.[21] But most of the projects are more complicated than that.

From the perspective of the Ministry of Land Management, most of these township development projects are illegal. In 2000, among 100,209 illegal cases regarding land use and transaction nationwide, 75 percent were related to unauthorized occupation of farmland (Xu 2004: 141). According to my interview with a high-ranking official in the Ministry of Land and Resources who was on the investigation team of the nationwide land auditing (*tudi qingcha*) in 2002, townships' projects accounted for more than half of all the total reported cases of "unauthorized occupation of farmland." And that was only the official figure.[22] On the other hand, the widespread illegal practices of land development at the township level require explanation, especially when townships seemed to have surpassed many higher-level urban governments in land development initiatives. According to Liu Neng's

(2000) survey of villages in Shandong, since 1995 there had been a visible decrease in both state expropriation and village household-initiated individual housing projects in the total farmland conversion to non-farm uses. Yet, township- and village collective-initiated projects increased from less than 20 percent to almost 80 percent of the total converted areas.

These figures for illegal cases show the frustration of high-level governments in their attempt to discipline local agents. But as the high-ranking official in the Ministry of Land Management suggested, the more difficult cases are those on the borderline between legal and illegal. In my research I found several examples of such borderline cases, like projects with township-granted ownership titles, the so-called "*xiangchanquan*" projects; and "small town construction" projects that were a part of rural development programs, but ended up providing a space for townships to maneuver between state and collective landownership and profit from it. In their exploration of the broad spectrum of legality at the moment of accelerated urban expansion, township governments have used their in-between position to operate in under-defined legal and administrative areas, and strategize to compete with the urban governments for land profits.

To begin with, because of the shortage of collective construction land and the high leasing fees of state-owned land, there are many cases of disguised farmland conversion and illegal leasing of collective land to bypass the regulation and fees. The so-called "*xiangchanquan*" ("township property rights") projects are a case in point. Township governments grant *xiangchanquan*, an extra-legal form of property rights to projects that mix illegal and legal practices. These projects are built on collective farmland that does not go through the formal procedure of ownership transfer from the collective to the state before leasing, or the approval process of farmland conversion. In suburban Beijing, the popularity of "family farms" is a telling example. Developers lease farmland from the collectives, and build so-called "family farms" that are marginally qualified as agricultural use of land. These "family farms" have large greenhouses or other decorative farm activities like a small animal farm in the middle of the complex for disguise, while the real focus is the multistory commercial housing units that occupy much of the complex (Wu 2000; Huang 2003). Buyers of such "family farm" housing units receive "housing ownership certificates" issued by township governments. Theoretically such "family farms" are illegal in two respects: using farmland for commercial housing without the urban government's approval of land-use conversion; and leasing collective land without first transferring the ownership from the collective to the state.[23] Because of these two illegal elements, the validity of "housing ownership certificates" issued by township governments becomes questionable. Also, as a township official stated, the township government never makes a clear statement in the (*xiangchanquan*) certificate about the land rights that the family farms are built on, so it is not "illegal": "We just use the collective farmland for agriculture-related projects."[24] In this gray zone, the townships have their own interpretation of legality, and find their space for brokering the meaning of property rights. The choice of the term "*xiangchanquan*" shows the townships' use of the formal word *chanquan*, to create the impression that the project is officially recognized. Yet such *chanquan* is granted by "*xiang*," which does not actually have the authority to grant property rights. The meaning of "*chanquan*" in this case, therefore, is to demonstrate townships' local influence over the actual disposal of village land. Because projects with *xiangchanquan* avoid the high fees of farmland conversion and land rights transfer, the cost of the land is much cheaper. It helps to bring down the total unit price of these family farms, making it popular with low-budget home buyers.[25]

Another example of townships' brokering of property rights comes from the role of township as a part of both the collective and the state. While townships are at the bottom of the state hierarchy, they are also at the top of the three-tier collectives that own rural land. The three tiers are: villagers' groups, which mostly coincide with natural villages, usually called *xiao-cun*, or small villages; administrative villages which include several villagers' groups, usually called *da-cun*, or large villages; and townships. Because townships are a part of the state, they can use their authority to acquire village land for specifically designated "small town construction" projects. But they are also a part of the collectives.[26] It is never clearly stated in the law whether townships, as a part of the collectives, need to go through the formal *zhengdi* process to convert ownership from the collectives to the state. And townships rarely did. Thus townships build on the collective land while avoiding the fees of rights transfer. As they avoid the approval process of ownership transfer, they also bypass the formal procedure of farmland conversion and the scrutiny of the supervising urban government. Consequently, in this gray zone of "small town construction," townships extend their projects from factories, development zones, roads, power plants, town halls, and staff housing, to commercial housing and retail and wholesale markets (Zhu 2003: 219). Again, townships use their role between the state and the collectives, in the in-between area of ownership rights, to find their own space in the competition for land profits.

Townships strategize in under-defined legal and administrative spaces to compete for land interests with the superior urban governments, but that is only half of the story. The other half is about townships' negotiation with the villages below them, and consolidating the control of scattered village land to launch large development projects.

Consolidating land control

Villages' collective land has become fragmented since the household contract system started in the early 1980s. This is mainly the result of dividing up the collective farm for individual households, and the practices of land adjustment. Based on the principle of equality, collective land lots are divided into small sections in different locations with different growing conditions. The customary leasing and renting arrangements between villagers were also highly complex and entangled throughout the 1980s and 1990s. But townships tend to build increasingly large industrial parks and commercial projects that require large areas of land. How do townships assemble fragmented pieces of land scattered in various villages, and consolidate them for large development projects?

Positioned in the ambiguous space between the state bureaucracy and the peasantry, and conditioned by financial and political imperatives, township leaders take advantage of the under-defined limits of their downward authority over villages. They would intensify and centralize their grip and try to extract resources more effectively from the village, with a focus on village collective land. In this section I will delineate townships' strategies of land control on regulatory, spatial, and organizational fronts.

Regulatory strategies: town planning

Urban and land-use planning is one of the most important tools of territorial governance. The process of planning provides an opportunity to restructure existing resource distribution and legitimizes power. In the name of modernization, rationality, and efficiency, a capitalistic urban planning apparatus is adopted to redistribute access to land in the fast-changing political economy of post-Mao China. As mentioned in the previous section, urban governments use urban planning to legitimize the incorporation of large areas of neighboring village land into planned urban areas. Resourceful and ambitious townships have tried to do the same. Township leaders and their planners draw development plans for the entire township, including both the town center (township seat) and the subordinate villages under the township's jurisdiction. Most of the township development plans that I have seen are highly focused on zoning, the use of land in the present and the future. A development plan usually includes the allocation of land for infrastructure, commercial, industrial, and residential uses for the following ten to twenty years, based on the projection of population and GDP growth. It seems to be commonly understood that plans themselves are not necessarily to be followed religiously, and they have not been. But the importance of the plans cannot be dismissed because of implementation lapses. The function of the township-wide development plans lies within their defining the reach of the township authority in the villages and substantiating a township's downward power. It gives the township the legitimacy to punish or fine the villages if they violate the plan, and provides the township with a bargaining leverage with villages.

The trend of townships making development plans for the villages independently from the urban government's general plans is found in many different regions, even in Dongguan. Dongguan, a city-region located in the fast-growing Pearl River Delta, has been well known for its villages that are active and aggressive, often more so than townships, in land development initiatives. Dongguan's village-based collective economies began with export processing for Hong Kong and Taiwanese manufacturers in the 1980s. To accommodate the growing need for factory and dormitory space, village collectives built industrial parks and housing complexes on the village collective land. The successful village enterprises contributed significantly to the revenue of both township and village governments in Dongguan in the 1980s, and many of the villages were financially stronger than townships at the time. By the mid-1990s, however, most collective enterprises had become privately owned, and their contribution to local government revenues dwindled. While villages continue to receive rental income from property projects like industrial parks to compensate for the loss in collective enterprises, towns without their own property projects feel a stronger pinch from the change. Although townships can still collect land conversion fees from villages and industrial taxes from enterprises, they have to share the revenues with higher-level governments. The highly scattered industrial parks located in different villages also make it costly for townships to collect fees and taxes from the enterprises.

The answer to the financial constraints is for the township to assert its administrative authority and centralize control over village land. Townships in the village-dominated Dongguan started to be more active in land development in the mid-1990s.[27] According to Liu Shiding's (2000) study of a town in Dongguan, the town government announced a new local policy called "one-pen approval" ("*yizhibi shenpi*") in 1994, to centralize the process of farmland conversion approval and development planning in the villages. This "one pen" was in the hands of the township party secretary. The township began with a thorough survey of the entire township jurisdiction, verified the boundaries of the villages, and counted the acreage of village land that could be used for construction. Following the ground survey, the township government drew a development plan of the entire township of 4,000 hectares, including both the township seat and all the villages. In the development plan, the township kept large areas of farmland in reserve for future conversion and property development, and started to expropriate village construction land for planned development projects undertaken by the township land development company. Under the same principle of integrated town planning and regularized development, the township government also drew a "unified land-use plan" for the township. The plan set the annual quota for farmland conversion in villages, standardized categories of village land, and set unified rates of land-lease sales.

In Liu's interview with the township mayor, the mayor emphasized the positive impact of the township's integrated development plan for all villages, and the township's effective coordination of resources that were scattered in individual villages. He proclaimed that, prior to the "one-pen approval" scheme, all thirteen villages under the township tried to establish or expand their own development zones. Yet none of them was able to raise enough funds for infrastructure projects like connecting roads. The township intervened at the right moment, put the zones under the township's management, and built roads of 120 km connecting the development zones to major transportation routes. Half of the funds for infrastructure investment came from the sale of land leases that were also managed by the township. The township also used its connection with the state banks to obtain bank loans for the projects. The rest were loans provided by contractors in the form of delayed and reduced construction costs, as well as rents and management fees collected from enterprises located in the industrial zones.

Not surprisingly, the centralized "one-pen approval" system created conflicts between the township and the villages. There was an incident in which a village had planned its own industrial development zone of 4 km without the approval of the township leader. The township party secretary intervened and halted the project after the construction had started. In another case, a village sold a lot of 12 km to an outside developer at a price lower than the standard rates set by the township. The township party secretary went to meet with the developer and returned the deposit (with interest) and got the land back. However, the township mayor stated in the interview that the villages eventually supported the "one-pen approval" system. This was because the township government was able to provide public infrastructure that could not be achieved easily by individual villages (Liu 2000: 136–40).[28]

Spatial strategies: concentration of development projects

Spatial concentration is another strategy aimed at consolidating the township's control of village land. By concentrating major construction and commercial activities in the space owned or designated by the township government, the township can gain more effective control over the commercial value generated from the activities. Ambitious township leaders would initiate several types of land development projects like town centers and retail and wholesale markets to advance their control of land.

Town centers

In many instances, township leaders try to concentrate the resources and investment right under their noses in the township seats. This is where the township government has the most immediate control. In the late 1980s, many rural towns tried to encourage peasants in the villages to move to the town seat to help build up a more urban-like town center, called "*nongmin jizi jianzhen*" (peasants raise funds for town building). Township development companies would build rows of residential–retail mixed projects in the town centers, and pre-sell the units to villagers to raise funds for the construction. In exchange, the township government would offer nonagricultural residency to the peasants. The township hoped that "*nongmin jizi jianzhen*" would help accelerate the pace of urbanization, create commercial opportunities, and boost land values in the town center from which the township government can profit directly. In addition, these development projects funded by villagers would boost the image of the township as an urbanized and modernized town. Highly visible projects serve to symbolize economic achievements, and legitimize local leadership. For many township leaders, this image could be converted into political credits and used for career advancement. Townships with modern buildings, higher density of population and commercial activities in the town center, and high GDP growth rates (also significantly derived from property development projects), have a better chance of being upgraded in the administrative hierarchy from *xiang* (township) to *zhen* (town), or from *zhen* to *zhongxin zhen* (central town). And the administrative upgrading of towns, sometimes just the rumor of upgrading, can boost the commercial value of land in the town center because of the widely believed connections between administrative status, government investment, and commercial opportunities.

Wholesale and retail markets

But real life does not always follow the plan. Despite the fact that many townships were successful in their expansionary plans for building up their town centers, quite a few ended up with rows of empty or half-finished housing and mixed-use projects in the town center. Some peasants might have purchased housing units in town centers in order to gain township residency, but many chose to remain living in the villages since there were few job or business opportunities in the town centers. This was particularly the case with those townships that are located too far away from major urban commercial activities or transportation nodes. These failed town center projects had brought the township government deeper into debt crises.

Some townships learned their lessons. If they are too far from large cities to take advantage of the commercial opportunities and boost the value of the residential property they build, they might as well create the commercial activities themselves in the town center. Or they could use administrative means to channel commercial activities to designated locations where the township has direct control. Wholesale and retail markets have thus become popular since the late 1990s. Large-scale, concentrated wholesale and retail markets have proved more effective than residential and mixed-use projects as a way to attract residents and boost commercial activities and land value in the township seats.

In both the town centers and the market projects, the townships themselves are not only the regulators but also active participants and initiators of the projects. The markets also served additional political functions. By gathering scattered shops into the concentration of the township-built markets, it is administratively easier for the township to monitor private and village-owned enterprises, and collect commercial and enterprise taxes and fees.

The political function of the markets can be illustrated by the case of a well-known wholesale market of handbags, backpacks, and suitcases in Xiaolong township in a northern province.[29] Xiaolong is a major center of handbag and suitcase production in northern China. The bag industry there started in the mid-1980s with small workshops scattered in the villages under Xiaolong. There were also workshops clustered in several streets in the town center, with storefronts.[30] As the handbag business grew in the mid-1990s, the neighboring towns and villages around Xiaolong formed an extensive network of bag production, while the streets in the town center became more specialized in retail and wholesale. The township, headed by an ambitious party secretary, decided to build a large indoor wholesale market specializing in bags, and demanded that all the bag shops in town relocate to the township-built wholesale market. At first the shop owners were reluctant to move. To discourage them from staying in their shops, the township government started to install underground pipelines in the areas where the shops had congregated. The ground around the shops was turned over, cutting off access to the shops. Shop owners finally left their streets and moved into the township market, and paid rents and management fees to the township government.

But the stone was thrown to kill more than one bird. After the shops moved into the market, the township party secretary announced that he would streamline tax collection by collecting both the state and the local (including township) taxes together. The state tax office in town protested and complained to the provincial government. The skillful township party secretary responded to the complaint with the rhetoric of the national policy of improving administrative efficiency. He also delivered the result of a more effective collection of both state and local taxes. His argument was persuasive because village and private enterprises were well known for tax evasion, and it had been costly for tax collectors to go after individual enterprises scattered in villages and town streets. Given the existing tax-sharing scheme, state and local taxes were collected separately by different tax offices in town. Yet there were many overlaps between the state and local taxes. The enterprise tax, one of the most important types of tax, was one of them. When an enterprise evaded the state tax, it would also evade the local tax. If the township was able to collect the local tax by putting all the shops in one market, it would also help state tax collection. The provincial government, the entity ultimately responsible for collecting state taxes, eventually decided not to intervene and left Xiaolong township alone. The township party secretary also offered to pay the salaries of the state tax office staff in town, in order to win their cooperation. The well-demarcated and guarded wholesale market has helped the township leaders to ensure their exclusive control of the market, where a significant portion of the town's wealth is generated.

But the politics between the township and the villages involves more than a straightforward relationship between the dominant and the dominated. As I have already mentioned, the "one-pen approval" scheme had provoked conflicts between township leaders and villages, when a village tried to sell the land lease without the township's approval. From Liu's report, it is unclear how the township leader managed to impose his authority on the village and stop the village's project, which was already under construction. Also, as the township mayor proclaimed the eventual compliance of the villages with the township's development plans, the actual process of such "consensus-building" is not presented in the report. How does the township solicit the cooperation of the villages in land projects? While the stories tell us about township leaders' relentless attempts to control village land, the question remains regarding the process and conditions of such exercise of power.

Organizational strategies: institutional control and social alliance with village leaders

Townships' control of village resources is supported by the organizational control of village finance. Since the late 1990s, as the township finance has grown tight, many township governments have placed the accounting and budgeting of villages, especially those of prosperous ones, under the direct control of townships. Townships would send accountants to villages to handle village bookkeeping. Major village expenditures are approved and sometimes reimbursed by the township controller (Hu 2002; Li 2005). Townships have also started to assert greater control over village personnel. Because villages are "autonomous organizations" that do not belong to the formal state system, village cadres are not part of the state bureaucracy; nor are they on the state payrolls. But in practice, as mentioned earlier, village administrations function as the extension of the state bureaucracy through its annexation to the township governments. Under the "one level down" cadre management regime implemented since the mid-1980s, village party secretaries are directly appointed by the township party branches. Village leader cadres also were assigned quantitative targets of tax collection and sterilization under family planning, similar to the cadre responsibility system at the higher level (Ren 2002).[31] Townships also persistently interfere with the process and results of village elections to ensure the villages' continuous cooperation with the townships (Tong 2002).

To reinforce the alliance between townships and village cadres, cross-appointments are common. Party secretaries of village party branches, especially those from prosperous villages, are often appointed to party committees or government positions at the township level. For example, village party secretaries can serve as a member of the standing committee of the township party branch, or as one of the vice-chiefs of the township. Key village cadres are also put on the township payroll and pension plans. Evidence shows that the cross-appointment of village and township cadres and the incorporation of the village in the township cadre management and benefit system have enhanced the control of key villages cadres.[32]

In addition to institutionalized connections, township cadres also use kinship and other social networks with villagers and village cadres to carry out policy tasks more effectively. Sun Linping and Guo Yuhua's (2000) analysis of the process of agricultural tax collection in a northern township is a good example. When carrying out unpopular policy tasks like collecting agricultural taxes, individual township cadres are assigned to villages with which they have social connections. When visiting less cooperative villagers' homes, they are accompanied by village cadres. While lending extra legitimacy to village cadres to collect taxes, they also use social pressure on the villagers and plead for their cooperation. If the villagers still do not relent, the township cadre pushes further by threatening the villagers with legal punishment. In this process of what Sun and Guo called "*ruanying jiansh,*" that is, combining both gentle ("*ruan*") and tough ("*ying*") approaches, it takes both the village's and the township cadres' collaboration, and both state authority and social pressure, to gain villagers' compliance. In my fieldwork I also found township and village cadres using similar approaches of "*ruanying jianshi*" when they tried to negotiate with villagers over relocation and farmland compensation.

Conclusion: brokering power and property rights

In this chapter I used the case of township governments' land development projects to examine the territorial power process in post-Mao China. I found that decentralization does not necessarily deliver a pre-fixed outcome of greater local state autonomy. Under the grand scheme of decentralization, there is a tendency towards concentration of resource control at each level of the local state. The persistent tension between decentralization and concentration characterizes territorial politics in post-reform China. While the terminology of "decentralization" seems to imply a policy package of power allocation from the central to the local state, the actual process of decentralization is in fact a highly contentious power reshuffling between different levels of the local state. In the case of land development, while urban governments try to use their administrative authority and legal rights to control rural land, rural townships respond by asserting their grip on rural land in the gray zone of extra-legality, as demonstrated by Beijing's *xiangchanquan* projects. Meanwhile, township governments take advantage of their under-defined state authority and stretch it downwards to intensify and centralize their control over villages below them, as demonstrated by the "one-pen approval" schemes of the township in Dongguan. Between the state and the peasantry, and between the urban governments above and the villages below, townships bear the characteristics of power brokers. These power brokers enjoy the advantage of operating in the ambiguous and under-defined space of power, and have to face the challenge of high levels of uncertainty with their borrowed authority. Township governments' land development strategies, such as controlling village-based industrial projects through one-pen approval, and finding a midway definition of property rights in *xiangchanquan* projects, reflect such ambiguity and uncertainty in their power brokerage.

This story of township power brokers in land development has two theoretical implications. One is conceptualizing the state as processes instead of a "consolidated outcome and unitary actor" (Crzymala-Busse and Luong 2002: 529). China's decentralization policies provide the platform for such processes of the state, without a preset course or predetermined outcome. Townships are of particular theoretical importance because of their position at the periphery of the state. They help to push this theoretical position of seeing the state as processes further by adding a spatial dimension to it; that is, the processes of the state at the periphery, where townships' power tends to be more uncertain and ambiguous. Townships' coping with and taking advantage of such ambiguity and uncertainty constitute an important part of the processes of the state.

In this study, I also used this empirical study of townships' land development to explore the theoretical connection between property relations and power relations. As township governments and their leaders act as power brokers between the state and the peasantry, their strategies for controlling village land are conditioned by such a position. Therefore, power brokers act as brokers of property rights.

These two theoretical concerns have converged in the historical moment of China's rapid urbanization and industrialization since the early 1980s. Land has been at the center of this great transformation. It has been one of the most important resources of which governments of all levels try to expand their control. As a result, it is the focal point of territorial politics and state processes. With the state land tenure system operating in the late-socialist market-oriented economy, property rights as a legal as well as a political concept have also been one of the most controversial subjects among policy-makers and scholars alike.

Finally, I hope to use this study of Chinese townships to lend support to those who have proposed a bottom-up approach to studying the state. Townships are often seen as a symbol of the modern Chinese state's attempt to penetrate further into rural society and extract resources from it more effectively. The agenda is about how the state as the principal disciplines and monitors the local state agents. But if we take the perspective of township leaders and cadres, the question becomes how local agents operate with specific conditions of power given by the township's position within and outside the state apparatus. By way of conclusion, I would borrow James Scott's (1998) term with a slight twist, and propose to "see like a local state" as a theoretical and methodological alternative in understanding the great transformation of China today.

Notes

1 For a discussion of fiscal decentralization policies and local state autonomy, see Oi (1992) and Montinola *et al.* (1997). For a more recent treatment of fiscal decentralization, see Tsui and Wang (2004). For the typology of Chinese local states, see Baum and Shevchenko (1999).
2 For example, Li's (1998) work on Guangdong provincial government, Wank (1998) on Xiamen municipal governments, Li (2005) on Yichang county in Hubei, Zweig (1992) and Edin (2003) on township governments.

3 In this chapter I use the term "townships" to refer to both *xiang* and *zhen*. Both *xiang* (townships) and *zhen* (towns) are at the same administrative level, under the county-level governments. For details of the difference, see Zweig (1992) and Ma (2000).

4 The general order of command in Chinese bureaucracy is hierarchical: all superior government agencies and officials have authority over those below them. But those immediately above have more direct influence. This is because of the "one step down" cadre management system. For discussion of "one step down" cadre management, see O'Brien and Li (1999).

5 Furthermore, the CCP's dominant position in the villages is formally stated in the Organic Law: the CCP party organization is the core of the village organization. See O'Brien and Li (1999).

6 Important work has been done on power brokering between the state and the peasantry in Chinese history. In addition to the earlier writing in the 1960s on gentry, there are works like the historian Duara's (1988) on state–gentry–broker–peasant quadruple.

7 Here I follow scholars whose work integrates legal and social factors in landed property rights issues, including those contributed to Jacobs (1998). Third World-focused research is represented by Santos (1977).These scholars of law, sociology, anthropology, and history have treated property as social relations; and share the view that law informs, and is informed by, the social and political evolution of the practices of landed property rights. See Singer (2000). For Eastern European post-socialist transition studies, see Verdery (1999).

8 The definition and calculation of China's urban expansion and urban population growth have always been controversial, due to the use of multiple criteria and reporting flaws. For discussion of the complexity, see Zhang and Zhao (1998). More recent work suggests that it is safe to take the figure of 36 to 40 percent as "urban"; that is, between 1980 and 2002 the urban population grew from 18–20 percent to 36–40 percent of the total population, or about 500 million in total were added to the urban population. See Lin (2002) and Zhou and Ma (2003).

9 Here "urban governments" are defined as those local governments at and above county levels, including counties, city districts, and all levels of cities.

10 PRC Constitution, Article 10. PRC Land Management Law (first adopted in 1986, amended in 1988, 1998, and 2004), Article 2.

11 There are two types of "cities" below the provinces: prefecture-level cities that have administrative authority over several districts (in urbanized areas) and counties (in rural areas); there are also county-level cities that have been upgraded to city status, mostly after 1986.

12 There are some differences between "city leading county" and "city governing county." For detailed discussion, see Chung and Lam (2004: 951–4) and Ma (2005).

13 Throughout the 1990s, local governments' irregular and illegal sales and conversion of farmland were rampant and approval could be given by the township government. In 2003, the land management system was restructured and the central ministry and its provincial bureaus took back from local governments much of the authority to approve land-lease sales and land conversion. It is too early to tell how effective the reinstallation of "vertical management" will be.

14 Since 2001, several provinces (e.g. Zhejiang, Jiangsu, Anhui, Guangdong, and Beijing) have chosen "testing-point" (*shidian*) cities and towns to experiment with the new policies of "rural construction land circulation" without the urban government's interference; see Xie *et al.* (2004).

15 According to a survey of the 200 largest projects in eleven counties of an unidentified province in 1992, only 21 percent of the appropriated land is used for public purposes like roads and schools, 5 percent for governmental agencies, and 74 percent for commercial projects; see Lin *et al.* (2004).

16 For the debate on rural governance reform and the necessity of township-level government, see Wu (2002).

17 George Lin has found in his fieldwork that in Yangtze River Delta over 98 percent of the total conveyance fee collected during the period 1989–97 was retained by the municipal government and none was handed over to the central government (Lin 2005: 430).

18 An official at the Finance Bureau of Kunshan city captures well the attitude of the urban government towards collective land: "land is owned by the state, so every level of the state is entitled to the profit from land" (Yang *et al.* 2004: 129).

19 In some cases, townships are made responsible for the expense of cultivating new agricultural land to make up for the farmland that is being expropriated, as a part of the national policy of "balancing between occupation (for non-farm uses) and expansion of farmland" ("*zhanbu pingheng*") (Yang *et al.* 2004).

20 The township gets a share of the compensation paid to the villages and villagers. But the overall compensation is so low that a small share pales in comparison with the share of the large conveyance fee that the urban governments take. The Land Law states that compensation fees belong to village collectives and individual households. A survey shows that, in practice, individual peasant households get only 5–10 percent of the total compensation, while the rest is retained by county and township governments (60–70 percent) and village collectives (25–30 percent). See Lin *et al.* (2004: 272).

21 Townships could also build factories and workers' dormitories on the construction land themselves, then rent the units to enterprises. See, for example, Zhang *et al.* (2004).

22 Interview in Beijing, August 2003. Also, a vice-director at the Hubei Procuratorate (*jianchayuan*) admitted in his investigative report that the number of unreported cases far exceeded that of reported cases. Most of the cases are resolved by fines instead of reconverting the land back to farm uses (Xu 2004: 140).

23 This is taking advantage of the ambiguous line between land leasing and renting in practice. When collective land is rented out to developers for non-farm projects, it is usually a long-term arrangement like a lease.

24 Interview in China, December 2003.

25 For homebuyers, family farms in the suburbs are much more spacious and less expensive. They also expect that in the event of urban government tearing down these illegal projects, the homeowners, as victims, can demand compensation from the government. The fact that this type of illegal housing with ambivalent "*xiangchanquan*" is popular in suburban areas means that township governments command enough legitimacy, if not legality, to issue the certificate, which carries a certain weight in the market.

26 Although it was commonly recognized that the principle of the "collective ownership" of village land is that "under the three-tiered ownership system, the team (villagers' groups) is the basis" (*sanji suoyou, yi dui wei jichu*). For a discussion of the ambiguity of the collective ownership of land, see Ho (2001).

27 Compared to Shenzhen and Guangzhou, where land control is in the hands of the district-county governments, Dongguan's townships have had greater control over village land. See Yang and Xu (2005).

28 The phenomenon of "*zhen-ya-cun*" ("the township dominates the village") is found in other research. In my own interviews with town planners in Zhongshan city-region in the Pearl River Delta region (in 2000) and another town near Shanghai (in 1997), both interviewees had boasted about the comprehensiveness of their plans for the villages under their jurisdiction.

29 Interview with a sociologist in Beijing, December 2001 and June 2002. Interview with the vice-mayor of Xiaolong (not the real name), June 2002.

30 The mixture of production and retail use of space is known as "stores in the front, workshops in the back" (*qiandian houchang*).

31 For the cadre responsibility system, see O'Brien and Li (1999) and Edin (2003). Most of their discussion of the cadre responsibility system focuses on the township leader cadres. Townships' responsibility in tax collection and population control, among other policy tasks, is further shared by villages below them. Tsui and Wang (2004: 76) reported that in recent years village leaders have also had to sign responsibility contracts with the superior township government.

32 See Edin (2003) for a discussion on overlapping appointments at different administrative levels as an important method of cadre management.

6 Diversity and evolution in the state-in-society

International influences in combating violence against women

Louise Edwards

This chapter examines the relational composition of the state by exploring the emergence of new actions on the pressing social problems of violence against women (VAW) and domestic violence (DV). The interactions between the matrix of interest groups concerned to eliminate VAW and DV in China support the notion central to this volume that a complex web of negotiations both propels changes in the state and comprises the very formation of the state. However, this chapter also argues that influences from outside China have increasingly important roles to play in influencing domestic actors in their production of the 'state-in-society'. Two prime agents seeking change in China on the issue of VAW and DV are the All China Women's Federation (ACWF) and the dispersed and loosely connected anti-VAW activist groups mobilising around V-day. The former is an arm of the Party-state, being an official Mass Organisation of the Chinese Communist Party (CCP). The latter is a loose group of university-based activists (including both students and staff) in key Chinese urban areas who have mobilised around an international movement to combat VAW called V-day. The ACWF carries the legitimating imprimatur of the Party-state and expresses the CCP's original intention to embed the state apparatus within broad societal contexts. In contrast, the V-day activists are a marginalised and often derided, ever-changing, multi-sited set of individuals with no official affiliation to each other. Both the ACWF and the V-day activists have complementary agendas on this issue of eradicating VAW and DV, yet both invoke different international partners. The weight of the international partners' influence helps keep both actors' agendas on the public stage – albeit appealing to different target audiences. The multiple differences in approach, appeal and style between the ACWF and the V-day activists present an opportunity for exploring the new mechanisms by which lobby groups contribute to the evolution of the state – reinforcing Migdal's notion of the importance of recognising the 'state-in-society' (Migdal 2001: 11).[1]

While focusing specifically on VAW and DV activism, the chapter supports Sharon Wesoky's point that international partnerships have become vital to Chinese women's activism (Wesoky 2002: 4) and proceeds to argue that these international influences need to be considered in any studies of China's 'state-in-society'. China's domestic processes are increasingly interwoven with international processes and if we accept that the state is not a monolithic, unchanging body above society, then we need also to consider that key influences on local actors impacting that evolving state, emerge from outside its borders. To this end, the chapter's first section provides an overview of the two main domestic actors on VAW and DV, outlining their similarities and differences in the domestic framework. It also introduces briefly a third group, the Domestic Violence Network, which serves an important intermediary role between the two. The second and third sections of this chapter examine the V-day activists' and ACWF's respective key international linkages and the implications of their different international partners in the effectiveness of their activities. The continuum of diverse actors, sometimes working independently of and other times in concert with each other, demonstrates the increasingly complex texture of the Chinese state-in-society. As we shall see in this case study on anti-VAW campaigns, it is no longer possible to discuss the 'state' as an oppositional force against 'society' in the People's Republic of China (PRC). Instead we see the complexity of conversations and activism now emerging with confidence within the Chinese 'state-in-society' around publicly recognised social problems, such as VAW and DV.

Diverse domestic actors

The largest domestic actor with the most far-reaching impact is the ACWF; its intimate ties to the Party-state place it in an important position in terms of effecting change in the 'state-in-society' process. Moreover, the ACWF's transformation over the issue of VAW is indicative of the manner in which 'state and society transform and constitute one another' (Migdal 2001). Officially formed in 1949, the ACWF's origins reach back through the preceding three decades to the Women's Bureau formed at the establishment of the CCP in 1921 (Edwards 2004b: 109–30). Charged by the CCP with providing the conduit for the implementation of CCP policy among women and mobilising women for the Communist cause, the ACWF and its predecessor body have often been regarded as irrelevant to women and perceived as merely a mouthpiece for the Party rather than an advocate for women's needs and interests (Jin 2001). In order to counter this charge, from the mid-1980s onwards the ACWF became more active and antagonistic – representing women rather than simply responding to CCP directives or disseminating Party policy to women (Howell 1996: 129–43; Edwards 2000: 64–8).

The eradication of DV has been one of the more influential of the ACWF's initiatives since the late 1980s and early 1990s. To this end they have undertaken a number of pragmatic initiatives such as mass education campaigns, support for women survivors of DV and building connections between the legal and policing sectors. Their main international links are forged with formal transnational bodies – primarily the United Nations (UN) through its UNIFEM initiatives. In 1993 the UN passed its Declaration on the Elimination of Violence against Women (DEVAW) and instigated a number of global campaigns in which China soon participated.[2] The ACWF's anti-DV movement received a major boost with the 1995 Fourth UN World Conference on Women, held in Beijing, by giving the campaign greater public exposure (Li Hongtao 2005: 64).

Central to the ACWF's impact are the large-scale research initiatives it is able to undertake as a result of its immense national reach and institutional structure. For example, in 1996 the ACWF conducted the 'Public Investigation into Domestic Violence' survey, which revealed that 11.2 per cent of wives had experienced physical violence from their husbands. A subsequent survey in 1998 revealed that 20 per cent of women surveyed had suffered physical injuries at the hands of their husbands. And, most significantly of all, 63.3 per cent of respondents thought that DV was one of the most significant current social problems (cited in Zhou Yunqing 2005: 441).[3]

In 2003 the ACWF opened 6,181 hotlines and 8,958 organisations charged with providing legal aid and consultation for DV victims ('Women look for ways', 2003). The programmes at the centre of the organisation are often implemented at the provincial and township levels. The ACWF model for effecting social change relies on stimulus from the top and draws on the weight of Party and government resources, both moral and financial, and the ACWF's concomitant access to official information dissemination mechanisms. Evidence of the ACWF's success came in the inclusion of an explicit prohibition on DV in the revised Marriage Law of April 2001 (see Wang Fengxian 2005: 162 for a discussion of the import of this provision).

Significantly, these recent moves by the ACWF were not the first efforts on the part of the CCP to tackle family violence. The Party had been active on this issue from its early years in the base-areas during the 1940s. Hinton talks about women communists in Long Bow Village mobilising village opinion against fathers-in-law and husbands known to beat or sexually abuse their daughters-in-law or wives (Hinton 1966: 538–59).[4] Yet, unlike the current campaigns, the earliest ones were highly localised and lacked international partner connections. Party cadres were crucial to the mediation process between family members and the system was underpinned by notions of the CCP as the key instrument of women's liberation. Neil Diamant notes that there were a number of problems with this process of mediation and that the cadres often found that their support among male peasants declined if they were seen to support women in family disputes (Diamant 2000: 8). The earlier CCP-centred approach contrasts sharply with the ACWF's current use of professional counselling, women's refuges and legal advisory structures beyond the reaches of the local Party cadres. Nonetheless, in 2003 the experience of women survivors of DV in China's villages still largely concurred with the earlier pattern. A survey noted that 50 per cent of women go to relatives or village leaders for mediation and only 7 per cent seek the support of law enforcement agencies ('Women Look for Ways', 2003).[5]

In contrast to the historical and political strength of the ACWF, the second domestic actor under consideration in this chapter, the V-day activists, is recent in origin and local in impact. Their existence points to important changes in the 'state-in-society' mix within the PRC. In contrast to previous decades, even as recently as the early 1990s the ACWF was the only body able to speak or act effectively on this issue. However, more recently, its efforts in combating VAW have been complemented by the emergence of groups like the V-day activists. China's V-day activists first emerged in 2003 in a series of activities around the Chinese-language performance in Guangzhou of *The Vagina Monologues* – a drama by American playwright Eve Ensler. The activists consist of a loose group of students, artists, actors and academics in China's urban centres who mobilise to raise consciousness about VAW. There is no sustained, formal organisation of China's V-day activists – there are no membership lists, membership fees or permanent, physical spaces dedicated to their campaign. The actions undertaken are *ad hoc* and evolving and usually occur on school or university campuses. The central impetus for their anti-VAW actions is the performance of *The Vagina Monologues* and a range of public lectures and roundtables. The sensational content of the play and the equally sensational willingness of young women to break longstanding social taboos on the public discussion of female sexuality and gendered sexual violence ensure the V-day events receive considerable publicity both on and off campus. As we will see in the following section, in performing the play they have formed dynamic transnational links with other groups of women staging the same performance in numerous locations around the globe. These other groups are also *ad hoc* and maintain limited organisational structures.

On the continuum of rich social activism on VAW and DV in China, positioned between the CCP's ACWF and the *ad hoc* V-day activists stands a group with official recognition, albeit less direct CCP connections than the ACWF – the Domestic Violence Network. While this network will not be a particular focus of this current chapter – which aims to explore different international connections with two different domestic actors – the existence of the Domestic Violence Network is significant for its official but extra-Party status. The Domestic Violence Network was formed in 2000 by the China Legal Studies Society (Zhongguo faxue hui) and draws together a wide range of professionals including social workers, police, doctors, cadres, academics and judges. From the international perspective the Domestic Violence Network fills the role normally performed by non-governmental organisations (NGOs) – even though its close cooperation with the ACWF undermines its technical 'non-governmental' status. Its semi-official status enables it to perform a vital role in relation to China's engagement with international agenda for eliminating VAW. To those international organisations unwilling to cooperate with a CCP organ – such as the ACWF – the Domestic Violence Network presents a credible NGO-like image.[6] The Domestic Violence Network's members are well informed about international academic, legal and political developments in VAW through their professional links. Nonetheless, its most intimate ties remain with the ACWF. It works closely with the ACWF to research DV in the China context and implement intervention strategies (Bu 2005a: 48; 'Fan jiating baoli' 2005). It is also active in taking the campaigns to rural areas using the ACWF's networks at all levels.[7] The Domestic Violence Network is also the key internet portal for DV in China since it hosts an extensive website at www.stopdv.org. cn supported by the USA's Ford Foundation, Sweden's Sida, Netherlands-based Oxfam and the University of Oslo. Its international connections include links between members and their peers in other nations as well as in the support provided by the aforementioned bodies in maintaining the web presence. Significantly, the website includes information on both ACWF initiatives and V-day activities. Participants in the Network include CCP members but their primary affiliation draws on their professional ties rather than, as is the case with the ACWF, their Party ties.

These groups, while different in structure, style, resources and vision, have seriously addressed the problems of VAW and DV in China. Together they are probably more effective than any one could be on its own. Moreover, their multifaceted approaches to combating VAW and DV indicate the evolution of a more complex 'state-in-society' composition compared to the CCP-dominated approached to social problems typical of the years prior to the early 1990s. The ACWF campaigns are marked by the moralism and heavy-handedness associated with the CCP's rule of China – its message appears 'grandmotherly' and potentially less interesting to a younger audience. Working closely with the ACWF, the Domestic Violence Network is primarily 'legal' in orientation – spending much time and energy promoting knowledge of laws prohibiting DV and increasing awareness among law enforcement agencies and the judiciary about appropriate handling of the cases. In this regard they are buttressing the state's new legal institutional structures. By contrast, the V-day activists are marked by their radical, risqué approach and their willingness to run counter to government proclamations banning the performance of the play their movement revolves around. The movement's explicit celebration of female sexuality places it on the dangerous fringe of social morals. Significantly, as Tamara Jacka points out, urban educated elites comprise the overwhelming majority of all three groups and, while they aim to address DV and VAW in rural areas, their main impact has been among urban communities (Tamara Jacka, personal correspondence, July 20, 2006).

The ACWF and the Domestic Violence Network promote knowledge about domestic violence, while the V-day activists explicitly address all violence against women – regardless of whether it is 'domestic' or otherwise. In this regard, the V-day activists are stretching the boundaries beyond the comparatively safe terrain established by the ACWF and the Domestic Violence Network. As we will see in this chapter, the ACWF's anti-VAW programmes tend to focus primarily on the more publicly and politically palatable issue of domestic violence, where, by definition the violence need not only be directed at women and where restoring harmony within a family is the central goal. In contrast the V-day activists tackle a wider range of violent acts perpetrated against women, including those related to women's bodies such as rape, prostitution, female genital mutilation, sexual slavery, forced pregnancy or abortion, female infanticide, as well as trafficking and kidnapping of women and girls.[8] This is not to say that the ACWF has been silent on some of these other issues, but rather to point out that the epistemological rationale behind the activism in each case differs fundamentally. Elaine Jeffreys has shown the ACWF can be highly influential in rescuing kidnapped women by using their extensive access to the media and provoking legal action against traffickers and brothel keepers (Jeffreys 2006). However, the ACWF's activism around kidnapping and sexual slavery emerges from within campaigns related to eliminating prostitution and rebuilding social morals – it is not positioned under the VAW umbrella. In contrast, the V-day activists promote opposition to these and other social menaces as part of a programme to win recognition for women about autonomy over their bodies, their sexuality and to develop a greater sense of women's dignity. Neither the family nor heterosexual monogamy is privileged within the campaigns of the V-day activists.

Most importantly, the ACWF and the V-day activists, as domestic Chinese actors, have dramatically different connections with international actors and thereby present a multifaceted Chinese face to the world. This expansion in the ways domestic Chinese actors could relate to the world is a recent and welcome phenomenon. Even into the 1990s, contacts between domestic and international bodies were closely monitored by the state and tended to present a monolithic CCP-oriented image imbued with official policies and exhortations akin to the 'non-interference in Chinese domestic affairs' mantra. Since the start of the twentieth century China's leaders have waged repeated campaigns to be 'taken seriously' by the USA and European powers and have been sensitive to humiliations, real or imagined, directed at China by international bodies or other nations. China's insecurity about her standing in the world created a contradictory stance of longing for international connections but remaining simultaneously resentful and suspicious of this need (see Tsu 2005). External criticism of problems in Chinese society is still greeted with accusations of 'China bashing' – rendering dialogue difficult. Currently, as the actions around eliminating VAW and DV show, this uniform and controlled form of international interactions has given way to a more relaxed approach. Indeed, international interactions garner considerable prestige rather than suspicion. Cecelia Milwertz has noted that 'in China governmental engagement with the UN system has provided legitimacy to the activities to combat and prevent domestic violence, as well as to scholarly engagement with the issue' (Milwertz 2005: 33).

It is in this transformation that key changes to China's political order are manifest. Chinese domestic actors can now criticise and publicise social problems (significantly, criticism of formal political matters remains taboo), often invoking international actors in their domestic campaigns. The support provided by international actors can now sometimes be harnessed without the dire negative consequences of the previous decades. The V-day activists' invocation of a radical, feminist international partner in making critiques of the continued oppression of women in China is one clear instance of the increasing domestic–international engagement.

The Vagina Monologues and global V-day activism in a Chinese context

Originally performed in 1996 in New York, Eve Ensler's play caused a storm and quickly attracted major American celebrities, such as Whoopie Goldberg, to its cast. Controversy has continued to follow the play wherever it has been performed because of the explicitly sexual nature of its content.[9] *The Vagina Monologues* consists of a changing number of monologues in which women discuss issues of VAW, sexuality and desire. The play is underscored by North American notions of sexual liberation in which the performers explain their progress towards feeling comfortable with and 'in charge of' their sexuality and sexual pleasure. Equally prevalent in the play is the narrative of women overcoming anxiety, shame or fear resulting from sexual violence. Together the monologues reclaim the vagina as a symbol of female power rather than female shame and vulnerability. Many of the dialogues narrate individual women's experiences of rape, abuse and sexual torture – and in so doing tackle the persistent global problem of VAW. Indeed, the monologues are deliberately international and draw on experiences of VAW from women around the world. The flexibility in the play's structure enables performers to include segments more relevant to their home audience and even add new segments if they so choose. *The Vagina Monologues* became an international phenomenon over the course of only two years and has been translated into 24 languages and performed in over 80 countries, including China.

The play has spawned a global movement of activists mobilising against VAW and also a charity organisation that raises funds to support groups fighting VAW across the globe. As early as 1998 it had become an international political movement with Valentine's Day (14 February) each year nominated as the focus for local action around the world and named 'V-day'. The V stands for 'Victory, Valentine and Vagina'. The movement serves as a focus to highlight the importance of eradicating VAW regardless of the location in which it occurs. The charity's main public face is its website and, while it is incorporated in the USA, it encourages activities all around the world without demanding direct control by the 'V-day core' – its key staff. The philosophy behind the movement presents an innovative vision for global movements for social change: 'V-day is a next-step philanthropy, housed in people's minds and hearts rather than one physical location'. Thus, V-day organisers, although centred in the USA, explicitly present a global invitation to all people keen to combat VAW and DV to join their movement:

> V-day is a global movement to stop violence against women and girls. V-day is a catalyst that promotes creative events to increase awareness, raise money and revitalise the spirit of existing anti-violence organisations. V-day generates broader attention for the fight to stop violence against women and girls, including rape, battery, incest, female genital mutilation (FGM) and sexual slavery. Through V-day campaigns, local volunteers and college students produce annual benefit performances of *The Vagina Monologues* to raise awareness and funds for anti-violence groups within their own communities. In 2006, over 2,700 V-day benefit events are taking place by volunteer activists in the U.S. and around the world, educating millions of people about the reality of violence against women and girls.
>
> ('About V-day' 2006)

By performing the play and engaging in V-day activities women around the world have created an international constituency wherein women's common unity of interests, conceived in terms of women's rights to control their bodies free from interference and violence, is emphasised. The movement is not directly coordinated and apart from a website appears to have no directives or ideological gatekeepers – yet millions of women worldwide have participated in V-day activities.

The V-day movement's evolution in the PRC has been both rapid and fraught with controversy. The performance of the play, which provides the focus for other related events, has faced official prohibition in some locations (public playhouses) and yet in others has proceeded unhindered (school and university campuses). Moreover, English-language performances have experienced no difficulties from censors, whereas Chinese-language ones attract more concern. This is indicative of the ambiguity with which the censoring authorities regard the VAW problem and also provides further evidence of the mutuality of the processes of 'state-in-society' formation. On the one hand, the state has the power to ban the play and on the other it allows it to appear in discrete educational or linguistic contexts. Its international origins are acknowledged through the unproblematic production of English-language performances, but anxiety clearly remains about the transference of this foreign material to an untutored Chinese audience. Chinese educational settings perhaps are perceived as being able to provide a level of 'ideological translation' not available to individuals in public audiences that self-select to attend a performance in a regular playhouse.

A history of the performance of the play provides evidence of the complexity of the interactions between the highly localised, domestic actors and their local state censoring authorities. The first performance of the play in Chinese – under the title *Yindao dubai* – took place in December 2003 at the Guangdong Art Academy. Students and staff from Guangzhou's Zhongshan

University performed the play to an audience comprised primarily of students from the University (*China Daily* 2004). However, this was not the play's first ever performance in the PRC. Its first PRC performances were in English. Nanjing University's Johns Hopkins Centre hosted the performance by local and overseas students in 2001. The American Club in Shanghai presented a second English-language performance in 2002 to a mainly expatriate audience (Zhang Yanjin 2004). In February of 2004 a second series of Chinese performances were planned in Shanghai and Beijing, but, before they opened, municipal authorities notified organisers that their productions were prohibited because the play 'did not fit with China's national situation' (*China Daily* 2004). The Shanghai performance had even reached the dress rehearsal stage when it was banned. At the time of the prohibition, director Lei Guohua declared rather hopefully that although the production had been banned in Shanghai this ruling did not mean it could not be performed in other cities (Li Xiaojing 2004). Lei Guohua's response reveals a further level of complexity in the mutuality of the 'state-in-society' process occurring in the PRC. The reach of the disciplining authorities is now publicly discussed as being partial and localised – far from the totalising or omnipotent force the state had in earlier periods narrated itself as being.

Indeed, the censorship of public performances in Beijing and Shanghai has not prevented women from performing the play in universities, schools or semi-public forums. For example, students at Shanghai's Fudan University performed the play in May 2004 on their campus (Fudan daxuesheng 2004) and accompanying the performance was a series of lectures on feminism, women's health and general consciousness-raising about women's rights. The students received support from DKT International, a Washington-based charity that focuses in particular on family planning and AIDS prevention (DKT International 2006). This flexibility and dynamism in the V-day activities demonstrate that the play and the V-day core are the catalysts for broader action rather than the sole focus or controllers of the programme. The students subsequently undertook an informal performance in June 2004 in conference facilities at a Shanghai hotel for delegates at a conference on 100 Years of Chinese Feminism jointly hosted by Fudan and Michigan Universities. In this instance, the audience comprised scholars of women's studies from around China and the world. During the performance conference delegates also viewed a DVD of the Zhongshan University performance and a documentary on the making of their show. The Fudan students' performance was also filmed. The 'expansionary' potential of the V-day movement was further confirmed when after the performance small focus groups of senior women's studies scholars from China were filmed discussing their opinions about the play and the issue of VAW.

Activists are clearly aware of the extent to which they are able to counter or evade their local state authority's discipline. At the June 2004 performance, although the performance and film viewing were announced in the conference programme, they were held in a smaller, upstairs room at the rear of the conference venue rather than the larger auditorium where most of the rest of the conference had been held. This gave a 'salon' milieu to the performance. Aware that the public performances of the plays had been banned in that very city only a few months earlier, the students and their staff supporters felt sufficiently empowered and impassioned about the issue of VAW to risk running foul of local state opinion on the suitability of this play for Chinese audiences – indeed they presented their play and conducted their ancillary activities at two separate venues. Their position as local actors, literally 'acting' in their performances of the play, revealed their willingness to distance themselves from local state discipline. Their informal links to broader social movements to eradicate VAW and DV internationally and nationally, combined with their adoption of a semi-public, education-oriented setting enabled their activities to continue. In this regard *The Vagina Monologues* is at once a symbol of ongoing state censorship and the dexterous engagement of local actors with their local and national state authorities.

Further evidence of the contradictory responses of the multiple Chinese state actors to the play and the issues it raised is provided by the 2005 performance of the play in a high-school setting. On 7 March 2005, the eve of the state-sponsored International Women's Day, the play was again performed in Chinese, yet this time to an even younger audience than in Guangzhou, Shanghai and Nanjing. Guangxi Huaguang Girls' Middle School in Nanning staged the first performance for school students in China under the directorship of the school's principle, Liu Guanghua (Zhang Qi 2005). Not only were the performers and audience younger than previous ones, but most of the students attending the school are from poorer regions around Nanning and many are from rural ethnic minorities. Huaguang is not a wealthy school and the production costs were a major hurdle for the performance but together staff and students eventually succeeded and even raised over 5,000 yuan to support students at the school from ticket receipts. The Guangxi students included their own monologue on girls' right to education within their production, reflecting a particular local interaction with the play's overarching advocacy of women's rights (stopdv wangzhan 2005).[10] The timing of the play's opening performance, just one day prior to March 8th, the official day on which the central Chinese state encourages recognition of women's contribution to society, linked the prohibited play with the state's women's agenda – asserting its confluence with a firmly established state programme.

The Guangxi Huaguang Girl's Middle School performance also provided insights into an important aspect of the impact of technology on the manner in which local domestic actors build from each others' initiatives, expand international actors' initiatives and in so doing further encourage challenges to local state discipline. The Huaguang school principal, Liu Guanghua, had previously viewed the video recording of the Zhongshan University production, just as had the Fudan–Michigan conference participants. Liu had been particularly inspired by the DVD's messages about engendering pride and confidence in women about their bodies and sexuality and their right to freedom from VAW. Seeing young Chinese women performing the play brought this North American product closer to a Chinese context and inspired her to provide a similar experience for the girls under her guidance. The existence and availability of the video version of the Zhongshan University production were crucial to the Guangxi school production because the students watched the video repeatedly and copied it line by line. No doubt the repeated viewing of this controversial content performed by Chinese university students also emboldened the young high-school students as well. Many said that they aspired to become university students. As I noted earlier, the Fudan students and conference participants also watched the Zhongshan production on video and similarly filmed their own production. Technology such as the easily copied and affordable DVD format has enabled connections and the dissemination of information and ideas from international actors to spread between local actors in China without excessive organisation or even direct contact with the international body. In turn these interactions bring new and powerful features to the domestic process of 'state-in-society' engagement.

The performance of the play in China, with all its sensational publicity, had a directly personal impact upon audience members. Audience comments published on an important news website, www.sina.com, reveal that the 'sexual liberation' message was as strong as the VAW message. Claiming control over their bodies through the celebration of the vagina appeared to be central to many viewers and was central to the Shanghai director's conception of the importance of the play. The latter declared that the play broke through the taboos women felt about speaking of their sexuality, sex organs and sexual experiences (Li and Sun 2004). Breaking the taboos on these topics was central to audience perception as well. One commentator on the Zhongshan University discussion board webpage, Xiao Fei, noted that some people felt that the message of the play was a good one but that the title should be changed because the word 'vagina' was problematic. Her response to this view was that such people clearly missed the meaning of the play because reclaiming the 'unspeakable' – the vagina – was central to the mission. Xiao Fei's comments were typical of those on the discussion board. She argued that

> the play enables us to be even more comfortable with our bodies, and that opposing sexual violence against women is not only about exposing the disastrous results of violence but even more important is that we change our traditions and culture in order that women's bodies achieve liberation, that we enable women to regard themselves positively, to strengthen ourselves and to recreate a female subjective consciousness.
>
> (Xiao Fei 2004)

Promoting the acceptability of an active and confident female sexuality also appealed to some audience members. In the same Zhongshan University bulletin board, Xiao Yan wrote that she thought the play told women about their bodies and sexuality and that this was important because 'many people don't understand what sex is and don't know what they should get out of their own sexual behaviour'. She also thought the play would tell men about the way women move from being children to mature women (Xiao Yan 2004). In another posting, reducing the shame about masturbation and sexual desire on the one hand and ignorance about childbirth on the other featured strongly in Xin Sun's response (Xin 2004).

The Domestic Violence Network's website also published responses from the Guangxi Middle School performers. These comments emphasised the importance of women's dignity, independence, confidence and certainty across a range of spheres – including their right to be proud of and not ashamed of their bodies and sexuality. For example, challenging centuries of thinking that menstruation is polluting, Liu Guanghua declared to her students 'Menstruation is our good friend' (Zhang Qi 2005). In each of the responses the overwhelming feeling is that more information and better information about female sexuality were vital to reducing the hardship of being a woman. Thus, the VAW theme has provided an acceptable umbrella under which audiences can engage with sexuality and sexual desire in a women-centred rubric.

China's V-day activists and their audiences appear cognisant of the North American middle-class ideological bias within the play that drives their campaign. Yet they are able to use the play's open-ended structure to target their particular concerns – as we saw in the case of the inclusion of education rights within the Guangxi performance. However, there is unease about the play's dominant critique of 'other cultures' practices and ways of conceiving of female sexuality among some audiences. Bu Wei notes that during one viewing a friend passed to her a sarcastic note saying, 'So, American vaginas are good' (*Haishi Meiguo yindao hao*). She also noted that the play's middle-class values are problematic – each performance in China has privileged urbanites speaking on behalf of rural women and in so doing risk subsuming their voices into those of the middle classes (Bu 2005b). Yet she also notes that just as Eve Ensler aimed to speak on behalf of women, so the Chinese performers were speaking on behalf of women whose perspectives would otherwise not be expressed in any form. Chinese performances of *The Vagina Monologues* are clearly interpreted in the full knowledge of their American bias – muted by the overt claim to internationalisation within the play's content. However, the flexibility of the play's multiple monologue structure allows for local input that implicates the performers equally in the role of 'othering' through representation. Moreover, the power of the many messages about sexuality, control over one's body and anti-VAW clearly resonates with middle-class Chinese women.

The rich mix of perspectives on VAW generated among audiences and performers of *The Vagina Monologues* coupled with the diverse and contradictory reactions to the play from various local state authorities serves to alert us to the dynamism currently present within the process by which Chinese society and Chinese state organs mutually constitute each other. Small, *ad hoc*, local actors in loose partnerships with international agents provide new perspectives on the particularities of the Chinese VAW problem. As will become clear in the next section, the engagement of directly state-sponsored bodies, specifically the ACWF, on the issue of VAW also provides important insights into the current process of narrating the state-in-society in China.

The ACWF's translation of international campaigns on VAW

As an official Mass Organisation of the CCP, the ACWF's engagement with VAW in the Chinese context illuminates the way in which in recent years the CCP has moved to absorb and improve upon perspectives from international bodies in their implementation in the PRC. In the years either side of the UN Women's Conference, the ACWF was able to bring DV well into the public arena by mobilising its considerable links with various media outlets, including its own newspapers and magazines. However, in contrast to the UN's initiatives – which encompass all VAW – the prime focus of the ACWF's campaigns has been DV. While this appears to narrow the frame of vision, in fact the ACWF's conception of DV is broader than that normally conceived of in Australia, Europe or the Americas. In the latter locations domestic violence conjures up notions of 'wife beating', yet in China the ACWF has also promoted the following within the domestic violence categories: child beating, parent beating, husband beating, daughter-in-law abuse and elder abuse (see the categorisation in Wei and Wang 2004). The 'domestic space' within the Chinese consciousness is a multigenerational space and the ACWF's conceptualisation of domestic violence thus includes this broader perspective. In this regard, the ACWF has absorbed the VAW message but gone beyond a sole focus on 'women'.

There are a number of reasons why this particular approach is effective within the Chinese 'state-in-society'. First, the centuries-old Confucian principle that harmony in the country is founded upon harmony in the family ensures that programmes aimed at building domestic stability are regarded favourably by a state structure concerned about social and political stability. As Bai Guimei, an academic at Beijing University, wrote: 'Family, the natural and basic unit of society, is regarded [as] essential for social stability and development in China. Promoting family harmony is an effective way to eliminate violence against women in [their] private life [*sic*]' (Bai 1997: 265). This sentiment was also explicitly revealed in Wei Hua and Wang Xin's 2004 volume titled *Domestic Violence* and they even extend invocations of the expanding impact of family harmony to the global arena. Wei and Wang write that only when men and women work together will the world be happy and peaceful, and the same principle stands for society and for the household (Wei and Wang 2004: preface; see also Zhang Zhongyou 1997).

Significantly, in reminding PRC citizens of the link between family harmony and broader social harmony the ACWF works towards an important perceptual shift required for the effective combating of DV. They have unsettled the long-held notion that 'the country has the country's laws and the family has the family rules' (*guo you guo fa, jia you jia gui*) – a notion that effectively kept family matters beyond the reach of the public purview.

The second reason why this family-focused, rather than women-focused approach is effective in China is because it ensures that the ACWF's activities and campaigns carry a reduced threat of 'bourgeois feminism'. This positioning ensures that they are more palatable to a wider range of people and political perspectives, including their sponsors, the CCP. Since the foundation of the CCP in 1921, women activists have been exhorted to beware bourgeois feminism since the latter was regarded as prioritising women's interests over class interests. The activities of the V-day activists show that fear of being labelled a bourgeois feminist are waning. Indeed, from about 1978 onwards, nationalism has presented the central ideological warning to women thinking of organising on women's issues. Assertions about the importance for Chinese women of establishing their own unique form of women's activism – a women's movement with Chinese characteristics – are commonplace (see Jaschok *et al.* 2001: 16–17). The women's movement and women's studies programmes in China have been vocal in their claims to indigenise feminism and distinguish the Chinese women's movement from that of Western feminism. Many women rejected the label 'feminist' since they regarded it as too radical and extreme for their tastes. As I discuss in more detail below, central to this promotion of an indigenised feminism is the assertion of the importance of men and women cooperating to combat social problems – including those that impact most commonly on women.[11]

Third, the ACWF's family-focused approach builds on longstanding Chinese Marxist conceptions of the root cause of DV. In this rubric, DV is a remnant of the feudal past with its inequitable marriage system of wives and concubines where women were little more than chattels traded between men. Sexuality and sexualised violence receive no explicit theorising within this rubric and are subsumed under the broad notion of a consciousness of male power. However, DV is not merely conceived as a product of patriarchy but rather is a result of a complex web of social relations generated by feudal modes of labour division that have privileged men. In this regard, for DV to be eliminated a whole raft of inequitable family and workplace relations must be transformed – and a single focus on women would not achieve this result. The overarching perspective is that as socialism improves relations between members of society by changing work relationships and structures, such inequities in family relationships will disappear. Zhou Yunqing explains that

> From the viewpoint of Socialist Feminism or Marxist feminism, the source of VAW lies in the patriarchal system's gendered division of labour, and this type of unequal division of labour between the two sexes leads to a

situation where notions of male power become a normalised state of consciousness and this permeates every part of society and social life.

(Zhou Yunqing 2005: 439)

DV is also commonly conceived as a consequence of the failure to achieve 'equality between men and women' (*nannü pingdeng*). Both academic and policy statements routinely describe DV as breaching the state's explicit laws on the equality of the sexes in the PRC (Xia 2002: 21; see also Liu Meng 2003: 22–3).

Explaining DV within classic Marxist notions of economic forces propelling change, on the one hand, and as a breach of the PRC's legal codes, on the other, is fundamental to ensuring that the ACWF has legitimacy and credibility with the dominant state actor, the CCP. The CCP has the power to change law, policy and funding related to DV so maintaining positive links with supporters within the Party is crucial to the success of all ACWF initiatives. Moreover, invoking Marxist rhetoric serves as a bridge, whereby the Western-style feminism emerging from the key international actors the ACWF connects with, such as UNIFEM, is made palatable to the Chinese state and more effective within the Chinese social and cultural setting. Where the ACWF was conceived at its inception as a bridge between the Party and the women of China, it has evolved in the twenty-first century to become a bridge between the Party and the international women's movement as expressed by the UN's agencies.

The ACWF's role as a domestic actor on VAW emerges in the context of these three points above as that of a conduit between key international actors and the state.[12] In this function it ensures that China has access to global resources and support in eradicating VAW. For example, in 1996 the United Nations General Assembly established a trust fund to support initiatives aimed to eliminate VAW and in July 2001 the ACWF was successful in winning funding for a large educational programme in China (Unifem 2006). Their programme included the production of videos and training materials for public broadcast and professional development.[13] In contrast to the other funded applications the Chinese project stressed that it would be working with 'women and men' to eliminate violence against women. Aiming for a national reach across multiple audiences, the ACWF stands as the only body with the credentials to undertake a programme of such a large scale. Its dual access to the state's authority and the women of China makes it the credible domestic actor to UNIFEM. Simultaneously, the ACWF also stands as a credible domestic actor to the CCP and the Chinese state through its dexterous translation of Western feminist rhetoric.

A clear example of the manner in which the ACWF serves as a bridge between international actors and the Chinese 'state-in-society' is provided by its mobilisation around White Ribbon Day – the International Day for the Elimination of Violence against Women. A group of Canadian men founded the event in 1991 and the UN has subsequently given 25 November formal international recognition. With men as its founders it is understandable that men are central in the publicity for this global campaign.[14] This contrasts with Western feminist actions against violence undertaken during the 1970s and 1980s, such as the 'Take Back the Night' marches – the latter were almost exclusively female. The enthusiasm with which the ACWF has embraced a movement that includes men is central to its effectiveness in engaging the PRC 'state-in-society' processes. News releases in 2002 explain that White Ribbon Day is designed to 'encourage men and women to work together against domestic violence' (*People's Daily* 2002b). In the 2003 campaign, six men were given awards for their work in eliminating DV (*People's Daily* 2003). Moreover, the event, like the UNIFEM trust fund programme, is jointly operated by the Department of Rights and White Ribbon Day is held in conjunction with International Human Rights Day on 10 December ('Fan jiating baoli ... ' 2005).

This confluence of campaigns further ensures that women's special rights in contrast to those of men are not overly emphasised but rather are framed by the notion that 'women's rights are human rights' – another UN-promoted slogan.[15] Where many feminist scholars around the world remain wary of the potential for the 'women's rights are human rights' campaign to collapse the gender-specific agenda, the opposite appears to have been the case in China. China faces largely negative international opinion and intense scrutiny for its human rights record and remains vulnerable to claims of abuse in this realm. By subsuming Human Rights Day into White Ribbon Day, the effect produced is one where China pronounces its support for human rights while subsuming them under an anti-VAW umbrella – with both initiatives sponsored by the UN. In this respect the state's actor on women's matters, the ACWF, performs an important role in mediating one of the more fraught aspects of China's international relations. The ACWF performs the CCP's 'human rights housework' in its DV campaigns. Human Rights are not just subsumed under women's rights but are further absorbed by the promotion of the all-encompassing campaign to build family harmony.

Conclusion

The two local actors discussed in detail in this chapter have clearly different styles and forms of interacting with the state and with international bodies despite their common agendas on VAW and DV. The V-day activists' connections to an international constituency are driven entirely by local Chinese actors even though the initial impetus came from outside China. Yet the indignation generated about the extent of VAW around the world through the play's monologues created a sense of global female unity against a particularly female problem. As local Chinese actors, their interactions with the international V-day movement are diverse and self-directed. Autonomy from international control for these particular local actors is maintained at all times. Support from the strength and vibrancy of the V-day movement internationally has produced scope within China for a women-centred consciousness to thrive among a certain segment of society. It also opens the VAW campaign to a younger audience that as yet lacks individual institutional status. Through its educational and entertainment mix, the V-day structure provides this group with access to a social cause that, in other guises, is supported by the state through the ACWF. Thus, China's local actors have harnessed international impetus for effecting social change within the rubric of the elimination of VAW. However, the emergence and continued existence of the V-day activists relies in large part on another, vastly different, domestic actor – the ACWF.

The ACWF has ensured that political movements calling for the elimination of VAW, such as the V-day activities, are able to continue in their *ad hoc* fashion because it has made the elimination of VAW (albeit in terms of a broad conception of DV) part of a wider public agenda, and, by the nature of the ACWF's affiliation to the CCP, this carries state authorisation. To achieve this integration the ACWF mobilised the programmes of the world's premier international organ – the UN. In linking China firmly with a major UN initiative through DEVAW, the ACWF has helped build the conditions in which more radical activities – such as those of the V-day activists and performers – are able to function. At the same time, in their engagement with the UN and building from their own extensive and impressive network of cadre, the ACWF is able to promote awareness of the DV problem throughout the country across multiple demographic sectors.

The various VAW activities in China reveal that local domestic actors are not necessarily divorced from the state but rather interact with it in multiple and diverse ways through complex webs of social and political relationships. The different styles of activism promote different reactions between the local actors themselves and between the local actors and the state. Moreover, the ACWF and the Domestic Violence Network maintain a dual relationship with the state – each is implicated in the state's apparatus to varying degrees yet they both serve as catalysts for change within the state. V-day promotes a global and grassroots-centred activism spurred by a loose and dynamic international movement. Their sensational agenda is furthered by the protection afforded the parallel agenda of the CCP's own organ – the ACWF.

The activism aimed to eliminate VAW and DV in the twenty-first century also reveals significant changes in the Chinese 'state-in-society'. This case study revealed how international actors, newly regarded more positively for their ability to bring prestige, respectability and global influence to the PRC, are able to connect in myriad different ways with diverse domestic actors to address a pressing social problem. Also, the anti-VAW and anti-DV campaigns of the PRC demonstrate that the PRC 'state-in-society' has grown increasingly comfortable with multiple approaches to tackling social problems. Significantly, these approaches no longer have to be derived directly from the CCP directives. *Ad hoc* actions by small groups of citizens have become vibrant and important parts of the increasingly rich 'state-in-society' composition. Ultimately, the anti-VAW and anti-DV campaigns in the PRC of the last few years reveal that the local, central and global are each powerful actors creating change in the Chinese 'state-in-society'. Moreover, combined together the complex interactions of these various actors present a strong programme for tackling VAW in China.

Notes

1 The author would like to thank Linda Li, Elaine Jeffreys and Tamara Jacka for their comments on earlier drafts of this chapter. Funding from the Australian Research Council made this research possible.
2 The Chinese translation of the Declaration is *Xiaochu dui funü baoli xuanyan*. DV is translated as *Jiating baoli*. For a discussion on the problems of VAW in other Asian nations, see Lenore Manderson and Linda Rae Bennett (2003).
3 See also the results of their 1990 survey *Zhongguo funü shehui diaocha* (Social investigation into China's women), where over 70 per cent of women said they had experienced some form of DV (cited in Wang Xingjuan 2005: 199).
4 Susan Glosser's translation of the cartoon of Li Fengjin, originally published in 1950 as part of the implementation of the new Marriage Laws, shows the CCP's focus on the cadres' roles in mediating DV – albeit under the nomenclature of 'oppressive, feudal marriage practices' (Glosser 2003).
5 However, a huge 33 per cent are reported as taking 'revenge with violence' on their attackers – suggesting a cycle of intra-family violence that supports the state's concern, that DV undermines broader social harmony rather than only women's safety.
6 There has been much debate about the existence of NGOs in China and at various points, including during the UN's Women's Conference at Beijing, the ACWF presented itself as an NGO. The Domestic Violence Network is clearly closer to an NGO than the ACWF in the former group's greater distance from the Party-state than the latter. For discussion on NGOs and women's organising in China, see Liu Bohong (2001) and Naihua Zhang (2001).
7 The Domestic Violence Network activists organised a series of traditional theatre activities to take their message to the countryside – including comic dialogues (*duikou ci*) and clapperboard rhymes (*kuaiban*) (see Bu 2005a). These avoided sexuality within their topics, preferring to alert their audiences to the legal protection afforded women and the services available to victims.
8 See the UN fact sheet on violence against women for the most succinct official summary of its range and conception (UN 2000). See Elaine Jeffreys (2004) for a discussion of the context of prostitution in China.
9 It gained particular notoriety for its positive portrayal of lesbian sex between an older woman and a female minor. Critics argued that sexual acts with minors were abhorrent regardless of the sexual orientation of the parties concerned.
10 The advocacy of women's and girls' right to education has been fundamental to women's activism in China from early in the twentieth century (see Edwards 2004a: 65–68).
11 Cooperation between men and women is central to the ACWF campaigns, whereas the V-day activists are often queried for the anti-men attitudes in *The Vagina Monologues*. For example, reporters Li and Sun asked the director of the banned Shanghai performance of *The Vagina Monologues* whether the play's aim to awaken a female consciousness could be considered a 'declaration of war against patriarchy' (Li and Sun 2004).

12 The ACWF's role as a bridge to the international community is also evident in its support for academic work on DV. The many published volumes and articles in recent years demonstrate an extensive knowledge and degree of interaction between Chinese and international researchers. Comparative volumes on the nature of DV and anti-DV campaigns around the world and in China are central features of the field and it is commonplace for authors to remind readers that DV is an international 'hot topic' (see Rong and Huang 2003: 1; Rong and Song 2002: 105–18; Wang Yixin 2004: 306–11). Under the protective parameters established by the ACWF with its prestigious international partner such scholarship thrives and presents a limited threat to the state (see Zhou Weiwen 2001). An early volume in the field edited by Ma Yuan and published in 1997 included numerous chapters on the implications of the UN's DEVAW programme on China, how China could address the problem and in the appendices included excerpts of various segments of Chinese legislation aimed at preventing VAW. These included laws prohibiting the kidnapping of women and children, anti-prostitution legislation, as well as the marriage law and laws on protection of the elderly (Ma 1997). The volume clearly positions China's burgeoning campaign against VAW within the UN's international campaign and within the central Chinese state's existing agendas.

13 The legal profession appears to be able to address more radical aspects of the DV agenda. In dealing with the cases that come before the judicial system they confront the ugly reality of violence rather than the positive perspective promoted in ACWF campaigns. For example, see the volume on rape within marriage published by the People's Court Publishing House (Ji 2005), the Legal Publishing House's recent volume on rape as a criminal offence (Zhu Mingshan 2004) or the People's Security University Press's volume on rape and indecent dealings with girls (Zhao Bingzhi 2004).

14 In some media reports on Human Rights Day and the International Day for the Elimination of Violence against Women distinctions between DV and VAW are blurred. For example, in writing of the 2002 campaign, the *People's Daily* declared, 'Nov. 25 marks International Day of no violence in families and speaks about the 1999 UN Declaration on the elimination of domestic violence against women' (*People's Daily* 2002a).

15 Cecelia Milwertz and Bu Wei provide an extended discussion of the human rights aspects of China's engagement with international VAW initiatives in their recent article (Milwertz and Bu 2007).

7 'Peaceful Rise' and China's new international contract

The state in change in transnational society

Chengxin Pan

Nearly three decades of breakneck economic growth have profoundly altered China's economic, social, cultural and political landscapes (Watson 1992; Tu 1993; F. Wang 1998; Tang 2005; Gittings 2005). Yet, despite these remarkable changes in China, many observers have identified evidence of major continuity. Domestically, the continuity is clearly reflected in the continued reign of the Chinese Communist Party (CCP). At the international level, it is related to a possible repetition of the recurring tragedy of great power politics (Mearsheimer 2001). Given that violent clashes between predominant status quo powers and their emerging challengers have been characteristic of international history, many realists believe that China's rise is no exception to this pattern. Consequently, the image of a Chinese dragon as a 'fire-breather', as former US Deputy Secretary of State Robert Zoellick (2005) puts it, is creating 'a cauldron of anxiety' among the rest of the world. Against this backdrop, partly in response to such widespread anxiety, China spelt out a strategy called 'Peaceful Rise' (*heping jueqi*) in late 2003.[1] Apparently aimed at reassuring the international community of China's peaceful intent, still this new strategy is greeted with much scepticism. As Zoellick (2005) notes, 'Uncertainties about how China will use its power will lead the United States – and others as well – to hedge relations with China. Many countries hope China will pursue a "Peaceful Rise", but none will bet their future on it'. For all its claim to a peaceful rise, China is thus seen by many as no different from previous rising major powers, notably Germany and Japan in the late nineteenth and early twentieth centuries.

Against such hunches about continuities, I suggest in this chapter that there have been a lot more fluidities and changes in terms of both China's domestic politics and international orientations, through a close examination of the 'Peaceful Rise' strategy. The notion of 'Peaceful Rise', I argue, denotes a new international contract,[2] so to speak, being struck between the Beijing regime and transnational actors. Within this contractual framework, the Chinese government promises responsible and peaceful foreign behaviour in accordance with international norms, in exchange for a largely favourable and stable international environment in which China could continue its rise or economic development. China of course insists that it has always behaved peacefully and responsibly in the international realm. But what is new in its 'Peaceful Rise' discourse, I argue, is Beijing's growing acceptance of international responsibility as defined by mainstream transnational actors, rather than on its own terms (as was previously the case). This ready acceptance of obligation, largely externally defined, is linked to changes in broader arenas, as many transnational actors have become instrumental in China's economic fortune and emerged as a new, if indirect, source of political legitimacy for the Chinese regime. Thus this new international contract, based on the changing meanings of state responsibility and legitimacy, reflects a transformation not only in China's international relations, but also in the Chinese state itself.

This chapter focuses on how such changes in the Chinese state have taken place, as exemplified in the domestic–global nexus underlining the formulation of the 'Peaceful Rise' strategy. In her study of the constitutive relationship between national interests and international society, Martha Finnemore (1996: 136) suggests that 'the particular form of the state is a result of both international and local factors'. This observation, I would say, applies also to the Chinese state in change. At one level, 'Peaceful Rise' was driven by domestic processes one of which was the regime's desire to carve out a new national identity and maintain domestic legitimacy. At the same time, such domestic processes are intersected with processes outside China's 'boundaries', so a better understanding of the change requires that the constitutive role played by the transnational society and its relevant components are addressed. Not only does transnational society often provide the backdrop of the 'Other' against which the Chinese state (re)defines its interests and identity, but, more importantly, multiple actors within transnational society, through their images, practices and interactions with Chinese 'domestic' actors, are constantly complicit in the production and reproduction of China as a state. As Gupta (1995: 377) points out, 'any theory of the state needs to take into account its constitution through a complex set of *spatially* intersecting representations and practices'.

Given the limitations of space, in this chapter I shall concentrate on the transnational dimension when discussing the emergence of the 'Peaceful Rise' strategy and its revelation of a state in change. This does not mean that domestic actors do not play an important part or that their role can be neatly detached from the transnational processes. Rather, I contend that only by examining the transnational context – and by clarifying the interactions between the transnational and the domestic – can we better appreciate the role of multiple domestic actors. This chapter cannot, nor does it purport to, provide a comprehensive answer to the question of why the Chinese state undergoes change the way it does – regarding its choice of strategy in projecting an international image. Instead, it only serves to catch a glimpse of the discursive nature as well as the fluidity of China as a state (Li 2006b), which, like all states, should be understood as nothing more than 'a historically constituted and constantly reconstituted form of political life' (Walker 1993: 46).

In what follows, I shall first examine how 'Peaceful Rise' embodies some significant changes in terms of the Chinese state's legitimacy base and its responsibility. Drawing on the 'state-in-society' approach (Migdal 2001), I shall survey how those changes have been effected by the constitutive influence of various transnational actors. Finally, I conclude that 'Peaceful Rise' is as much a foreign policy initiative *of* the Chinese government as it is a social construct *from* transnational society, an understanding which is contingent on our interpretation regarding what China's 'rise' may mean for the world.

Expanding the social contract: 'Peaceful Rise' and a state in change

On the surface, 'Peaceful Rise' is primarily a foreign policy statement aimed at reassuring the outside world of China's peaceful intent and the non-violent nature of its economic expansion. The phrase was first used by former Vice-President of the Central Party School Zheng Bijian, now chairman of the government-affiliated think-tank China Reform Forum. In November 2003, in his address to a plenary session of the Boao Forum in China's Hainan province, Zheng (2003) stated that China has blazed a new strategic path which is 'peaceful rise through independently building socialism with Chinese characteristics, while participating in rather than detaching from economic globalization'. Once coined, the phrase was quickly endorsed by the top Chinese leadership, appearing both in Premier Wen Jiabao's speech at Harvard University in December 2003, and in President Hu Jintao's address at the forum marking Mao Zedong's 110th birthday (Wen 2003; Hu Jintao 2003). As far as Beijing is concerned, the notion of 'Peaceful Rise', which appears to be both an accurate description of China's developmental trajectory hitherto and a sensible strategy for the future, can be employed to reinforce a positive image of the Chinese state in international society. This image, as Wen Jiabao told his audience at Harvard University, portrays China as 'a country in reform and opening-up and a rising power dedicated to peace' (Wen 2003).

In this context, the international scholarly community has often treated 'Peaceful Rise' as a new foreign policy paradigm (Medeiros 2004; Suettinger 2004; Sutter 2004; Jia 2005), raising questions such as: Can it work? Will China be able to rise peacefully, even if such is the intention? To what extent is it *new*? While these questions – all focusing on the policy itself – are important to ponder, what has been less fully recognised is that 'Peaceful Rise' also reveals significant change in the Chinese state itself – a new social contract on the horizon. It is well known that since the beginning of the 'reform and opening' policy in the late 1970s, the Chinese state has been predicated on 'an unwritten social contract between the party and the people where the people do not compete with the party for political power as long as the party looks after their economic fortunes' (Breslin 2005: 749). Today, what is implied in 'Peaceful Rise' is the expansion of that social contract from a domestic to a transnational level, in which China makes an explicit commitment to 'peace' to reassure the international community, which in return could continue facilitating China's 'rise' or economic development.

Two changes are observed here. The first is the expansion of state responsibility from serving the people to serving transnational capital. To be sure, this is not the first time that China has stressed its role as a peace-loving, responsible member of the interstate system. As Richard Bernstein and Ross Munro (1997: 51) pointed out, the slogan 'We will never seek hegemony' is 'one of the few that has remained in use in China as the country passed through its various political stages'. But that slogan largely expresses a 'passive' attitude, outlining what China will *not* do. 'Peaceful Rise', on the other hand, explicitly underlines what China will do – maintain peace. This suggests a growing recognition in the Chinese leadership that in the globalisation era peace means more than the absence of conflict, but requires its own explicit acceptance of international norms and active participation in the maintenance of the international order. As a consequence, the leadership is no longer as suspicious of US global hegemony as in the past. In the words of Zheng Bijian (2005), the CCP 'does not intend to challenge the existing international order, let alone to break it by violent forces'.

Consequently, 'Peaceful Rise' not only is a foreign policy initiative but also indicates a new official discourse on state responsibility. For example, speaking at the APEC Chief Executive Officers' Summit in November 2004, President Hu Jintao promised that the Chinese government would 'create new ways of attracting foreign investment, and push for greater reform in government administrative system by building a predictable and more transparent management system for sectors open to foreign investment' (quoted in Jia Qingguo 2005: 498). Another example of this new discourse of responsibility is the unusual manner in which Chinese authorities conducted their World Trade Organisation (WTO) entry negotiations. In order to fast-track the negotiations and accelerate China's entry, the chief negotiator Long Yongtu and other negotiators were instructed to insulate themselves not only from Chinese interested parties, but even from their own colleagues in Beijing (Breslin 2004: 665). In a sense, this reveals the extraordinary lengths to which the Chinese leaders have gone in order to meet international 'obligations' and be seen as 'responsible' players in the international economic system.

Associated with this new sense of responsibility, the second change embodied in 'Peaceful Rise' is a broadened legitimacy base for the state. Within the 'Peaceful Rise' discourse, two sources of legitimacy for the Chinese government are evident, one domestic and the other transnational, which are intertwined through Beijing's fixation on economic development. While partly designed to boost domestic legitimacy, economic development has led to deepening ties between China and the outside world. As a result, in the eyes of the Chinese government, by playing an increasingly significant role in the Chinese economy, transnational actors have become also important for the state's legitimacy and political survival.

This added role comes as an unintended consequence of transnational actors' participation in China's economy. However, as many transnational actors directly benefit from China's economic boom, some have come to openly endorse the performance of the Chinese government. The international business community, for instance, has increasingly looked favourably at China as a valuable trading partner and investment destination, even to the point of treating it as 'the leading neoliberal poster country' (Hart-Landsberg and Burkett 2004). The president of the world's largest media company Time Warner once praised China as 'an ideal cooperative partner in the global economy' in terms of its steady economic growth and good prospects (quoted in Knight 2003: 330). Perhaps nowhere is the international acceptance of the Chinese state more evident than the warm reception its leaders now receive abroad. A recent example is Hu Jintao's April 2006 visit to the US, where on one occasion he was treated to a lavish banquet at Microsoft Chief Bill Gates' $100 million lakeside mansion in Seattle. Executives from Starbucks, Costco, Weyerhaeuser and Amazon.com were among the guests, 'all eager to show the Chinese leader their appreciation for his efforts in providing American businesses with an ample supply of cheap labor, a stable currency exchange and an affable investment climate' (Kwong 2006: 1).

Not only has Beijing gained more respect in the business world, but it is making friends far and wide among world leaders as well. When Hu Jintao visited France in 2004, French President Jacques Chirac had the Eiffel Tower illuminated red in his honour. And his visit to Australia in 2003, as one commentator put it, 'was such a sanitized affair that he seemed to be visiting a vassal state' (Seth 2005: 8). For a country highly sensitive to 'face' and national image, increasing global acceptance thus provides an additional layer of legitimacy for the Chinese government, both on the world stage and in the eyes of local political and economic elites. By this, I do not mean that the Chinese government and transnational actors have completely converged, as the fine details of the 'international contract' are often open to different interpretations and contestations. Nevertheless, it is fair to say that international business has now become integral to the state's legitimacy; this in itself constitutes a remarkable change in the ways in which the Chinese state has traditionally legitimised itself.

The changing ways in which state responsibility and legitimacy are perceived by the Chinese leaders underline the changing nature of the Chinese state, especially in terms of the ways it operates and functions in various aspects of Chinese political and economic life. For example, Chinese cadres at almost every level have come to realise that their career advancement is linked to their ability to attract foreign investment (Zha 2005: 784). In this context, it is not difficult to imagine the implications for other dimensions of work, such as 'party construction' (*dangjian*) and 'political and ideological work' (*sixiang zhengzhi gongzuo*), as well as for the organisation and operation of the party-state more broadly. In 2000, even before the formal articulation of the 'Peaceful Rise' strategy, the tectonic plate of party politics had already begun to shift, as the CCP rewrote its mission statement in the order of the so-called 'Three Represents' (*sange daibiao*).[3] In 2001, the CCP amended its constitution for the first time to open its membership to private entrepreneurs. Noting the significance of this change for China, a RAND analyst wrote:

> The defining event in China in the first year of the 21st century is probably not the aircraft collision near Hainan and its aftermath, or the trial and release of Chinese–American scholars, or the repression of the Falun Gong, or the award of the 2008 Olympics to Beijing. The defining event is the decision of the Chinese leadership to admit capitalists as members of the Communist Party. This decision raises the possibility of Communists co-opting capitalists – or of capitalists co-opting the party.
>
> (Wolf 2001: A17)

Whether it is communists co-opting capitalists or the other way round, what is not in doubt is a party-state in historic transition, as a China committed to 'Peaceful Rise' seeks to redefine its legitimacy, responsibility and identity *vis-à-vis* market, capital, great global powers and its own people. What is ironic is that 'Peaceful Rise' is aimed primarily at the stability and continuity of the state; but, to that end, the state has been compelled to significantly transform itself. One may indeed argue that the apparent continuity of having the CCP in power in China merely masks the abundance and depth of change, to which the next section now turns.

The transnational sources of China's 'rise' and state legitimacy

In one way or another, changes in contemporary China tend to be linked to its economic development since the late 1970s. This economic miracle, in turn, had its origins in the end of the decade-long Cultural Revolution in 1976. Those upheavals not only devastated the Chinese economy and social life, but also significantly alienated the political leadership from much of Chinese society (Goldman *et al.* 1993). With the foundation of state legitimacy seriously weakened, the image and practice of the state badly needed a facelift to reclaim its political mandate. It was against this background that the reformist camp led by Deng Xiaoping came to the fore. Effectively replacing the old doctrine of 'class struggle' with the immediately pragmatic appeal that 'getting rich is glorious', the reformers set China on a path of economic rehabilitation, reform and development.

From the outset, the economic reform was aimed not at bringing about fundamental change in the state's political structure, but, quite the opposite, at keeping it largely intact – by way of a 'mundane' objective of continually raising people's living standards. In this sense, it can be said that China's rise owes much to the desire of the CCP to stay in power, as well as to various sub-state and local actors, and China's indigenous conditions, such as low wages, low costs, high savings rates and, some would add, Confucian culture. And yet these constitute only part of the complex picture of the rise of China. As the country's integration with the outside world deepens, local initiatives are increasingly inseparable from transnational influences. Consequently, the picture cannot be completed unless we bring in transnational actors and understand their roles in China's economic development. Thus far, two conditions are especially noteworthy for the country's impressive economic performance: a favourable international economic environment and a normative change on the part of the Chinese leadership in its attitudes towards the free market and the capitalist economic system in general. In both respects, as will be illustrated in this chapter, transnational actors have played a significant role.

First, transnational actors contribute to China's rise through the channels of investment, trade and technology transfer. Increasing access to global capital, foreign markets and production know-how has been instrumental in China's soaring economic growth. As Nicholas Lardy (2003: 1) suggests, the volume of foreign direct investment (FDI) flowing into China has been a key 'indicator of its economic rise'. In 1979 China passed a joint venture law, signalling its intention to open its economy to foreign investment. In order to attract investment, the following year it created four special economic zones on its southeast coast. Although the initial inflows of foreign investment were modest, it was those special economic zones, where about 90 per cent of FDI went between 1986 and 1999, that helped jumpstart China's economic growth. To date, tens of thousands of corporations from 190 countries and regions have invested in China, which include 450 of the Fortune global top 500 multinational corporations (Xinhua News Agency 2006). Since 1993, it has consistently been the largest recipient of FDI among developing countries. Annual net FDI inflows into China grew from US$1 billion in 1985 to US$52.7 billion by 2002, the year when it overtook the US to become the world's largest FDI destination (Li 2005: 435; Hart-Landsberg and Burkett 2004: 13).

Like foreign investment, China's export-led economy is also at the centre of its remarkable success story. Foreign trade as a share of GDP increased from 12.68 per cent in 1980 to 60.3 per cent in 2003 (Xu Jianguo 2004), making the country a major export centre in East Asia. With most FDI in China going to the manufacturing sector, the export activities of foreign transnational corporations are becoming increasingly crucial to China's economic growth (Hart-Landsberg and Burkett 2004: 48–9). In 2003, foreign invested enterprises (FIEs) accounted for 55.81 per cent of all Chinese exports, or close to 70 per cent if domestic Chinese producers who produce under contract for export using foreign components are included (Breslin 2005: 743). Thus Stephen Roach at Morgan Stanley argues that 'the vigor of Chinese export growth has come far more from the deliberate outsourcing strategies of western multinational companies than from the rapid growth of indigenous Chinese companies' (quoted in Hart-Landsberg and Burkett 2004: 83).

As foreign trade as a share of China's GDP grows, so does the importance of the foreign market for the Chinese economy. This is especially true with the American market. During the booming decade of the American economy between 1991 and 2001, the United States acted as a 'dynamic absorber of East Asian manufactured products, which were a main source of economic growth in export-oriented East Asian countries', including China (Ohashi 2005: 72). Such access to overseas markets has helped produce, among other things, a huge trade surplus for the Chinese economy, whose foreign currency reserves have recently passed the US$1 trillion milestone. Consequently, the 'FDI trade nexus', as Ohashi (2005: 71) notes, has been 'boosting economic growth in China since the early 1990s and resulted in China becoming the "factory of the world" and the world's largest supplier of sixty-six products in ten manufacturing industries in 2001'.

Meanwhile, Western, especially US, technology has also made an important contribution. In the mid-nineteenth century, European science and technology were one of the first things that shocked the Middle Kingdom and opened its eyes to the outside world. Since the late 1970s, science and technology were once again back on the state policy agenda. As *Newsweek* contributing editor Robert J. Samuelson (2004: A21) wrote, China wants to be 'more than the world's sweatshop' and so it wants to attract not only investment, but also technology. In 1984 alone, over 1,000 contracts were signed to import advanced Western technology and equipment (Stoessinger 1994: 110). Meanwhile, China's scholarly exchange programme in the early reform period enabled foreign countries to transfer technology to China on a scale triple that of the comparable programme in the 1950s (Harding 1987: 155). And thanks to the inflows of FDI, foreign investors have now established more than 700 research and development centres across the country (Xinhua News Agency 2006).

Of course, in all these processes we should not overlook the active role played by the Chinese state and numerous local actors. Without their initiatives and cooperation, transnational forces, be they foreign investment or the market, cannot on their own steer China's transformation. As Wang Hui (2003: 119) notes, 'the actualities of market economics and the process of globalization cannot be implemented other than by state intervention'. In this sense, the state has indeed played the role of 'midwife of capitalism' (Robison and Goodman 1996: 4). Having said that, I argue that the Chinese state did not take on this role as a matter of course; rather, this has been largely a result of a cognitive learning process. While the state was keen to revive its economy in order to salvage its waning legitimacy, it had no readymade blueprint at hand, and had no choice but to adopt a highly pragmatic approach. As Deng Xiaoping once explained: 'We are engaged in an experiment. For us, it [reform] is something new, and we have to grope around to find our way' (quoted in Harding 1987: 87). Given this 'ideational vacuum', the Chinese state understood that it was in need of new ideas and norms to liberate thought (*jiefang sixiang*) so as to carry out the monumental task of economic reform, or the 'second revolution' as Deng once aptly described it.

This is where transnational actors' normative influence comes in. Indeed, if we are to understand the ideational forces behind China's rise, the fact should not be lost that China's economic reform has largely coincided with the ascendancy of neoliberalism on the world stage as the new economic orthodoxy known as the 'Washington Consensus'. Deng's 'let some get rich first (so others can follow suit)' is widely credited with helping unleash China's force of production. But this doctrine, for all its apparent 'Chinese characteristics', has a conspicuous international pedigree. As Peter Kwong (2006: 1) points out, if Deng's slogan 'sounds like Ronald Reagan's neoliberal "trickle down economics", it's because that's exactly what it is: both Ronald Reagan and Deng Xiaoping were great fans of the neoliberal guru Milton Friedman'. Indeed, as Kwong recalled, there was a great public fanfare among Chinese liberal intellectuals when Friedman first visited China in 1980. His lecture given at the Chinese People's Political Consultative Conference was attended not only by intellectuals and ministerial-level officials, but also by top Communist Party leaders (Kwong 2006: 1).

Friedman was not the only neoliberal thinker who captivated Chinese leaders and intellectuals; Friedrich von Hayek was another. The joint winner of the 1974 Nobel Prize for Economics argued that because governments always receive limited information, they should not interfere with the market's spontaneous order. His book *The Road to Serfdom* was treated as a classic and its Chinese version sold tens of thousands of copies (Terrill 2006: 15).[4] According to one of China's most influential public intellectuals, Hayek's theory was instrumental in China's decision to gradually dismantle the economic structure of central planning and to accord market forces a decisive role (Wang Hui 2003: 120). The Hayekian idea of 'small government, big society' (*xiao zhengfu, da shehui*) has now been internalised as an almost sacred principle in China, underpinning a range of social and economic reforms in areas such as health care, housing, state-owned enterprises and the financial system.

In a similar vein, the neoliberal notion of export and the attraction of FDI as key components of successful development has been dutifully observed in China since the early days of its reform. Indeed, it was the faith in the centrality of FDI in economic growth that was behind China's determination to join the WTO, especially in the wake of the Asian financial crisis in 1997–8 when FDI activities stagnated across the region (Hart-Landsberg and Burkett 2004: 49). In a widely circulated article, Long Yongtu (1999) explained that joining the organisation is necessary for China to become part of mainstream international society. The chief negotiator for WTO entry insisted that 'China's economy must become a market economy in order to become part of the global economic system, as well as the economic globalization process' (quoted in Lardy 2002: 21). Predictably, the process of joining the WTO further intensified China's 'socialisation' into the global economic system. Given its role in China's WTO entry, the Ministry of Foreign Trade and Economic Cooperation (MOFTEC) was at the forefront of such socialisation. In recent years, institutional norms within MOFTEC have become 'increasingly aligned with the norms of the international regime, and its officials became the strongest advocates within the government of China's adoption of international practices' (Pearson 2001: 355). Such changes, as Pearson (2001: 355–6) notes, would have been unlikely without pressure from US and European negotiators in the lead-up to WTO entry, for most of those changes had not been considered seriously by Chinese officials back in the 1980s.

As cognitive learning and normative change pave the way for China's economic integration with the international system, integration in turn helps accelerate its economic expansion. The rapid growth in China's foreign trade in the immediate aftermath of its accession to the WTO exceeded already high expectations. Within three years, China surpassed Japan to become the world's third largest trading nation in 2004. In the meantime, its outward FDI also gathered pace, with the average annual investment (in 160 countries) rising nearly tenfold from the 1980s to US$3 billion during the four years of 2000–3 (Zhang 2005: x, 5).

To the extent that various transnational actors are behind this economic expansion, there has been 'an ideational acceptance' among Chinese authorities that 'dependence on the capitalist global economy is the best or at least the quickest way of promoting economic growth' (Breslin 2005: 749). After all, underlying this acceptance is a growing recognition within the key state actors of the important contribution of transnational actors to the maintenance of the state's legitimacy. For the most part, transnational society is interested not in boosting the legitimacy of the Chinese state *per se*, but rather in taking advantage of the commercial opportunity on offer, with some even harbouring the hope of a Chinese democracy along the way. And yet, in practice, by contributing to China's economic development transnational society has, if only unwittingly, helped enhance the state's legitimacy.

Transnational actors, norm diffusion and China's 'peace' commitment

Insofar as the state's legitimacy has been boosted by its engagement with transnational actors, it is logical that the government would want to behave more 'responsibly' in the international realm – that is, to meet somewhat the international expectations of it. In this sense, its commitment to peace should also be seen as a transnational construct. Sure, such a commitment has its roots in Beijing's domestic concern with economic development and internal stability, a concern which is increasingly shared by a new middle class in China. Nevertheless, I argue that China's renewed sense of international responsibility cannot be fully explained unless we also take into account the constitutive influence of international normative structures on the Chinese state.

By international normative structures, I refer to two types of discursive or normative structures at the transnational level, one of a realist stripe, the other of a liberal persuasion. The realist normative structure is characterised by an overriding strategic concern with what realists see as the highly destabilising effect of a rising great power on the international system. The liberal structure, meanwhile, is based on a belief in the state's cognitive learning capacity and the inherent malleability of state preferences and interests in an interdependent and increasingly institutionalised world. Accordingly, these structures have two distinct sets of questions about China, with the former centring on how better to respond to an almost inevitable China threat, and the latter asking how better to facilitate 'positive' change in China (Mearsheimer and Brzezinski 2005: 46–50). As will be illustrated below, by way of their different images and practices both structures have shaped, in one way or another, China's renewed 'peace' commitment.

Associated with the realist normative structure is its 'China threat' image. With a long dominance in international politics, realism sees the world as an anarchical system in which states are engaged in a constant struggle for power or supremacy. From this perspective, with the demise of the Soviet 'evil empire', China emerged as its natural successor in this 'dangerous' world. An early example of this 'China threat' argument can be found in Samuel Huntington's 'Clash of Civilizations' thesis, which portrays an emerging threat from a Confucian–Islamic alliance to the Christian West (Huntington 1993). What has followed is an explosion of 'China threat' discourses, in which China is seen variously as a cultural, military, economic, environmental, resource or ideological threat, or various combinations of those aspects. The China threat image, moreover, is never far away from the policy of containment strenuously advocated and implemented by hardline commentators and practitioners, particularly in the United States (Pan 2004). Even with the US preoccupied with the 'war on terror', the Pentagon has continued to see China as having 'the greatest potential to compete militarily with the United States' (U.S. Department of Defense 2006: 29).

This China image and the containment policy based upon it thus constitute an international environment that is potentially detrimental to China's economic development and, by extension, its legitimacy. How to address this international concern over China's rise becomes 'one of the most important challenges China has been facing since the mid-1990s' (Jia Qingguo 2005: 493). Having tried without success to dismiss the 'China threat' argument, Beijing has resorted to reinventing its 'peace' image and commitment. Jiang Changbin, Director of the Central Party School's Centre for International Strategic Studies, provides a telling account of how the discursive practice of the 'China threat' at the international level relates to the birth of 'Peaceful Rise' in China. He suggests that it was against the backdrop of the heated debate over the 'China threat' that a research team led by Zheng Bijian was assembled to study the 'Peaceful Rise' project. After all, he argues, 'we cannot tolerate the continued absence of our own voice' in that global debate (Jiang Changbin 2005: 46). Zheng Bijian himself added weight to this explanation in an interview in 2004. He said that his determination to explore 'Peaceful Rise' was aroused after his trip in December 2002 to the US, where he encountered first hand the ubiquitous presence of the 'China threat' and 'China collapse' arguments (see Zheng and Tok 2005).

However, the realist structure alone cannot satisfactorily account for China's revamped 'peace' commitment. Otherwise we are unable to fully to explain why 'Peaceful Rise' emerged in late 2003 when the 'China threat' theory, though still visible, had largely subsided and been overshadowed by America's fear of terrorism. Indeed, if the 'China threat' image and practice were the only significant point of reference for Chinese policy-makers, the latter could well have come up with equally hostile rhetoric and response, as is frequently suggested in the notion of 'self-fulfilling prophecy'.

Thus, while realism might have provided some direct impetus for the emergence of the notion of 'Peaceful Rise' *per se*, to the extent that 'Peaceful Rise' signifies a new international contract for the Chinese state it should be seen as *more* than a counterargument against the realist construction. Rather, as Beijing's repeated efforts to join the WTO can attest, this peace commitment has a deeper normative root. On the eve of China's accession to the WTO, Long Yongtu reassured the international community that 'China will be a responsible member that will play a constructive role, abide by the rules, and do its best to contribute to the improvement of the multilateral trading system' (*People's Daily* 2001a). In a speech to an economic forum attended by foreign delegates in March 2001, then Vice-Premier Wen Jiabao highlighted the 'important changes' already made to the Chinese government's functions and responsibilities. As he put it, 'economic globalization does not imply less government responsibility and role. In the process of participating in economic globalization, the Chinese government will shoulder the responsibilities, further convert its functions, and improve the way for playing its role' (quoted in Knight 2003: 331). These statements clearly demonstrate that since the mid- to late 1990s China's attitudes towards international institutions have shifted from suspicion and indifference to enthusiastic participation and a heightened sense of responsibility.

Such a 'thick' commitment to peace can best be explained as a result of transnational norm diffusion, a process in which liberal international norms, institutions and actors help to reshape Chinese perceptions of global politics and attitudes towards international norms. There has now been a steady stream of literature on norm diffusion and changes in China's foreign behaviour (Foot 2000; Zhang 2003; Carlson 2005; H. Wang 2003). In the pages that follow, I want to sketch out some of the major transnational actors, channels and processes through which liberal norm diffusion in relation to China's 'peace' commitment has occurred and state responsibility has been reconstructed.

The United States

The United States is arguably the most important single international actor in China's global perceptual change. Given its continued dominance on the world stage and the importance of its vast market for China's exports, among other things, it is perhaps no exaggeration to say that a US constructive engagement of China is essential to the formation and continuation of an international environment conducive to China's development. In this equation, to be sure, the US is not the only state actor that matters; other Western powers as well as China's neighbours have played a similar role. Nor is the United States a unitary actor; hardline US rhetoric and policy on China are rarely in short supply. Nevertheless, overall the foreign policy establishment of recent US administrations has followed a largely neoliberal policy of 'constructive engagement'. This should not be surprising, given that 'to change China' has been seen as a major goal and responsibility of Western liberals all along (Spence 1969). Madeleine Albright (1998), for example, has argued that 'the manner in which we engage China will have an important bearing on whether China becomes integrated as a constructive participant in international institutions'. Similarly, Condoleezza Rice insisted that 'Knowing that China has the potential for good or bad, ... it is our responsibility to try and push and prod and persuade China to a more positive course' (Kessler 2005: A16).

Given such open desire to promote change in the Middle Kingdom, a link between China's 'positive course' and US engagement is not difficult to discern. For instance, 'Peaceful Rise' was first floated at a time when the Bush Jr administration, preoccupied with its 'war on terror', quietly discarded its earlier designation of China as a 'strategic competitor' and treated it once again as a partner. More precisely, Zheng Bijian's 'Peaceful Rise' speech in November 2003 was delivered two months after then US Secretary of State Colin Powell unequivocally asserted that 'U.S. relations with China are the best they have been since President Nixon's first visit in 1972' (Kessler 2003: A15). In December 2003, visiting Chinese Premier Wen Jiabao made his 'Peaceful Rise' speech at Harvard one day after George W. Bush declared that Washington and Beijing were now 'partners in diplomacy' and bluntly warned Taiwan that he opposed any attempt to unilaterally change its relationship with the mainland (Sanger 2003). In both cases, the message of 'Peaceful Rise' edged into being China's response to a US-dominated world order which the Chinese leaders perceived to be favourable to Chinese developments, so that they harboured no intention of becoming an antagonistic challenger. Wang Jisi (2005: 15), Dean of the School of International Studies at Peking University, explains the rationale behind China's response this way: 'under the global hegemonic system built by the United States, there is still a quite large space for China to rise'. If anything, all this seems to testify to 'a beneficial interactive relationship between America's dove camp with a pragmatic China policy and the moderate foreign policy of the Chinese government' (Xiao Gongqin 2001: 46).

This kind of 'positive' interaction was also evident in the previous decade. For example, some scholars have suggested that China's change of self-perception and worldview during Jiang Zemin's leadership had much to do with Jiang's meeting with Bill Clinton in 1998 as well as the smooth handover of Hong Kong the year before. Both experiences were very 'rewarding', in a subjective sense at least, for the Chinese leaders, which allegedly fuelled Beijing's desire to join the game of formulating international norms (Shi 2005: 763). Indeed, even in the wake of the 1989 Tiananmen crackdown, US engagement efforts did not stop. Shortly after the dramatic events in June, US President George H. W. Bush secretly sent his National Security Advisor Brent Scowcroft to Beijing to convey Washington's hope that China's pre-Tiananmen policy of reform would continue. 'President Bush still regards you as his friend, a friend forever', Scowcroft reportedly told Deng Xiaoping on 11 December 1989 (Mirsky 1990: 21). In response, Deng praised the visit, and expressed his confidence that Sino–US relations would improve in the long run. A few months after the visit, Deng made the following sanguine assessment of China's international environment at the time: 'We should not think that the situation has deteriorated seriously or that we are in a very unfavourable position. Things are not so bad as they seem. In this world there are ... contradictions that we can use, conditions that are favourable to us, opportunities that we can take advantage of' (Deng Xiaoping 1990). In a word, Deng believed that peace and development remained the order of the day. It is hard to know the precise extent to which US engagement actually contributed to Deng's continued faith in 'peace and development' as the main themes of the international system. Yet it is fair to propose that Washington's prompt reassurance and continued engagement significantly helped the cause of neoliberal reform in China.

International institutions

Apart from Washington's engagement policy, the role of international institutions is also worth noting. International norms reside in an array of transnational actors, but international institutions are likely the most powerful standard-bearers in international society. Despite a wide array of rules and norms, international institutions are commonly characterised by their prescriptions of normative boundaries to distinguish unacceptable from acceptable state behaviour. Thus the socialisation of states as 'responsible' members of the international community is a primary function of most international institutions. A case in point here is the ASEAN (Association of South-East Asian Nations) Regional Forum (ARF), which is regarded by many ARF participants as 'a tool for socializing China to accept the legitimacy of multilateralism, transparency and reassurance as a basis for security' (Johnston 2003: 126).

Now that China is part of most international economic, security and human rights regimes, the 'socialising' influence of international institutions on China has become more clearly identifiable. As Samuel Kim (1994: 433) observes, 'In varying ways and degrees international organisations shortened [the] Chinese global learning curve'. Similarly, in their study of the role of multilateral economic institutions (MEIs) in China, Thomas Moore and Dixia Yang (2001: 194) argue that in an effort to 'transmit the principles and rules of economic liberalism to China ... MEIs have served as a significant source of domestic and foreign policy change in China'.

Beijing's engagement with those institutions has not always been a smooth ride. Nevertheless, once inside, for the most part it has seemingly come to accept relevant international norms, develop vested interests in maintaining the international system, and at times modify its interests and preferences along the way. The net effect is that, although Chinese leaders often called for the establishment of 'a fair and reasonable new international political and economic order', in practice they seemed to have become increasingly status quo players in the international economic system. Ann Kent (1997/8: 132) suggests that China's growing participation in international organisations is clearly 'a measure of its increased global commitments and responsibility'. Thomas Moore (2005: 145) also notes that 'however dissatisfied China may be with various inequities in the international economic system, it seeks neither to undermine specific regimes nor to weaken their norms in any substantial way'. He goes on to say that, 'while China still pursues its own interests, this pursuit of self-interest leads Beijing to accept policies that entail unprecedented levels of interdependence' (Moore 2005: 149).

China's accession to the WTO again provides a good example of this metamorphosis. Even before the eventual entry, the negotiation process had already led Beijing to 'change its self-image to one that reflected more what other great powers expected of China, than a proactive image that grew out of China's own conscious quest for recognition as a great power' (Shi 2005: 758). Another example can be found in Beijing's changing attitude towards the Group of Eight (G8). Realising that it is the 'beneficiary' of economic globalisation and the current international order, the Chinese state has now sought to gradually integrate with G8 countries, selectively participate in G8 discussions and undertake international responsibility in accordance with its status and practical interests (Jiang Yong 2006). The point is not that the Chinese state would not cooperate or behave responsibly in the absence of the 'socialisation' effect of international institutions, but that the way in which international cooperation and responsibility are defined within China is, and has been, increasingly influenced by the predominantly Western international institutions.

International NGOs and academia

To fully understand this 'learning' process, it is now necessary to turn to a third kind of liberal transnational actor, namely international non-governmental organisations (NGOs) and academia in largely Western societies.

These actors frequently operate alongside state and formal institutional actors, but as innovators, proliferators and unofficial reinforcers of 'international norms' in a transnational society they have played distinctive roles in 'socialising' China or segments of Chinese society into the international community. According to China Development Brief, there are now over 200 International NGOs operating in the country. This is in addition to a growing presence of NGOs on Chinese-language websites. For instance, the Carnegie Endowment for International Peace, an influential US-based liberal think-tank, recently opened both its Chinese-language website and its office in Beijing.

Given the growing presence of international NGOs, it is not surprising that since the 1990s their influence on China's internalisation of international norms has been steadily on the rise. Rosemary Foot (2000) explains, for example, how NGOs have influenced Chinese attitudes towards human rights, particularly through shaming human rights abusers. In other cases, some organisations foster so-called 'epistemic communities' in China through promoting scholarly exchanges. As early as 1979, the Ford Foundation identified three areas (international relations, economics and law) for support in scholarly exchanges between the US and China (Zhang 2003: 101). Through its International Fellowships Program, the Ford Foundation sponsored a total of more than 168 candidates from 24 Chinese provinces to continue postgraduate study overseas. And since the opening of its Beijing office in 1988, the Foundation has made grants totalling about US$206 million, sponsoring numerous projects in areas ranging from economics, educational reform, governance and public policy to civil society and international cooperation (*Industry Updates* 2006).

Like international NGOs, Western scholars, through their work, are also important agents for China's new 'peace' commitment. Take the field of international relations (IR), for example: in recent years, there has been an explosion in the number of Western books being translated and published in Chinese. Today, nearly a dozen leading Chinese publishers are geared up in a race to bring even more Western IR literature to the Chinese audience.[5] As those books make their way to China, so do their theoretical frameworks and concepts, inevitably affecting the ways the Chinese come to perceive the world. Even with a cursory search through Chinese IR journals and articles, one can easily run into largely favourable discussions of such concepts as 'interdependence' (*xianghu yicun*), 'responsible power' (*fu zeren de daguo*), 'international norms' (*guoji guifan*), 'democratic peace' (*minzhu heping*), 'global governance' (*quanqiu zhili*), 'multilateralism' (*duobian zhuyi*) and 'constructivism' (*goujian zhuyi*). Given the apparent American/Western origins of those concepts, this seems to confirm what Shaun Breslin (2002: 7) describes as 'the over-dependence on the US as a source of ideas' in the Chinese IR community. And the field of international relations is just a microcosm of the growing influence of international NGOs and scholars on China's changing perceptions of the world.

Of course, not all the normative influences from transnational actors have been welcomed by the Chinese government. After the 'colour' revolutions in Central Asia, and for fear that its political legitimacy might be undermined by the NGOs' activities, Beijing has acted swiftly to put restrictions on both local and international NGOs. Yet, just as China's economic rise and the state's increased legitimacy cannot be separated from transnational actors, its commitment to becoming a 'peaceful', 'responsible' power has been in large measure influenced by the abovementioned transnational actors and normative structures which they constitute – thus supplying some degree of warranty of their continuous interactions with domestic Chinese state and social actors.

Conclusion

In this chapter, I have dealt with a much-debated topic in China's international relations, 'Peaceful Rise'. In doing so, however, I did not follow the conventional route of examining 'Peaceful Rise' within foreign policy parameters. Rather, I am interested more in understanding how 'Peaceful Rise' reveals a state in change, and how such change has come into being. 'Peaceful Rise', as I have argued, represents a new social contract being 'written' between the Chinese state and transnational actors. With this new contract, the Chinese state is changing in terms of both how it defines its responsibility and how it legitimises itself. From a state-in-society perspective, those changes cannot be fully understood unless we locate them in a transnational social context. As I have illustrated, transnational actors have played important roles in both China's rise and its commitment to peace. Thus I argue that they, together with domestic actors within the Chinese state and society, are responsible for the emergence of the new international contract in the Chinese state.

The chapter has not directly addressed the implications of China's peaceful rise for global politics; the ways in which China's change has been effected in transnational society does have an important bearing on our understanding of China's international implications, nevertheless. So long as the Chinese leadership continues to place a premium on domestic stability and political legitimacy, Chinese foreign policy is more likely than not to reflect this domestic priority. Indeed, as manifested in the declaration of 'Peaceful Rise', a regime that relies partly on the international community for legitimacy can ill afford to behave irresponsibly in the international realm. Thus the new international contract, while revealing many of the dynamics of China's change process, is useful also for assessing the global implications of China's rise, which might well have begun to depart from the pattern of earlier rising powers.

The focus on largely liberal transnational actors in this discussion does not imply that these are the only actors that matter. Certainly domestic actors and processes have a large role, and their interactions with transnational actors are an important part of the story – dimensions that are beyond the scope of this current analysis. Bearing this in mind, we are not surprised that the formation, and future trajectory, of the new international contract as reflected in 'Peaceful Rise' has not been, and will not be, a smooth, unilinear development. What China is and how it (re)writes its contract with the outside world always depend on how a variety of actors, 'domestic' and otherwise, interact and negotiate in the (re)production of the Chinese state as a fluid social construct. This chapter, hopefully, has captured a glimpse of a part of the processes involved.

Notes

1 'Peaceful Rise' was later modified to 'peaceful development' (*heping fazhan*). Despite the modified wording, the basic tenet does not seem to have changed. If anything, the change from 'rise' to the more modest word 'development' only highlights China's growing sensitivity to its image in the international community. For the sake of analytical convenience, I will use 'Peaceful Rise' to refer to both terms in this chapter.
2 In this chapter, the notion 'social contract' is used in a loose sense. It therefore does not imply that there are two formal, independent parties to the 'new international contract', nor that the 'contract' is struck as a result of equal consent.
3 The idea of 'Three Represents' was put forward by former CCP General Secretary Jiang Zemin in February 2000. It states that the CCP must always represent 'the development trend of China's advanced productive forces, the orientation of China's advanced culture and the fundamental interests of the overwhelming majority of the Chinese people'.
4 On a personal note, when I studied International Relations at Peking University in the late 1980s, the undergraduate subject of 'international relations theory' was taught by an American called Wilson (I can't remember his first name). While he taught little theory during his class except showing us Hollywood movies throughout the semester, one of the few textbooks he gave us was (oddly) Hayek's *Road to Serfdom*.
5 For example, Shanghai Renmin Chubanshe (Shanghai People's Press), Shijie Zhishi Chubanshe (World Affairs Press), Changzheng Chubanshe (Long March Press), Beijingdaxue Chubanshe (Peking University Press) and Zhejiang Renmin Chubanshe (Zhejiang People's Press) all have published series in international studies and international relations theories. See Wang Yizhou (2003: 10).

8   Conclusion

News from the front

David S. G. Goodman

One of the more commonly and widely held beliefs outside the People's Republic of China (PRC) about the changes wrought by the reform era during the three decades since 1978 is that there has been no political change. The noted Washington commentator James Mann made this the central theme of his address to the US China Economic and Security Review Commission in early 2007 (Mann 2007b; also Mann 2007a). The equally well-established US China scholar Elizabeth Perry published an article around the same time, arguing that the PRC has seen no fundamental political change in the last three decades, particularly because it remains dominated by the discourses of revolutionary authoritarianism (Perry 2007).

While one must be careful not to take these and other comments out of context, so strongly is the general argument often made that observers sometimes like to contrast the PRC's transition from state socialism with that which has, or probably more accurately has not, occurred in the former Soviet Union. It is often said that the PRC's economic success has come because the government of that country prioritised economic reform over political change, in contrast to the Soviet Union's successor Russian Federation, which emphasised the move towards political pluralism (White 1994; McFaul 1997).

Certainly there can be no doubt that the PRC remains a Party-state dominated by the Chinese Communist Party (CCP). Certainly too there is no institutionalised open national-level political competition in the PRC. At the same time, these rather bald statements mask as much as they reveal. Most significantly, the state itself has changed its own view of the relationship between state and society. From the mid-1950s until the end of 1978 the state saw itself in something akin to a totalitarian perspective. It had a holistic view of state and society in which the state directly managed the economy and society, and was the initiator of social and economic change. Since the end of 1978 the PRC has become a more recognisably authoritarian regime where the state regulates society and the economy indirectly, and intervenes directly in social and economic increasingly less.

One of the results is necessarily that state and society are in some senses now more clearly differentiated, at least to the extent that the government increasingly comes to recognise certain activities as not its responsibility and even possibly not even in its purview. A whole range of institutions have moved into the political space created by these changes, including chambers of commerce; non-governmental organisations (NGOs); and even loose organisations which might loosely be described as 'rights organisations' protecting either self-interest (for example in disputes over land usage) or more altruistic concerns (as, for example, domestic violence.) Necessarily, given the PRC's founding principles and methods of operation (however much these may be changing) the boundaries between state and society remain not clearly defined, are constantly changing and are in any case hotly contested.

At the same time, in this context the 'state' is a difficult concept to operationalise, not least because it is not strictly comparable to a situation where a system of governance (the regime) can be clearly differentiated from that particular expression of authority currently responsible for leadership or government, as is more usually the case in a multi-party democracy. This lack of operational distinction between a specific government and the regime is of course a common feature of party-states. It is virtually impossible to regard any move away from one-party dominance as anything less than a fundamental change in the state, and one-party states have always had a tendency in practice (though not in principle) to avoid governance–government distinctions, not least because they are teleologically driven (Ionescu 1967).

The contributions to this volume clearly and convincingly demonstrate that the state and politics in China have changed considerably since the beginning of the 1980s. Decentralisation was discussed before, and even partially implemented during the mid-1950s and the early 1960s (Solinger 1993), but not in such far-reaching, system-altering ways. In that process the separation of government from much economic administration is as fundamental as the devolution of decision-making from the centre to the provinces to the localities within the territorial administrative hierarchy (Montinola *et al.* 1995). Moreover, it is a far cry from the politics of the Mao-dominated years to a China where a discourse of corruption plays such a large role (as highlighted by Ting Gong) or a China where there is a public movement to counter violence against women, let alone one in which part of the PRC state apparatus (the Women's Federation) is involved (as Louise Edwards details in Chapter 6).

The attention of the outside world focuses inevitably on Beijing and national-level politics. Nonetheless, it may actually be at the more local levels that changes in politics and the state are most obviously made manifest. Decentralisation over economic decision-making has placed discretion over resource allocation, licensing and taxation at the local levels, and in the hands of officials who may well see themselves more as local leaders than as agents of the central state. Indeed, these are central and common themes of the chapters in this volume by Ting Gong on the emergence of corruption

(Chapter 4); of You-tien Hsing on property allocation (Chapter 5); of James Lee and Yapeng Zhu on housing reform (Chapter 2); of Linda Chelan Li on tax reform (Chapter 3); and of Tim Oakes on the management of culture (Chapter 1).

Local change is explicitly described and analysed, yet possibly the most far-reaching conclusion from this volume is one that is far more implicit: the need and the means to further conceptualise the 'state' in China. All the chapters are centrally concerned with the state in transition, yet its definition is unclear. This is neither undesirable nor not a viable strategy for explaining change. The 'state' generally can of course be, and is, understood in many different ways. It is sometimes equated with a society's political structure and the exercise of sovereign authority in the territory of that society, and sometimes with specific governments in that area. For political scientists the notion of the state is usually more specifically some definition of the system of governance within which politics occurs; for economists, it is more usually a black box of regulatory decision-making or an economic actor.

A definition of the state in China which goes little beyond the description of one-party rule and the hegemony of the Chinese Communist Party's once revolutionary authoritarianism says something fundamental about the PRC but is at the same time too static: it is in danger of failing to identify let alone even to interpret the dynamic aspects of change. Like the concept of the nation, with which it is often associated and sometimes confused, the state is most usefully understood as a project, constructed by social interaction (Migdal 2001). Of necessity this entails that the state is not static but is in a constant process of change. Not all change is the violent and dramatic change usually described as revolution, but nonetheless change remains a constant (Wertheim 1974).

The chapters in this volume highlight six different dimensions of the state in transition. While each is presented and considered separately, they are necessarily overlapping and mutually reinforcing in presenting a model of the state, which while imperfect provides a sound working hypothesis on which further research can be based. Moreover and more immediately, in the process recognising the different dimensions of the state also assists in explaining the extent of change.

The starting point is the system of governance: the formal and informal rules and regulations for the operation of the political system (regime). One way in which the state has started to change in the reform era is that, even allowing for earlier comments about the difficulties of distinguishing government from governance in a party-state, as the system has become more institutionalised after Mao authoritative decision-makers (government) have become conceptually distinct. One might even argue that separating government from governance was in some sense a primary goal of the reforms overseen by Deng Xiaoping. In turn, both governance and government are to be distinguished from the administrative structures (bureaucracy) that implement policy and the decisions of government.

While these aspects of the state are clearly crucial to its operation, they do not exist in a power vacuum. The justification for the state and the direction of policy is provided by the values and beliefs that shape the exercise of political power (ideology). This dimension of the state is particularly high profile and important where there is or has been a commitment to revolution. Similarly, a large part of the legitimacy of any state rests on its social foundations (social base); hence the importance in the modern era generally of the emergence of the idea of the nation-state. This, though, is not to say that there may not be significant differences in the state's interactions with the political nation as a whole, and a more narrowly based ruling class. Finally, the operation of the state is clearly influenced by the extent of its interactions with sources of power and influence based beyond its territorial borders: other states, international institutions and global economic interests.

Regime

It is abundantly clear that the PRC remains a CCP party-state. Many of the pre-reform structures of governance necessarily remain in place, including crucially the pre-eminence of the CCP's Political Bureau and its subordinate units. At the same time, it is not necessary to go as far as Chengxin Pan's argument that 'the apparent continuity of having the CCP in power in China merely masks the abundance and depth of change' to see that there has nonetheless been significant change in the system of governance. The local studies contained in this volume provide evidence that there have been significant changes in the conceptualisation and operationalisation of state–society relations; in the CCP's control of state activities; and in the spatial distribution of power.

One of the key characteristics of much scholarship on pre-reform China was its assumption of an opposition between state and society. The CCP for its part took a somewhat different view in its insistence that it could and should speak for society as well as control it. As both Edwards, and Lee and Zhu argue (if for different reasons and in different ways), the reform era has fundamentally altered the state–society relationship. For Lee and Zhu, their analysis of housing reform fits well into a series of changes that include the introduction of marketisation, and the commercialisation of welfare. In their view these changes have 'fundamentally realigned the long-existing paradigm of the state–society relationship', not least because the state is no longer responsible, as was previously the case, for the individual life chances of the individual. As Edwards outlines in her analysis of the movement to counter domestic violence against women, while the state remains a political actor in its own right to some extent, the system of governance also now allows partial interests to become involved in the political process in ways that were previously unthinkable. From the external viewpoint state and society are no longer in contradistinction; internally, other voices may be heard in a kind of lobby process alongside the CCP, even if the latter may still occasionally have the louder voice and remain the framework for decision-making.

It would be a mistake to see the emergence of social interests, of NGOs or even of local interests in opposition to central dictates (as detailed in particular by Ting Gong (Chapter 4) and You-tien Hsing (Chapter 5)) as the emergence of any kind of political pluralism. Much of it is sanctioned by the CCP in the interests of ensuring the greater efficiency of socialism, rather than due to a belief in the virtue of pluralist diversity (Goodman 1985). At the same time, the ways in which the CCP exercises control have clearly changed. In the past CCP control over lower levels of the state structure was ensured though the tight management of appointments to leadership positions; and through the fear of expressions of local interest being regarded as the political crime of 'localism'. In the reforms of the last thirty years, first the number of leadership appointments subject to appointment was dramatically reduced; and, as Tim Oakes (Chapter 1) highlights, from 1990 on localism has almost been de rigueur in the promotion of local development, after the CCP gave the signal for the reproduction of local folk culture, commercialisable in its own right and as the development of a form of symbolic capital.

The role of decentralisation in fundamentally altering the system of governance in China has already been mentioned. Remarkably for those waiting for more cataclysmic change this has occurred because of, not despite, the actions of the CCP. While Ting Gong criticises the extent to which decentralisation remains incomplete and the problems that this causes, nonetheless she highlights both the extent of the change and the executive role of the CCP in initiating this process:

> The economic reforms and administrative reorganization since 1978 have resulted in a diffusion of state power to local governments as reformers have taken important steps to structurally and functionally differentiate government authority. The party gradually abolished within its organization those departments that duplicated the administrative institutions to loosen its control over local affairs. A wide range of decision-making powers were devolved from the central government to lower levels to promote local incentives and effective governance. Local governments acquired greater managerial power over state enterprises, more flexibility in local budgetary processes, increased freedom to approve foreign investment and to engage in international trade, and expanded jurisdiction over resource distribution and taxation.
>
> (Chapter 4, p. 76)

This is a view shared by Hsing, who goes on to argue that at the same time these processes have had two even more dramatic results. One is that devolutionary pressures have left county, township and village in contest for control of 'the local state'. The other is that there has been an equally important governance change in the relationship between rural and urban areas. Regional development policies since the late 1980s that have been designed to mitigate the worst effects of unequal development through the 'regional integration of rural and urban areas' (the establishment of city regions, city-run-counties and the like) have resulted in the movement of 'control of rural areas and resources from rural to urban governments'.

Government

These fundamental governance changes, and in particular the introduction of decentralisation, have had a profound impact on the location and exercise of government. The territorial administrative hierarchy of the PRC identifies three basic levels of government: central, provincial and local. The provincial level of jurisdiction includes municipalities directly under the State Council (Beijing, Shanghai, Tianjin and Chongqing) and the autonomous regions (Xinjiang Uighur, Xizang Tibetan, Guangxi Zhuang, Ningxia Hui and Inner Mongolia). The local levels include counties and city-level counties, townships and villages. Before the 1980s, of these only the county level was regarded as a part of the formal system of government.

Decentralisation in the reform era has had three separate consequences for the operation of government, all centred at local levels. Significant economic decision-making has been localised; local leaders, in townships and villages as well as at the county level, have become economic actors in their own right and not simply state agents; and the CCP operates differently at the local level. The essence of these changes is that local government and local government leaders now exercise considerably more authority in their own right.

Almost all the contributions to this volume highlight the ways in which the changes of the reform era, and in particular decentralisation, have resulted in increased and significant decision-making now occurring at local levels. Gong details how decentralisation in economic decision-making has brought discretion over resource allocation, licensing, investment and taxation to the local levels. Hsing analyses the increased capacity of localities to be involved in the processes of land management, which have of course been crucial in industrial and real estate development. Lee and Zhu deal with local experimentation with housing reform in Guiyang. Oakes details how localities have the ability to choose specific settings and directions for their individual cultural development strategies.

Important as this degree of decentralisation would be in its own right, as Gong argues, the imperfect process of decentralisation has effectively meant that local leaders have become significant economic actors and not simply local agents of the state (sometimes described as agents of the local state (Oi 1995, 1999)). Gong's case is that effective decentralisation requires power deconcentration, increased accountability and greater representation. While the first has clearly been part of recent PRC decentralisation, increased accountability and greater representation have been considerably more muted.

One result is that local government leaders have been able to build up not only extra-budgetary revenues (which central government sanctions to some extent outside the formal plan process) but also off-budgetary revenue (which higher levels of government know nothing about at all). These resources enable local officials to move beyond the formal budgetary boundaries which are the apparent control mechanism available to higher levels of the state.

With the political and economic pressures that they face to deliver economic growth, local leaders effectively act to maintain and develop local interests. Their primary concern is now the development of the local economy, and, as Hsing adds in her contribution (Chapter 5), while they rarely own economic enterprises themselves they are significant brokers and dispensers of influence and support. Moreover, in Gong's view this is a significant governmental change because now, as opposed to in earlier years, the PRC central government has 'to rely heavily on its local "agents" to rule in an increasingly cellularized power structure' – a process which, as Hsing points out, may often lead to considerable higher-level 'frustration'.

In some ways these observations suggest that the party-state may be fraying at the edges, or at least in the localities. Although the CCP remains central to politics at central and provincial levels, at local levels, while the CCP still exists, it is much less of a political organisation than is the case at higher levels of the system. While in the contributions to this volume the CCP is much in evidence when matters of PRC policy or strategic direction are being discussed, in the examination of case studies in specific localities the CCP has either no or only a shadowy existence.

Bureaucracy

The 9–10 per cent annual growth rate of the PRC economy since 1978 is frequently remarked on by external commentators of all kinds. Less often mentioned but no less significant, not least as the foundation for current success, was the average 6 per cent per annum growth rate achieved overall between 1952 and 1978 (State Statistical Bureau 1990). While that figure masks some severe fluctuations, especially during the aftermath of the Great Leap Forward, it did mean that especially during the 1950s the PRC established a working administrative system. In particular, the bureaucracy supplied and managed education, health and welfare services in line with the dictates of the state planning process.

As described in several of the contributions to this volume, the principal change to bureaucracy with the advent of reform has been the introduction of market principles in the allocation of resources and services. The state's administrative structures now provide less directly by way of public services and instead increasingly have a role as a market regulator. The experiments with the introduction of the Housing Monetarisation Policy in Guiyang in and after 1998 to reform the housing market, described by Lee and Zhu in Chapter 2, indicate the extent and the impact of this change on both bureaucracy and the wider society. Under the influence of market pressures, and with no state (in whatever form) intervention, the results appear to be increased urban poverty, greater social inequalities and the ghettoisation of the housing market on lines of wealth.

One clear corollary of these changes in bureaucracy is, then, that social welfare is increasingly passing from the state bureaucracy to other social institutions, often established by villagers themselves. Oakes, in his description of village adoption of cultural development strategies in Guizhou, details the activities of the 18th Festival Association in Jin Family Fort. Through its various activities and the promotion of tourism this association raises enough funds to substitute for the state in the provision of basic village welfare and public goods.

Less predictable perhaps, and certainly less intended, has been the impact of the marketisation of public services on local bureaucracy. As might be expected given earlier comments on the growing strength of local government in its relationship with higher levels of the system, the evidence from the local studies presented in this volume is that local bureaucracy has to some extent been captured by local government. Hsing's analysis of the new land management bureaux and their activities is particularly acute in this respect:

> The stated mission of land bureaus is farmland conservation. Yet under the growth-minded urban government leaders, local land management bureaus have become an important channel for the urban government to control rural land inventories, and oversee farmland conversion and land-lease sales.
>
> (Chapter 4, p. 92)

The tendency now would appear to be that local bureaucracy is likely to become part of the local power constellation controlled by local leaders. This may not always be in opposition to other parts of the state administration, but the potential for that kind of conflict is clearly there, even if it may still be contained within the framework of the party-state.

One final observation about the ways in which the state bureaucracy is no longer as it was can be drawn from the contribution of Linda Chelan Li (Chapter 3). The pre-reform era state bureaucracy operated on principles and procedures crystallised during the early 1950s but inherited from earlier CCP experiences (Barnett 1967; Lieberthal and Oksenberg 1988). The path dependence of the bureaucracy was taken for granted by the leaders of the CCP and even to some extent desired, representing a form of reliability. This has changed, though, with the advent of reform, where the bureaucracy has been required to learn new tricks, not just once, but several times as even the reforms of twenty or ten years ago have had to be replaced. As Linda Chelan Li indicates in her study of rural tax reform in Hubei, this requires new strategies in order to ensure not only that specific reforms are implemented but also that a climate that welcomes change and improvement is sustained.

Unsurprisingly, it is clear that the state bureaucracy has been somewhat more successful in the former than the latter.

Ideology

The official ideology of the People's Republic of China, enshrined in the most recent (1982) constitution, remains Marxism–Leninism–Mao Zedong Thought, as it was before the advent of the reform era. At the same time, as many of the contributions to this volume argue, there is apparently a neoliberalist agenda to be found in the values and belief system of the contemporary state. While the contradiction between these two ideologies is clearly acute, the apparent attenuation of the CCP's value system suggests that there has been a major change in the construction of state power.

Drawing on the work of David Harvey (2005), Lee and Zhu explicate the neoliberalist state agenda in terms of: neoclassical economics; market regulation replacing state intervention; economic distribution favouring capital; moral authoritarianism centred on the nuclear family; international free trade; and opposition to unionised labour. Through their study of Guiyang's housing reform they argue that the Chinese state has taken a distinct neoliberalist turn, most especially by allowing the market to determine the allocation of housing resources and through encouraging China's integration into the global economy.

According to Chengxin Pan the CCP has exchanged revolution for the more peaceful and nationalist goal of wealth creation. In the process he sees neoliberalism at home leading to neoliberalism in the PRC's international affairs. The description of domestic value change is blunt:

> The changing ways in which state responsibility and legitimacy are perceived by the Chinese leaders underline the changing nature of the Chinese state, especially in terms of the ways it operates and functions in various aspects of Chinese political and economic life. For example, Chinese cadres at almost every level have come to realise that their career advancement is linked to their ability to attract foreign investment (Zha 2005: 784). In this context, it is not difficult to imagine the implications for other dimensions of work, such as 'party construction' (*dangjian*) and 'political and ideological work' (*sixiang zhengzhi gongzuo*), as well as for the organisation and operation of the party-state more broadly.
>
> (Chapter 7, p. 131)

Tim Oakes, in his discussion of local cultural development strategies (Chapter 1), takes the analysis of neoliberalism in the Chinese state even further. His starting point is the recognition, common to all but one of the contributions to this volume, that wealth creation has become the state's number one priority. As Oakes indicates, echoing Gong, Hsing and Pan in particular, local governments have become of necessity more entrepreneurial as central funds have not kept pace with population and economic growth. Particularly in the poorer parts of China (and there are fewer poorer parts of the PRC than the villages in Guizhou where Oakes's research is grounded) local cultural practices can with appropriate support and mobilisation become a significant financial resource for local government. In terms which will resonate in other parts of the world that have experienced a neoliberal turn, the apparent 'shrinking' of the state also entailed a closer relationship between government and the private sector than an espousal of market principles might have suggested.

Although the potential for encouraging localism may seem to be dangerously unlimited, the ideological sanction for the commodifiable development of local culture came in fact from the highest levels of state authority. In the wake of the events of June 1989 the leadership of the CCP saw a need to reinforce its nationalist credentials, emphasising its commitment to 'China's broad and profound traditional culture', a formula which went further than any statements of that kind since the early 1950s in relating contemporary China to its pre-1949 development. In January 1990 the then Minister of Culture proceeded to unpack the idea of 'traditional culture' in terms of China's local and folk cultures (Guo 2004). As Oakes points out, this provided the impetus for the widespread emergence of local cultural development strategies. As the case of Shanxi Province indicates, while there is no necessary conflict between the local and the national, the encouragement of local culture does significantly shift the balance underlying the exercise of state power (Goodman 2002).

Social base

As might be expected, changes in the construction of the Chinese state's social base are as dramatic as the ideological contrasts just described. Entrepreneurs and business people had been excluded from CCP membership since at least the early 1940s, well before the establishment of the PRC. Yet since 2000 they have been accepted in the redefinition of the political nation, and encouraged in practical terms since the mid-1990s to serve as leaders, especially at local levels of government.

The CCP has long seen the explicit identification of the political nation – those social classes who are formally sanctioned to participate in politics, and who might generally be regarded as the beneficiaries of the state – as an important part of its appeal. Thus, during the Cultural Revolution the political nation was restricted to the 'workers, peasants and soldiers'. Not only were business people excluded as 'capitalists', but even intellectuals were for the most part dismissed as a 'stinking ninth category' of counter-revolutionaries.

Then President of the PRC and General Secretary of the CCP Jiang Zemin first publicly articulated the notion that entrepreneurs and business people should be included in the conceptualisation of the political nation in 2000. This was the principal innovation of his theory of the 'Three Represents' – business people representing the 'most advanced' elements in Chinese society. This came after a period of several years which had seen successful business people often being co-opted by local government into taking local leadership positions in return for some freedom of manoeuvre.

Chengxin Pan, in Chapter 7, sees the reincorporation of the capitalist class as one of the most important symbolic acts of all the reform acts undertaken by the state. Certainly the symbolism of these changes that emphasises not only the roles of entrepreneurs and enterprise, but also the importance of wealth in its own right, cannot be underestimated. Tim Oakes repeats the statement from a village head in Ox Market Fort, Guizhou Province, which would previously have been unutterable without severe political consequences:

> Before liberation, this was a very cultured village. Over one-third of the households were landlords! ... These days, Jiang Zemin and Deng Xiaoping consider the landlords the advanced representatives of economic progress. We should understand this. To me, they weren't landlords, they weren't exploiters. They were people who worked hard, saved their money, and advanced the village along with themselves.
>
> (Chapter 1, p. 23)

Apart from this fairly obvious change in the state's social base, the contributions to this volume highlight three further aspects of change in the social power constellations of the state:

1   As Gong in her discussion of imperfect decentralisation, Hsing in her analysis of land management, and Oakes in examining the emergence of local cultural development strategies all detail is that local leadership now not only includes local business people in addition to local officials, but is in large measure based on the local partnership of cadres and entrepreneurs.
2   As highlighted by Lee and Zhu in their investigation of housing reform, and Oakes, current policy settings will almost inevitably lead to social polarisation, not least because they are implicitly designed to do so, or at least to encourage wealth creation almost no matter what. As Oakes points out, this social polarisation may actually be more acute because of the government–business alliance at local levels.
3   As Edwards points out in her study of the movement against domestic violence against women, social change has ensured that there is now a greater diversity of political actors. In the case she examines these include elements who are safely within the party-state (members of the Women's Federation) as well as those who are so far outside that they do not even constitute an organisation of any sort, only coming together for specific acts and events.

International interaction

The contributions to this volume are mainly concerned with the domestic development of the Chinese state. Nonetheless, as might be expected, there are still indications of the ways in which the construction of state power has altered as a result of its international interactions. As already discussed, the pursuit of investment and particularly of foreign-sourced investment is a major priority for local leaders. In addition, there is also evidence that the construction of state power is shaped by interaction with international institutions and other states.

Edwards, in her discussion of the interplay of forces that have helped shape China's movement against domestic violence against women (Chapter 6), details how neither the party-state's Women's Federation nor the informal coalition of women's groups also involved would be able to operate so effectively without the support of the international women's rights movements. In comments which later resonate with those made by Chengxin Pan about China's economic development, she argues that global integration across a range of activities, but especially those related to women's rights, requires a degree of domestic compliance, regardless of the level of priority male officials might otherwise think appropriate.

Pan's contribution to this volume (Chapter 7) is more centrally concerned with the ways in which China's external engagement have shaped the development of the state. The extent to which 1978 constitutes a watershed in China's external relations can easily be exaggerated. Isolationism had already started to thaw from the extremes of the late 1960s, well before reform was on the CCP's agenda. Nonetheless, it is clear that the abandonment of a revolutionary stance in external affairs has been more complete since the start of reform and the end of Communist Party rule in the USSR and Eastern Europe.

Pan's argument is that the PRC has now adopted international interdependence to such a degree, because of its neoliberalist stance, that it is prepared to entertain actions that previously would have been regarded as 'interference'. China is no longer in the game of undermining international agencies and agreements, even when it disagrees with the outcomes of their actions or the principles on which they are based. This applies across the board, from matters of climate and environmental regulation, to issues of rights protection, to membership of international trade and financial regulation bodies. Though it is not quite expressed this way, the argument seems very definitely to be that the state has exchanged being right for being powerful in the international arena. Necessarily this has domestic repercussions.

Bibliography

"About V-day" (2006) "About V-day." Available at: http://www.vday.org/contents/vday/aboutvday (accessed June 12, 2006).

Abrams, Philip (1988) "Notes on the Difficulty of Studying the State," *Journal of Historical Sociology*, 1(1): 58–89.

Albright, Madeline (1998) "Engaging China Is Not Endorsing China: Policy Must Reflect American Values," June 22. Online. Available at: http://www.nyu.edu/global beat/asia/china/06221998albright.html.

Anshun Shi Wenhuaju (2002) *Tuxiang Renleixue Shiyezongde Anshun Tunpu* [The Folkloric Heritage of Anshun Tunpu], Guiyang: Renmin Chubanshe.

Archer, Margaret (1988) *Culture and Agency*, Cambridge: Cambridge University Press.

—— (1995) *Realist Social Theory: The Morphogenetic Approach*, Cambridge: Cambridge University Press.

—— (2000) *Being Human: The Problem of Agency*, Cambridge: Cambridge University Press.

—— (2003) *Agency and the Internal Conversation*, Cambridge: Cambridge University Press.

Arikan, Gulsun G. (2004) "Fiscal Decentralization: A Remedy for Corruption?," *International Tax and Public Finance*, 11: 175–95.

Arthur, W. Brian (1989) "Competing Technologies, Increasing Returns, and Lock-in by Historical Events," *Economic Journal*, 99 (March): 116–31.

Bai, Guimei (1997) "The UN Declaration on the Elimination of Violence against Women and Its Practice in China," in Ma Yuan (ed.) *Jianjue zhizhi he xiaochu dui funü de baoli* (Resolutely curb and eliminate VAW), Beijing: Renmin Fayuan Chubanshe.

Barnett, A. Doak (1967) *Cadres, Bureaucracy, and Political Power in Communist China*, New York: Columbia University Press.

Bassanini, Andrea P. and Dosi, Giovanni (2001) "When and How Chance and Human Will Can Twist the Arms of Clio: An Essay on Path-dependence in a World of Irreversibilities," in Raghu Garud and Peter Karoe (eds.) *Path Dependence and Creation*, Hillsdale, N.J., and London: Lawrence Erlbaum Associates.

Baum, Richard and Shevchenko, Alexei (1999) "The State of the State," in Merle Goldman and Roderick McFarquhar (eds.) *The Paradox of China's Post-Mao Reforms*, Cambridge, MA: Harvard University Press.

Bernstein, Richard and Munro, Ross H. (1997) *The Coming Conflict with China*, New York: Alfred A. Knopf.

Bernstein, Thomas P. and Lu, Xiaobo (2003) *Taxation without Representation in Contemporary Rural China*, New York: Cambridge University Press.

Bian, Y. and Logan, J. (1997) "Work Units and Housing Reform in Two Chinese Cities," in X. Lu and E. J. Perry (eds.) *Danwei: The Changing Chinese Workplace in Historical and Comparative Perspective*, Armonk: M. E. Sharpe.

Bourdieu, P. (1998a) *Acts of Resistance: Against the Tyranny of the Market*, New York: Free Press.

—— (1998b) *Practical Reason: On the Theory of Action*, Stanford, CA: Stanford University Press.

—— and Nice, R. (1998) *Acts of Resistance: Against the New Myths of Our Times*, Cambridge, England: Polity Press.

Brehm, John and Gates, Scott (2000) *Working, Shirking, and Sabotage: Bureaucratic Response to a Democratic Public*, Ann Arbor, MI: University of Michigan Press.

Brenner, N. and Theodore, N. (2002) *Spaces of Neoliberalism: Urban Restructuring in North America and Western Europe*, Oxford: Blackwell.

Breslin, Shaun (2002) *IR, Area Studies and IPE: Rethinking the Study of China's International Relations*, Centre for the Study of Globalisation and Regionalisation (CSGR) Working Paper No. 94/02, Coventry, England: University of Warwick, April.

—— (2004) "Globalization, International Coalitions, and Domestic Reform," *Critical Asian Studies*, 36(4): 657–75.

—— (2005) "Power and Production: Rethinking China's Global Economic Role," *Review of International Studies*, 31(4): 735–53.

Brodsgaard, Kield Erik (2002) "Institutional Reform and the *Bianzhi* System in China," *China Quarterly*, 170 (June): 361–86.

Brueckner, Jan (2000) "Fiscal Decentralization in Developing Countries: The Effects of Local Corruption and Tax Evasion," *Annals of Economics and Finance*, 1: 1–18.

Bu, Wei (2005a) "Organising Against Domestic Violence – Exploring the Use of a Popular Theatre Troupe as Alternative Media in Rural China," in Nicola Spakowski and Cecelia Milwertz (eds.) *Women and Gender in Chinese Studies: Berliner China Hefte*, vol. 29, Berlin: LIT Verlag.

—— (2005b) "Shuochu ziji de gushi" (Telling one's own story). Online. Available at: http://stopdv.org.cn/article.asp?id=2170 (accessed July 8, 2006).

Burchell, Graham, Gordon, Colin, and Miller, Peter (eds.) (1991) *The Foucault Effect: Studies in Governmentality*, London: Harvester and Wheatsheaf.

Bureau of Real Estate of Ministry of Construction (2003) *Zhu fang huo bi hua ji lian zu zhu fang zhi dou* (Housing monetarization and the social rental housing system), Beijing: Bureau of Real Estate of Ministry of Construction.

Carlson, Allen (2005) *Unifying China, Integrating with the World: Securing Chinese Sovereignty in the Reform Era*, Stanford, CA: Stanford University Press.

Chang, Gordon G. (2001) *Coming Collapse of China*, New York: Random House.

Chen, A. (1998) "China's Urban Housing Market Development: Problems and Prospect." *Journal of Contemporary China*, 7(17): 43–60.

Chen, Jian (1998) *Liushi de zhongguo* (*Loss of Chinese Property*), Beijing: Zhongguo Chengshi Chubanshe.

Chen, Kang, Hillmand, Arye L., and Gu, Qingyang (2002) "From the Helping Hand to the Grabbing Hand: Fiscal Federalism and Corruption in China," in John Wong and Lu Ding (eds.) *China's Economy into the New Century: Structural Issues and Problems*, Singapore: Singapore University Press.

Chen, Rousseau (2002) "The Trouble with All this New Money," *Shanghai Star*, May 23.

Cheung, Peter T. Y., Chung, Jae Ho, and Lin, Zhimin (eds.) (1998) *Provincial Strategies of Economic Reform in Post-Mao China*, New York and London: M. E. Sharpe.

China Daily (2004) "Stage Drama 'Vagina Monologues' Banned in China," *China Daily*, February 8. Available at: http://www.chinadaily.com.cn/english/doc/2004-02/08/content_304238.htm. Accessed July 8, 2006

Chung, Jae Ho (2000) *Central Control and Local Discretion in China: Leadership and Implementation during Post-Mao Decollectivization*, New York: Oxford University Press.

—— and Lam, Tao-chiu (2004) "'City System' in Flux: Explaining Post-Mao Administrative Changes," *China Quarterly*, 180: 945–64.

Corrigan, Philip and Sayer, Derek (1985) *The Great Arch: English State Formation as Cultural Revolution*, Oxford: Basil Blackwell.

Croll, Elisabeth (1994) *From Heaven to Earth: Images and Experiences of Development, in China*, London: Routledge.

Crzymala-Busse, Anna and Luong, Pauline Jones (2002) "Reconceptualizing the State: Lessons from Post Communism," *Politics and Society*, 30(4): 529–54.

David, Paul (1985) "Clio and the Economics of QWERTY," *American Economic Review*, 75(2): 332–7.

—— (1986) "Understanding the Economics of QWERTY: The Necessity of History," in W. Parker (ed.) *Economic History and the Modern Historian*, Oxford: Blackwell.

Davis, D. S. (2003) "From Welfare Benefit to Capitalized Asset: The Recommodification of Residential Space in Urban China," in R. Forrest and L. James (eds.) *Housing and Social Change*, London: Routledge.

Deng, Frederic (2003) "The Political Economy of Public Land Leasing in Beijing, China," in Steven C. Bourassa and Yu-Hung Hong (eds.) *Public Leasehold: Policy Debates and International Experience*, Cambridge, MA: Lincoln Institute of Land Policy.

Deng Xiaoping (1990) "The International Situation and Economic Problems," March 3. Online. Available at: http://english.peopledaily.com.cn/dengxp/vol3/text/d1130.html.

Diamant, Neil J. (2000) *Revolutionizing the Family: Politics, Love and Divorce in Urban and Rural China 1949–1968*, Berkeley, CA: University of California Press.

DiMaggio, Paul (1988) "Interest and Agency in Institutional Theory," in *Institutional Patterns and Organizations: Culture and Environment*, Cambridge, MA: Ballinger Publishing.

Ding, X. L. (2000) "The Illicit Asset Stripping of Chinese State Firms," *China Journal* 43: 1–27.

DKT International (2006) "Social Marketing: Focus on Family Planning and AIDS Prevention." Available at: http://www.dktinternational.org/default.htm (accessed July 8, 2006).

Drache, Daniel (ed.) (2001) *The Market or the Public Domain? Global Governance and the Asymmetry of Power*, London: Routledge.

Du Gay, Paul and Pryke, Michael (2002) "Cultural Economy: An Introduction," in P. du Gay and M. Pryke (eds.) *Cultural Economy*, London: Sage.

Duara, Prasenjit (1988) *Culture, Power and the State: Rural North China, 1900–1942*, Stanford, CA: Stanford University Press.

Edin, Maria (2003) "State Capacity and Local Agent Control in China: CCP Cadre Management from a Township Perspective," *China Quarterly*, 173: 35–52.

Edwards, Louise (2000) "Women in the People's Republic of China: New Challenges to the Grand Gender Narrative," in Louise Edwards and Mina Roces (eds.)

Women in Asia: Tradition, Modernity and Globalisation, Sydney: Allen and Unwin; Ann Arbor: University of Michigan Press.

—— (2004a) "Chinese Women's Campaigns for Suffrage: Nationalism, Confucianism and Political Agency," in Louise Edwards and Mina Roces (eds.) *Women's Suffrage in Asia: Gender, Nationalism and Democracy*, London: RoutledgeCurzon.

—— (2004b) "Constraining 'Women's Political Work' with 'Women's Work': The Chinese Communist Party and Women's Participation in Politics," in Anne E. McLaren (ed.) *Chinese Women: Living and Working*, London: RoutledgeCurzon.

"Fan jiating baoli lifa yanjiu hui juxing" (2005) "Fan jiating baoli lifa yanjiu hui juxing" (Legal research association hold meeting to eliminate domestic violence). Available at: http://life.people.com.cn/GB/3931716.html (accessed June 12, 2006).

Feng, Chongyi (1999a) "Seeking Lost Codes in the Wilderness: The Search for a Hainanese Culture," *China Quarterly*, 160: 1,037–56.

—— (1999b) "Jianxi in Reform: The Fear of Exclusion and the Search for a New Identity," in H. Hendrischke and C. Feng (eds.) *The Political Economy of China's Provinces*, London: Routledge.

Fewsmith, Joseph (1994) *Dilemmas of Reform in China: Political Conflict and Economic Debate*, New York and London: M. E. Sharpe.

Finnemore, Martha (1996) *National Interests in International Society*, Ithaca, N.Y.: Cornell University Press.

Fisman, Raymond and Gatti, Roberta (2002) "Decentralization and Corruption: Evidence across Countries," *Journal of Public Economics*, 83: 325–45.

Fitzgerald, John (1995) "The Nationless State: The Search for a Nation in Modern Chinese Nationalism," *Australian Journal of Chinese Affairs*, 33 (January): 74–104.

—— (ed.) (2002) *Rethinking China's Provinces*, New York and London: Routledge.

Foot, Rosemary (2000) *Rights beyond Borders: The Global Community and the Struggle over Human Rights in China*, Oxford: Oxford University Press.

Forrest, R., Murie, A., and Williams, P. (1990) *Home Ownership: Fragmentation & Segmentation*, London: Routledge.

Foucault, Michel (1982) "The Subject and Power," in Hubert Dreyfus and Paul Rabinow (eds.) *Michel Foucault, Beyond Structuralism and Hermeneutics*, Brighton: Harvester.

Fraser, D. (2000) "Inventing Oasis: Luxury Housing Advertisements and Reconfiguring Domestic Space in Shanghai," in D. Davis (ed.) *The Consumer Revolution in Urban China*, Berkeley: University of California Press.

Friedland, Roger and Alford, Robert R. (1991) "Bringing Society Back in: Symbols, Practices, and Institutional Contradictions," in Walter W. Powell and Paul J. DiMaggio (eds.) *The New Institutionalism in Organizational Analysis*, Chicago: University of Chicago Press.

Friedman, Edward (1994) "Reconstructing China's National Identity: A Southern Alternative to Mao-era Anti-imperialist Nationalism," *Journal of Asian Studies*, 53 (1): 67–91.

Fudan daxuesheng (2004) "Fudan daxuesheng yanchu Zhongwen ban *Yindao dubai*: Zhongguo xiaoyuan V-day xingdong kailu xianfeng" (Fudan University students perform the Chinese language version of *The Vagina Monologues*: Pioneers for V-day activities on a Chinese campus). Online. Available at: http://stopdv.org.cn/article. asp?id=1911 (accessed July 8, 2006).

Gao, Chuyuan, Ouyang, Benzhang, and Li, Anhua (2003) "Jianren, jianshi, jianzhi de lilun fenxi yu yige shiqian yangbe" (Trimming staff size, responsibilities and expenditures: theory and implementation), in Wang, Huaxin (ed.) *2003 nian zhongguo defang caizheng yanjiu baogao: Hubeisheng nongcui shuifei gaige shijian yu tansuo* (Local finance research report, 2003: practice and research on the tax reform in the rural area of Hubei Province), Beijing: Jingji Kexue Chubanshe.

Garud, Raghu and Karnoe, Peter (eds.) (2001) *Path Dependence and Creation*, Hillsdale, N.J., and London: Lawrence Erlbaum Associates.

Gilbert, N. (2002) *Transformation of the Welfare State: Silent Surrender of Public Responsibility*, Oxford: Oxford University Press.

Gittings, John (2005) *The Changing Face of China: From Mao to Market*, Oxford: Oxford University Press.

Glosser, S. (ed. and trans.) (2003) *Li Feng Jin: How the New Marriage Law Helped One Woman Stand Up*, Portland: Opal Mogus Books.

Goldman, Merle, Link, Perry, and Su, Wei (1993) "China's Intellectuals in the Deng Era: Loss of Identity with the State," in Lowell Dittmer and Samuel S. Kim (eds.) *China's Quest for National Identity*, Ithaca, N.Y.: Cornell University Press.

Gong, Ting (1996) "Jumping into the Sea: Cadre Entrepreneurs in China," *Problems of Post-Communism*, 43(4): 26–34.

Goodman, David S. G. (1985) "The Chinese Political Order after Mao: 'Socialist Democracy' and the Exercise of State Power," *Political Studies*, 33(2): 218–35.

—— (ed.) (1997) *China's Provinces in Reform: Class, Community and Political Culture*, New York and London: Routledge.

—— (2002) "Structuring Local Identity: Nation, Province, and County in Shanxi during the 1990s," *China Quarterly*, 172: 837–62.

Gough, J. (2002) "Neoliberalism and Socialization in the Contemporary City: Opposites, Complements and Instabilities," *Antipodes*, 34(3): 405–26.

Guiyang Business Bureau (2006) "Guiyang is Hopeful to Achieve the Initial Stage of Modernization," news release. Online. Available at: http://www.gzcom.gov.cn/guiyang/info/Article.jsp?a_no=3999&col_no=276.

Guiyang Municipal Housing Reform Office (1992) *The Directory for Housing Reform in Guiyang*, Publication No. 75 [Guiyang Fangai Jinan], Guiyang: Construction Bureau of Guizhou Province.

Guizhou Provincial Housing Reform Office of Construction Bureau of Guizhou Province (2003) *Guan yu wo sheng zhu fang fen pei huo bi hua gai ge you guan qing kuang de bao gao* [Report on situations of housing monetarization reform in our province], Guiyang: Construction Bureau of Guizhou Province.

Guizhou Sheng Luyou Wenhua Yanjiu Zhuanbo Zhongxin [Guizhou Tourism Culture Research Dissemination Center] (2001) *Tuxiang Renleixue Sheyezhong de Guizhou Guzhen Mingzhai* [The folkloric heritage of Guizhou villages], Guiyang: Guizhou Renmin Chubanshe.

Guo, S. (1999) *1996–1998 de jing ji he zheng ce* (Economy and policy 1996–98), Guiyang: Guizhou Renmin Chubanshe (Guizhou People's Press).

—— (2000) (ed.) *Guizhou zhu fang fen pei huo bi hua gai ge* (Housing reform of monetarization distribution in Guizhou), Beijing: Zhongguo Caizheng Jingji Chubanshe (China Finance and Economy Press).

—— (2005) *Wen ding de bian qian guoshuqing wen ji* (Stable transformation: collected essays of Guo Shuqing), Hong Kong: Peace Book.

Guo, Yingjie (2004) *Cultural Nationalism in Contemporary China: The Search for National Identity under Reform*, London: Routledge.

Gupta, Akhil (1995) "Blurred Boundaries: The Discourse of Corruption, the Culture of Politics, and the Imagined State," *American Ethnologist*, 22(2): 375–402.

Hall, Stuart (1997) "The Centrality of Culture: Notes on the Cultural Revolutions of Our Time," in K. Thompson (ed.) *Media and Cultural Regulation*, London: Sage.

Harding, Harry (1987) *China's Second Revolution: Reform after Mao*, Sydney: Allen & Unwin.

Harloe, M. (2001) "Social Justice and the City: The New Liberal Formulation," *International Journal of Urban and Regional Research*, 25(4): 889–97.

Hart-Landsberg, Martin and Burkett, Paul (2004) "China and Socialism: Market Reforms and Class Struggle," *Monthly Review*, 56(3): 1–160.

Harvey, D. (1982) *The Limits to Capital*, Oxford: Blackwell.

—— (1989a) *The Urban Experience*, Oxford: Blackwell.

—— (1989b) "From Managerialism to Entrepreneurialism: The Transformation in Urban Governance in Late Capitalism," *Geografiska Annaler*, 71B: 3–17.

—— (2005) *A Brief History of Neoliberalism*, Oxford University Press.

Hendrischke, Hans and Feng, Chongyi (eds.) (1999) *The Political Economy of China's Provinces: Comparative and Competitive Advantage*, London: Routledge.

Hinton, William (1966) *Fanshen: A Documentary of Revolution in a Chinese Village*, Harmondsworth: Penguin; reprint 1972.

Hirschman, Alberto O. (1970) "The Search for Paradigms as a Hindrance to Understanding," *World Politics*, 22(3): 329–43.

Ho, Peter (2001) "Who Owns China's Land? Policies, Property Rights and Deliberate Institutional Ambiguity," *China Quarterly*, 166: 394–421.

Howell, Jude (1996) "The Struggle for Survival: Prospects for the Women's Federation in Post-Mao China," *World Development*, 24(1): 129–43.

Hu, Jintao (2003) "Zai jinian Mao Zedong tongzhi danchen 110 zhounian zuotanhui shang de jianghua" (speech at a CPC Central Committee symposium to commemorate the 110th anniversary of the birth of Comrade Mao Zedong), *People's Daily*, December 27.

Hu, Yifan (2002) "Nongfu zhibia" (Changes in agricultural taxes), *Caijing*, August 5.

Huang, Peijian (2003) "Jiti tudi liuzhuan: zouxiang bianfa" (Circulation of collective land: moving towards a policy change), *Economic Observer*, 11 August.

Huang, Tu and Qui, Yue (1997) *Zhongguo dangdai tanguan xianxingji* (The exposure of corrupt officials in contemporary China), Haerbin: Heilongjiang Chubanshe.

Huang, Weiding (1998) *Shiluo de zhunyan* (*The Lost Dignity*), Beijing: Zuojia Chubanshe.

Huntington, Samuel (1993) "Clash of Civilizations?," *Foreign Affairs*, 72(3): 22–49.

Industry Updates (2006) "Ford Foundation Adapted with Changing Country," *Industry Updates*, August 15, China Daily Information Company.

Ionescu, Ghita (1967) *The Politics of the Eastern European Communist Party States*, London: Weidenfeld and Nicholson.

Jacobs, Harvey (ed.) (1998) *Who Owns America? Social Conflicts over Property Rights*, Madison: University of Wisconsin Press.

Jaschok, Maria, Milwertz, Cecelia, and Hsiung, Ping-Chun (2001) "Introduction," in Hsiung Ping-chen, Maria Jaschok, Cecelia Milwertz, and Red Chan (eds.) *Chinese Women Organizing: Cadres, Feminists, Muslims, Queers*, Oxford: Berg.

Jeffreys, Elaine (2004) *China, Sex and Prostitution*, London: RoutledgeCurzon.

—— (2006) "Over My Dead Body!: Media Constructions of Forced Prostitution in the People's Republic of China," *Portal: Journal of Multidisciplinary International Studies*, 3(2).

Jepperson, Ronald L. (1991) "Institutions, Institutional Effects, and Institutionalism," in Walter W. Powell and Paul J. DiMaggio (eds.) *The New Institutionalism in Organizational Analysis*, Chicago: University of Chicago Press.

Ji, Xiangde (2005) *Hunnei qiangjian wenti yanjiu* (Research into the problem of rape within marriage), Beijing: Renmin Fayuan Chubanshe.

Jia, Kang (1999) "Feigaishui xiangguan wenti fenxi ji jiben duice silu tantao" (Problems and solutions of transforming fees to taxes), in Peiyong Gao (ed.) *Feigaishui* (Converting Fees into Taxation), Beijing: Jingji Chubanshe.

Jia, Qingguo (2005) "Peaceful Development: China's Policy of Reassurance," *Australian Journal of International Affairs*, 59(4): 493–507.

Jiang, Changbin (2005) "Lun Zhongguo heping jueqi yu Meiguo guoji zhanlue" On China's Peace Rise and America's International Strategy, *Guoji jingji pinglun* International Economic Review, 1–2: 45–51.

Jiang, Lisong (2004) "Cong wanggong deng minjian xinyang kan tunpuren de zhuti laiyuan" The origin of tunpu: a new study based on the Wanggong faith, *Guizhou Minzu Yanjiu* Guizhou Nationalities Research, 24(1): 45–50.

Jiang, Yong (2006) "Moving Closer: China and G8 Nurture Dialogue," *Beijing Review*, July 13. Online. Available at: http://www.bjreview.com.cn/06-28-e/w-1.htm.

Jin, Yihong (2001) "The ACWF: Challenges and Trends," in Hsiung Ping-chen, Maria Jaschok, Cecelia Milwertz, and Red Chan (eds.) *Chinese Women Organizing: Cadres, Feminists, Muslims, Queers*, Oxford: Berg.

Johnston, Alastair Iain (2003) "Socialization in International Institutions: The ASEAN Way and the International Relations Theory," in G. John Ikenberry and Michael Mastanduno (eds.) *International Relations Theory and the Asia-Pacific*, New York: Columbia University Press.

Jonas, Andrew and Wilson, D. (eds.) (1999) *The Urban Growth Machine*, Albany, N.Y.: State University of New York Press.

Jones, M. and Ward, K. (2002) "Excavating the Logic of British Urban Policy: Neoliberalism as the 'Crisis of Crisis-Management,'" *Antipode*, 34(3): 473–94.

Keane, Michael (2004) "Bringing Culture Back in," in J. Howell (ed.) *Governance in China*, Lanham, MD: Rowman & Littlefield.

Kelliher, Daniel (1992) *Peasant Power in China: The Era of Rural Reform, 1979–1989*, New Haven, CT, and London: Yale University Press.

Kent, Ann (1997/8) "China, International Organizations and Regimes: The ILO as a Case Study in Organizational Learning," *Pacific Affairs*, 70(4): 517–32.

Kessler, Glenn (2003) "Powell Strongly Defends Bush's Foreign Policy," *Washington Post*, September 6: A15.

—— (2005) "Rice Puts Japan at Center of New US Vision of Asia," *Washington Post*, March 19: A16.

Khan, A., Griffins, K., and Riskin, C. (1999) "Income Distribution in Urban China during the Period of Economic Reform and Globalization," *American Economic Review*, 89: 296–300.

Kim, Samuel S. (1994) "China's International Organizational Behaviour," in Thomas W. Robinson and David Shambaugh (eds.) *Chinese Foreign Policy: Theory and Practice*, Oxford: Clarendon Press.

Klitgaard, Robert (1988) *Controlling Corruption*, Berkeley, CA: University of California Press.

Knight, Nick (2003) "Imagining Globalisation: The World and Nation in Chinese Communist Party Ideology," *Journal of Contemporary Asia*, 33(3): 318–37.

Kraus, Richard (2000) "Public Monuments and Private Pleasures in the Parks of Nanjing," in D. Davis (ed.) *The Consumer Revolution in Urban China*, Berkeley, CA: University of California Press.

Kwong, Peter (2006) "The Chinese Face of Neo-Liberalism," *Counter Punch*, 13(12): 1–3.

Lardy, Nicholas. R. (1998) *China's Unfinished Economic Revolution,*Washington, D. C.: Brooking Institution Press.

—— (2002) *Integrating China into the Global Economy*, Washington, D.C.: Brookings Institution Press.

—— (2003) "The Economic Rise of China: Threat or Opportunity?," Federal Reserve Bank of Cleveland, August.

Lary, Diana (1996) "The Tomb of the King of Nanyue – The Contemporary Agenda of History: Scholarship and Identity," *Modern China*, 22(1): 3–27.

Lash, Scott and Urry, John (1994) *Economies of Signs and Spaces*, London: Sage.

Layder, Derek (1994) *Understanding Social Theory*, London: Sage.

Lee, Y.-s. F. (1988) "The Urban Housing Problem in China," *China Quarterly*, 115: 387–407.

Li, Hongtao (2005) "Intervention and Counseling Strategies for Men's Domestic Violence against Women in Beijing," in Nicola Spakowski and Cecelia Milwertz (eds.) *Women and Gender in Chinese Studies: Berliner China Hefte*, vol. 29, Berlin: LIT Verlag.

Li, Linda Chelan (1997) "Towards a Non-Zero-Sum Interactive Framework of Spatial Politics: The Case of Centre–Province in Contemporary China," *Political Studies*, 45(1): 49–65.

—— (1998) *Centre and Provinces: China, 1978–1993. Power as Non-Zero-Sum*, Oxford: Clarendon Press; reprint 2002.

—— (2004) "The Prelude to Government Reform in China? The Big Sale in Shunde," *China Information*, 18(1): 29–65.

—— (2005) "Understanding Institutional Change: Fiscal Management in Local China," *Journal of Contemporary Asia*, 35(1): 87–108.

—— (2006a) "Differentiated Actors: Central–Local Politics in China's Rural Tax Reforms," *Modern Asian Studies*, 40(1): 151–74.

—— (2006b) "'The State' in Change: Processes and Contestations in Local China," *Pacific Review*, 19(1): 1–12.

—— (forthcoming) *Towards Responsible Government in East Asia: Trajectories, Intentions and Meanings*, Abingdon, England: Routledge.

Li, Minqi (2005) "The Rise of China and the Demise of the Capitalist World-Economy: Exploring Historical Possibilities in the 21st Century," *Science & Society*, 69(3): 420–48.

Li, Qing and Sun, Ling (2004) "'Zhongguo shi' nüxing yijue xingle" "Chinese style" women's consciousness awakes, *Qingnian bao* Youth news. Online. Available at: http://news.sina.com.cn/0/2004-01-09/17091547694s.shtml (accessed July 6, 2006).

Li, Xiaojing (2004) "Shanghai jinji tingyan huaju *Yindao dubai*" Shanghai suddenly puts a stop to the performance of *The Vagina Monologues*. Online. Available at: http://ent.sina.com.cn/2004-02-12/0913299631.html (accessed July 6, 2006).

Lieberthal, Kenneth and Oksenberg, Michel (1988) *Policy Making in China: Leaders, Structures and Processes*, Princeton: Princeton University Press.

Lin, George (2002) "The Growth and Structural Change of Chinese Cities: A Contextual and Geographic Analysis," *Cities*, 19(5): 299–316.

—— (2005) "The State, Land System, and Land Development Processes in Contemporary China," *Annals of the Association of American Geographers*, 95(2): 411–36.

Lin, Min and Galikowski, Maria (1999) *The Search for Modernity: Chinese Intellectuals and the Cultural Discourse of the Post-Mao Era*, New York: St. Martin's Press.

Lin, Mingyi, Yuejin, Lu, and Zhenglu, Zhou (2004) *"Shiluan jinjiao chengshihua jingcheng zhongde nongmin jiti tudi chanquan zhidu jianshe"* Establishing a peasants' collective landed property rights system in the process of urbanization in suburban areas, *Turang* Soil, 26(3): 27–35.

Lin, Suanglin (2002) "Too Many Fees and Too Many Charges: China Streamlines Fiscal System," in John Wong and Lu Ding (eds.) *China's Economy into the New Century: Structural Issues and Problems*, Singapore: Singapore University Press.

Ling, Fei (2004) *Xiayige shishui?* (Who is Next?), Beijing: Dazhong Chubanshe.

Liu, Bohong (2001) "The All China Women's Federation and Women's NGOs," in Hsiung Ping-chen, Maria Jaschok, Cecelia Milwertz, and Red Chan (eds.) *Chinese Women Organizing: Cadres, Feminists, Muslims, Queers*, Oxford: Berg.

Liu, Hua (2000) "Gonggong caizheng yu 'cifan caizheng' bianxi" An analysis of public finance and "subsistence finance", *Sichuan Caizheng* 2: 16–18.

Liu, Meng (2003) *Zhongguo hunyin baoli* Marital violence in China, Beijing: Shangwu Yinshuguan.

Liu, Neng (2000) "Xiangzhen yunxing jizhide yici jiepo" An analysis of the operational mechanism of the township, in Rong Ma, Liu Shiding, and Qiu Zeqi (eds.) *Zhongguo xiangzhen zuzhi bianqian yanjiu* Study of the changes of township organizations of China, Beijing: Huaxia Publisher.

Liu, Shiding (2000) "Xiangzhen caizheng shouru jiegou" Financial structure of townships, in Rong Ma, Liu Shiding, and Qiu Zeqi (eds.) *Zhongguo xiangzhen zuzhi bianqian yenjiu Transformation of Chinese Township Organization*, Beijing: Huaxia.

Liu, Z. (2003) "Promote Healthy and Sustainable Development of Housing and Real Estate," speech made at the 2003 Annual Housing and Property Conference, Wuhan, Hubei Province.

Logan, J., Bian, V., and Bian, F. (1999) "Housing Inequality in Urban China in the 1990s," *International Journal of Urban and Regional Research*, 23(1): 7–25.

Logan, J. R. and Molotch, H. L. (1987) "The City as Growth Machine," in S. Fainstein and S. Campbell (eds.) *Urban Fortunes: The Political Economy of Place*, Berkeley, CA: University of California Press.

Long, Yongtu (1999) "Jiaru Shimao zuzhi, rongru guoji shehui zhuliu" Joining the WTO, melting into mainstream international society, *Guoji maoyi wenti* Issues of international trade, 9: 1–3.

Long, Z. (ed.) (2003) *Kouxiang Guizhou Lishi Zhi Men Knocking on the Door of Guizhou's History*, Guiyang: Renmin Chubanshe.

Ma, Laurence (2005) "Urban Administrative Restructuring, Changing Scale Relations and Local Economic Development in China," *Political Geography*, 24: 477–97.

Ma, Rong (2000) "Introduction," in Rong Ma, Liu Shiding, and Qiu Zeqi (eds.) *Zhongguo xiangzhen zuzhi diaocha* Survey on China's township organization, Beijing: Huaxia.

Ma, Yuan (ed.) (1997) *Jianjue zhizhi he xiaochu dui funü de baoli* Resolutely curb and eliminate VAW, Beijing: Renmin Fayuan Chubanshe.

McFaul, Michael (1997) "Russia's Rough Ride," in Larry Diamond, Marc F Plattner, Yun-han Chu, and Hung-mao Tien (ed.) *Consolidating the Third Wave Democracies: Regional Challenges*, Baltimore, MD: Johns Hopkins University Press.

Malpass, P. (2004) "Fifty Years of British Housing Policy: Leaving or Leading the Welfare State?," *European Journal of Housing Policy*, 4(2): 209–27.

Manderson, Lenore and Bennett, Linda Rae (eds.) (2003) *Violence against Women in Asian Societies*, London: RouteldgeCurzon.

Mann, James (2007a) *The China Fantasy*, Viking.

—— (2007b) "U.S. China Relationship: Economics and Security in Perspective," Hearings of the U.S.-China Economic and Security Review Commission, February 1.

Massey, D. B. (1995) *Spatial Divisions of Labour: Social Structures and the Geography of Production*, New York: Routledge.

Matarasso, Francois (ed.) (2001) *Recognizing Culture: A Series of Briefing Papers on Culture and Development*, London: Comedia and UNESCO.

Mearsheimer, John J. (2001) *The Tragedy of Great Power Politics*, New York: W. W. Norton.

Mearsheimer, John J. and Brzezinski, Zbigniew (2005) "Debate: Clash of the Titans," *Foreign Policy*, 146: 46–50.

Medeiros, Evan S. (2004) "China Debates Its "Peaceful Rise" Strategy," *YaleGlobal*, June 22. Online. Available at: http://yaleglobal.yale.edu/display.article?id=4118.

Migdal, Joel (2001) *State-in-Society: Studying How States and Societies Transform and Constitute One Another*, New York: Cambridge University Press.

Miller, Daniel (2002) "The Unintended Political Economy," in P. du Gay and M. Pryke (eds.) *Cultural Economy*, London: Sage.

Milwertz, Cecelia (2005) "Domestic Violence – Three Reports on Research and Activism," in Nicola Spakowski and Cecelia Milwertz (eds.) *Women and Gender in Chinese Studies: Berliner China Hefte*, vol. 29, Berlin: LIT Verlag.

Milwertz, Cecelia and Bu, Wei (2007) "Non-Governmental Organising for Gender Equality in China – Joining a Global Emancipatory Epistemic Community," *International Journal of Human Rights*, 11(1–2): 131–49.

Ministry of Construction (1998) *Selected Documents of State's Policies about the Real Estate 1985–1987*, Beijing: Nengyuan Chubanshe Energy Press.

—— (2006) *About Implementing the Construction Ratio for New Housings. Policy No. 165*. Online. Available at: http://www.realestate.gov.cn/file.asp?recordno=44571&team no=22&line=1 (accessed August 8, 2006).

Ministry of Finance (ed.) (2002) *Difang Caizheng Tongji Ziliu, 2001* [Statistical information of local finance, 2001], Beijing: Zhongguo Caisheng Jingji Chubanshe.

Mirsky, Jonathan (1990) "The Empire Strikes Back," *New York Review of Books*, 37 (1): 21–5.

Montinola, Gabriella, Qian, Tingyi, and Weingast, Barry R. (1995) "Federalism, Chinese Style: The Political Basis for Economic Success in China," *World Politics*, 48 (October): 50–81.

—— (1997) "Federalism as Incentives to Preserving Market Incentives," *Journal of Economic Perspectives*, 11: 82–92.

Moddy, K. (1997) *Workers in a Lean World*, New York: Verso.

Moore, Thomas G. (2005) "Chinese Foreign Policy in the Age of Globalization," in Yong Deng and Fei-ling Wang (eds.) *China Rising: Power and Motivation in Chinese Foreign Policy*, Lanham, MD: Rowman & Littlefield.

Moore, Thomas G. and Yang, Dixia (2001) "Empowered and Restrained: Chinese Foreign Policy in the Age of Economic Interdependence," in David M. Lampton (ed.) *The Making of Chinese Foreign and Security Policy in the Era of Reform, 1978–2000*, Stanford, CA: Stanford University Press.

Muldavin, Joshua (1997) "Environmental Degradation in Heilongjiang: Policy Reform and Agrarian Dynamics in China's New Hybrid Economy," *Annals of the Association of American Geographers*, 87(4): 579–613.

Negus, Keith (1997) "The Production of Culture," in P. du Gay (ed.) *Production of Culture/Cultures of Production*, London: Sage.

Niebuhr, H. Richard (1963) *The Responsible Self: An Essay in Christian Moral Philosophy*, New York: Harper and Row.

O'Brien, Kevin and Li, Lianjiang (1999) "Selective Policy Implementation in Rural China," *Comparative Politics*, 99(1): 167–86.

Oakes, Tim (2000) "China's Provincial Identities: Reviving Regionalism and Reinventing 'Chineseness,'" *Journal of Asian Studies*, 59(3): 667–92.

Ohashi, Hideo (2005) "China's Regional Trade and Investment Profile," in David Shambaugh (ed.) *Power Shift: China and Asia's New Dynamics*, Berkeley, CA: University of California Press.

Oi, Jean C. (1992) "Fiscal Reform and the Economic Foundations of Local State Corporatism in China," *World Politics*, 45(1): 99–126.

—— (1995) "The Role of the Local State in China's Transitional Economy," *China Quarterly*, 144 (December): 1,132–49.

—— (1999) *Rural China Takes Off: Institutional Foundations of Economic Reform*, Berkeley, CA: University of California Press.

Oi, Jean C. and Walder, Andrew (eds.) (1999) *Property Rights and Economic Reform in China*, Stanford, CA: Stanford University Press.

Oksenberg, Michel and Tong, James (1991) "The Evolution of Central–Provincial Fiscal Relations in China, 1971–84," *China Quarterly*, 125: 1–32.

Pan, Chengxin (2004) "The "China Threat" in American Self-Imagination: The Discursive Construction of Other as Power Politics," *Alternatives*, 29(3): 305–31.

Pearson, Margaret M. (2001) "The Case of China's Accession to GATT/WTO," in David M. Lampton (ed.) *The Making of Chinese Foreign and Security Policy in the Era of Reform, 1978–2000*, Stanford, CA: Stanford University Press.

Peck, J. and Tickell, A. (1995) "The Social Regulation of Uneven Development: "Regulatory Deficit," "England" South East and the Collapse of Thatcherism," *Environment and Planning*, 27: 15–40.

Pei, Minxin (2003) "China's Governance Crisis," *Foreign Affairs*, 81(5) (September/October): 96–109.

People's Daily (2001a) "China Will Be Responsible WTO Member: Senior Trade Official," *People's Daily*, September 9. Available at: http://english1.people.com.cn/english/200109/09/eng20010909_79692.html.

—— (2001b) "Guizhou Effort to Eradicate Poverty in 5 Hears," *People's Daily*, October 9.

—— (2002a) "China Says No to Domestic Violence," *People's Daily*, November 27. Available at: http://english.people.com.cn/200211/27/eng20021127_107559.shtml (accessed June 12, 2006).

—— (2002b) "White Ribbons to End Violence against Women in Beijing," *People's Daily*, November 30. Available at: http://english.people.com.cn/200211/30/eng20021130_107691.shtml (accessed June 12, 2006).

—— (2003) "China Invites International Involvement in Eliminating Violence against Women," *People's Daily*, December 10. Available at: http://english.people.com.cn/200312/10/eng20031210_130121.shtml (accessed June 12, 2006).

Perry, Elizabeth J. (2007) "Studying Chinese Politics: Farewell to Revolution?," *China Journal*, 57 (January): 1–22.

"Province View" (2006) "Province View." Online. Available at: http://www.china.org. cn/english/features/provinceview/167774.htm (accessed July 17, 2006).

Prud'homme, Remy (1994) "On the Dangers of Decentralization," World Bank Policy Research Working Paper No. 1252, Washington, D.C.: World Bank.

Public Governance and Territorial Development Directorate Public Management Committee (2002) *Highlights of Public Sector Pay and Employment Trends: 2002 Update*, Paris: OECD.

Qi, Z. (2003) "Zhong guo guo wu yuan zhong zhi yao qiu gu li ju min huang gou zhu fang" China's State Council urged urban residents to change their flats, *Jing ji ri bao* Economic Daily, September 1.

Qin, Hui (1997) "Nongmin Fudan wenti de fanzhan chushi: Qinghua daxue xuesheng nongcui diaocha baogao zi fenxi" How the issue of "peasants' burden" is developing? – an analysis of rural survey from Tsinghua University students, *Reform*, 2. Online. Available at: http://wwwguoxue.com/economics/ReadNews.asp? NewsID=426&BigclassName (accessed May 3, 2004).

—— (2000) "Binshuishi gaige yu 'Huangzhongxi' dilu" Merging fees-into-tax reform and the "Huangzhongxi" rule, *China Economic Times*. Online. Available at: http:// www.guxiang.com/xueshu/others/jingji/200209/200209210023.htm (accessed May 3, 2004).

—— (2003) "Divising the big family assets," *New Left Review*, 20 (March–April): 83–110.

Raco, M. (2005) "Sustainable Development, Rolled-out Neoliberalism and Sustainable Communities," *Antipode*, 37(2): 324–47.

Ramo, Joshua Cooper (1998) "The Shanghai bubble," *Foreign Policy*, 111 (summer): 64–75.

Ren, Baoyu (2002) "Caizheng shijiao xiade xiangji zhili" Township governance from a fiscal perspective, in *Zhongguio nongcun yanjiu* China rural studies, Beijing: China Social Science Publishers.

Robison, Richard and Goodman, David S. G. (1996) "The New Rich in Asia: Economic Development, Social Status and Political Consciousness," in *The New Rich in Asia: Mobile Phones, McDonald's and Middle-Class Revolution*, London: Routledge.

Rong, Weiyi and Huang, Lie (eds.) (2003) *Jiating baoli duice yanjiu yu ganyu: Guoji shijiao yu shizheng yanjiu* Research and intervention on counteracting domestic violence: international perspectives and evidence, Beijing: Zhongguo Shehui Kexue Chubanshe.

Rong, Weiyi and Song, Meiya (eds.) (2002) *Fandui zhendui funü de jiating baoli: Zhongguo de lilun yu shijian* Opposing domestic violence against women: theory and practice in China, Beijing: Zhongguo Shehui Kexue Chubanshe.

Rose-Ackerman, Susan (1978) *Corruption: A Study in Political Economy*, New York: Academic Press.

Samuelson, Robert J. (2004) "The China Riddle," *Washington Post*, January 30: A21.

Sanger, David E. (2003) "Bush Lauds China Leader as 'Partner' in Diplomacy," *New York Times*, December 10: 6.

Santos, de Sousa (1977) "The Law of the Oppressed: The Construction and Reproduction of Legality in Pasargada," *Law and Society Review*, 12(1): 5–126.

Scott, Allen (2000) *The Cultural Economy of Cities: Essays on the Geography of Image-Producing Industries*, London: Sage.

Scott, James C. (1990) *Domination and the Arts of Resistance: Hidden Transcripts*, New Haven, CT, and London: Yale University Press.

—— (1998) *Seeing Like a State: How Certain Schemes to Improve the Human Condition Have Failed*, New Haven, CT: Yale University Press.

Seth, Sushil (2005) "China's Middle Class Falls into Line," *Taipei Times*, March 1: 8.

Shi, Chih-Yu (2005) "Breeding a Reluctant Dragon: Can China Rise into Partnership and away from Antagonism?," *Review of International Studies*, 31(4): 755–74.

Singer, Josef (2000) *Entitlement: The Paradoxes of Property*, New Haven, CT: Yale University Press.

Solinger, Dorothy J. (1993) "Economic Reform via Reformulation: Where Do Rightists' Ideas Come From?," in *China's Transition from Socialism: Statist Legacies and Market Reforms, 1980–1990*, New York: M. E. Sharpe.

Sorkin, Michael (ed.) (1992) *Variations on a Theme Park: The New American City and the End of Public Space*, New York: Hill & Wang.

Spence, Jonathan D. (1969) *To Change China: Western Advisers in China 1620–1960*, Boston, MA: Little, Brown.

State Council (1991) *Regulations on the Management of Fees and Corvee Services Shouldered by Peasants*, Document No. 92, issued 7 December.

State Council (1994) "Guo wu yuan guan yu shen hua cheng zhen zhu fang zhi du gai ge de tong zhi" [Notice of State Council on deepening housing reform in cities and towns], Document of State Council No. 43 [1994], in Office of Leading Group of Housing.

State Council (1998) "Guan yu jin yi bu sheng hua cheng zhen zhu fan zhi gai ge jia kuai zhu fang jian she de tong zhi" [Notice No. 23, concerning moving a further step in housing system reform]; reprinted in S. C. Kuo (ed.) (2000) *Guizhou Housing Monetarization Reform* (*Guizhou Zhufang Fenpei Huobihua Gaige*), Beijing: China Finance and Economic Press.

State Statistical Bureau (1990) "Quanguo guomin shouru zhishu" [Index of national income], in *Lishi tongji ziliao huibian 1949–1989* [Collection of historical statistical materials 1949–89], Beijing: Zhongguo Tongji Chubanshe.

Stoessinger, John G. (1994) *Nations at Dawn: China, Russia, and America*, New York: McGraw-Hill.

State Council (1998) "Guan yu jin yi bu sheng hua cheng zhen zhu fang zhi du gai ge jia kuai zhu fang jian she de tong zhi" [Notice on further deepening urban housing reform and speeding up housing construction], in Editorial Committee (ed.) *Chang yong zhu fang zhi du gai ge fa lu fa gui* [Commonly used laws and regulations on housing system reform], Beijing: Renmin Fayuan Chubanshe [People's Court of Justice Press].

stopdv wangzhan (2005) "*Yindao dubai* Guangxi gaoxiao xunyan" [*The Vagina Monologues* tours a Guangxi highschool]. Available at: http://stopdv.org.cn/article.asp?id=2087 (accessed July 8, 2006).

Storper, Michael (1997) *The Regional World: Territorial Development in a Global Economy*, London: Guilford.

Suettinger, Robert L. (2004) "The Rise and Descent of 'Peaceful Rise,'" *China Leadership Monitor*, 12: 1–10.

Sun, Linping and Guo, Yuhua (2000) "Ruanying jianshi: zhengshi quanli fezhengshi yunzuode guocheng fenxi" [Combination of soft and hard approaches: a process analysis of informal exercise of formal power], *Tsinghua Sociological Review*, May: 21–46.

Sun, L. and He, X. (2000) "Zhu fang huo bi hua shi zui jia de gai ge zhi lu" [Housing monetarization is the best way to reform the housing system], in S. Guo (ed.)

Guizhou zhu fang fen pei huo bi hua gai ge [Housing Monetarisation Reform in Guizhou], Beijing: Zhongguo Caizheng Jingji Chubanshe [China Finance and Economy Press].

Sun, Tao (2001) "Evolution of Central–Local Relations and Fiscal Decentralization in China's Economic Reform," paper for the International Consultation on Decentralization, Bhopal, India, August 25–26.

Sutter, Robert (2004) "Asia in the Balance: America and China's 'Peaceful Rise,'" *Current History*, 103(674): 284–9.

System Reform of the State Council and Institution of China Housing System Reform (eds.) *Zhong guo zhu fang zhi du gai ge* [China housing system reform], Beijing: Gaige Chubanshe [Reform Press].

Tang, Wenfang (2005) *Public Opinion and Political Change in China*, Stanford, CA: Stanford University Press.

Tanzi, Vito (1998) "Corruption around the World – Causes, Consequences, Scope and Cures," *IMF Staff Papers*, 45(4): 559–94.

Terrill, Ross (2006) "China Is Not Just Rising, but also Changing," *New York Times*, September 9: 15.

Tickell, A. and Peck, J. (2003) "Making Global Rules: Globalization or Neoliberalization?," in J. Peck and H. W.-C. Yeung (eds.) *Remaking the Global Economy: Economic Geographical Perspectives*, London: Sage.

Tong, Zhihui (2002) "Cunmin zhijie xuanju zhongde xiangzhengfu" [Township government in villages' direct election], in *Zhongguio nongcun yanjiu* [*China Rural Studies*], Beijing: China Social Science Publishers.

Tsai, Lily (2002) "Cadres, Temple and Lineage Institutions, and Governance in Rural China," *China Journal*, 48 (July): 1–27.

Tsu, Jing (2005) *Failure, Nationalism and Literature: The Making of Modern Chinese Identity, 1895–1937*, Stanford, CA: Stanford University Press.

Tsui, Kai-yuen and Wang, Youqiang (2004) "Between Separate Stoves and a Single Menu: Fiscal Decentralization in China," *China Quarterly*, 177: 71–90.

Tu, Wei-ming (1993) *China in Transformation*, Cambridge, MA: Harvard University Press.

UN (2000) "Fact Sheet No. 4: Violence against Women." Available at: http://www.un.org/womenwatch/daw/followup/session/presskit/fs4.htm (accessed June 12, 2006).

Unger, Jonathan and Xiong, Jean (1990) "Life in the Chinese Hinterlands under the Rural Economic Reforms," *Bulletin of Concerned Asian Scholars*, 22(2): 4–17.

Unifem (2006) "Unifem trust fund in support of actions to eliminate violence against women EVAW." Available at: http://www.unifem-eseasia.org/projects/evaw/vawfund.htm (accessed June 12, 2006).

U.S. Department of Defense (2006) *Quadrennial Defense Review Report*, February 6, Washington D.C.: U.S. Government Printing Office.

Verdery, Katherine (1999) "Tuzzy Property: Rights, Power and Identity in Transylvania's Decollectivization," in Michael Burawoy and Katherine Verdery (eds.) *Uncertain Transition: Ethnographies of Change in the Postsocialist World*, Lanham, MD: Rowman & Littlefield.

Walder, Andrew (1995) "Local Governments as Industrial Firms: An Organizational Analysis of China's Transitional Economy?," *American Journal of Sociology*, 101 (2): 263–301.

Walker, R.B.J. (1993) *Inside/Outside: International Relations as Political Theory*, Cambridge, England: Cambridge University Press.

Wang, Fei-ling (1998) *Institutions and Institutional Changes in China: Premodernity and Modernization*, New York: St. Martin's Press.

Wang, Fengxian (2005) "Zenme baodao jiating baoli" [How to report domestic violence], in Tan Lin and Liu Bohong (eds.) *Zhongguo funü yanjiu shinian* [Ten years of research into China's women], Beijing: Shehui Kexue Wenxian Chubanshe.

Wang, G., Zhang, S., and Zhang, X. (2002) *Guizhou zhu fang huo bi hua gai ge yan jiu* [A research to housing monetarization reform in Guizhou], Guiyang: Guizhou Renmin Chubanshe [Guizhou People's Press].

Wang, Hongying (2003) "National Image Building and Chinese Foreign Policy," *China: An International Journal*, 1(1): 46–72.

Wang, Huaxin (ed.) (2003a) "Jingchu dadi jinxin 'sange daibiao' de weida shijian: Hubeisheng nongcun shuifei gaige de jiben zuofa yu chengxiao" [Implementing the spirit of "the Three Representations": practice and results of the rural tax reforms in Hubei], in H. Wang (ed.) *2003 nian zhongguo defang caizheng yanjiu baogao: Hubeisheng nongcui shuifei gaige shijian yu tansuo* [Local finance research report, 2003: practice and research on the tax reform in the rural area of Hubei Province], Beijing: Jingji Kexue Chubanshe.

—— (ed.) (2003b) *2003 nian zhongguo defang caizheng yanjiu baogao: Hubeisheng nongcui shuifei gaige shijian yu tansuo* [Local finance research report, 2003: practice and research on the tax reform in the rural area of Hubei Province], Beijing: Jingji Kexue Chubanshe.

—— (2004) "Hubeisheng fazhan xuanyu jingji caizheng zhengce yanjiu" [A study of the fiscal policy on developing the county-level economy of Hubei Province], *Caizheng Yu Fazhen*, 1: 21–30.

Wang, Hui (1998) "Contemporary Chinese Thought and the Question of Chinese Modernity," *Social Text 55*, 16(2) (summer): 9–44.

—— (2003) *China's New Order: Society, Politics, and Economy in Transition*, Cambridge, MA: Harvard University Press.

Wang, Jing (2001) "Culture as Leisure and Culture as Capital," *Positions*, 9(1): 69–104.

—— (2003) "Framing Policy Research on Chinese 'Culture Industry': Cultural Goods, Market–State Relations, and the International Free Trade Regime," paper presented at the Workshop on Critical Policy Studies, Cambridge, MA, November 15–16.

Wang, Jisi (2005) "Meiguo baquan yu Zhongguo jueqi" [American hegemony and China's rise], *Waijiao pinglun* [Foreign affairs review], 84: 13–16.

Wang, Shaoguang (1994) "Central–Local Fiscal Politics in China," in Hao Jia and Zhimin Lin (eds.) *Changing Central–Local Relations in China: Reform and State Capacity*, Boulder, CO: Westview Press.

Wang, Xingjuan (2005) "Jiating baoli zai Zhongguo" [Domestic violence in China], in Zheng Bijun and Tao Jie (eds.) *Zhongguo nüxing de guoqu, xianzai yu weilai* [Chinese women: past, present and future], Beijing: Beijing Daxue Chubanshe.

Wang, Y. P. (2004) *Urban Poverty, Housing and Social Change in China*, London: Routledge.

Wang, Y. P. and Murie, A. (1996) "The Process of Commercialisation of Urban Housing in China," *Urban Studies*, 33(6): 971–89.

Wang, Yixin (2004) "Guo neiwai jiating baoli de xianzhuang yi ji duice" [Policies and the present situation of DV nationally and internationally], in Beijingshi funü lianhehui (eds.) *Pingdeng, youxian, fazhan* [Equality, priorities, development], Beijing: Beijing Shehui Kexue Chubanshe.

Wang, Yizhou (2003) "Zhongguo guojiguanxi yanjiu: Dui chengjiu yu queshi de jidian ganshou" [The study of international relations in China: some reflections on its achievements and shortcomings], *Shijie jingji yu zhengzhi* [World economics and international politics], 4: 10–12.

Wang, Zhuo (1998) "Lun guojia caizheng de shencengci maodun" [On the deeper contradictions of government finance], *Southern Economy*, 6: 7–9.

Wank, David (1998) *Commodifying Communism: Business, Trust, and Politics in a Chinese City*, Cambridge, England: Cambridge University Press.

Watson, Andrew (1992) *Economic Reform and Social Change in China*, London: Routledge.

Wedeman, Andrew (1997) "Stealing from the Farmers: Institutional Corruption and the 1992IOU Crisis," *China Quarterly*, 152 (December): 805–31.

—— (1999) "Agency and Fiscal Dependence in Central–Provincial Relations. in China," *Journal of Contemporary China*, 8(20): 103–22.

—— (2000) "Budgets, Extra-Budgets, and Small Treasuries: Illegal Monies and Local Autonomy in China," *Journal of Contemporary China*, 25 (9): 489–511.

Wei, Hua and Wang, Xin (2004) *Jiating baoli* [Domestic violence], Ji'nan: Ji'nan Chubanshe.

Wen, Jiabao (2003) "Remarks of Chinese Premier Wen Jiabao: Turn Your Eyes to China," Harvard University, December 10. Online. Available at: http://english. people.com.cn/200312/12/eng20031212_130267.shtml.

Wertheim, W. F. (1974) *Evolution and Revolution*, Harmondsworth: Penguin.

Wesoky, Sharon (2002) *Chinese Feminism Faces Globalisation*, London: Routledge.

White, Gordon (1994) "Prospects for Civil Society," in David S. G. Goodman and Beverley Hooper (eds.) *China's Quiet Revolution*, Melbourne: Longman Cheshire.

Wilson, Alexander (1992) "Technological Utopias: World's Fairs and Theme Parks," in *The Culture of Nature: North American Landscape from Disney to the Exxon Valdez*, Oxford: Blackwell.

Wolf, Charles, Jr. (2001) "China's Capitalists Join the Party," *New York Times*, August 13: A17.

"Women look for ways" (2003) "Women look for ways to defeat domestic violence," *Xinhua News Agency*, November 26. Available at http://www.china.org.cn/english/ 2003/nov/80939.htm [Accessed July 8, 2006].

Wong, Christine. P. W. (1991) "Central–Local Relations in an Era of Fiscal Decline: The Paradox of Fiscal Decentralization in Post-Mao China," *China Quarterly*, 128: 691–715.

—— (ed.) (1997) *Financing Local Government in the People's Republic of China*, New York: Oxford University Press.

—— (2000) "Central–Local relations Revisited: The 1994 Tax Sharing Reform and Public Expenditure Management in China," paper for the International Conference on Central–Periphery Relations in China: Integration, Disintegration or Reshaping of an Empire? Chinese University of Hong Kong, March 24–25.

Wong, Christine. P. W., Heady, Christopher, and Woo, Wing T. (1995) *Fiscal Management and Economic Reform in the People's Republic of China*, Hong Kong: Oxford University Press.

Wong, L. (2001) "Welfare Reform Policy," in L. Wong and N. Flynn (eds.) *The Market in Chinese Social Policy*, New York: Palgrave.

World Bank (2005) "East Asia Decentralizes: Making Local Government Work." Online. Available at: http://siteresources.worldbank.org/INTEAPDECEN/Resources/ dc-full-report.pdf (accessed July 14, 2005).

Wu, Alun (2000) "Jiating nongchang ganbugan zhu" [Dare to live in a "family farm"], *Caijing*, August 5.

Wu, Fulong (1998) "The New Structure of Building Provision and the Transformation of the Urban Landscape in Metropolitan Guangzhou, China," *Urban Studies*, 35(2): 259–72.

Wu, Licai (2002) "Zhipei, chongtu yu hezuo: shilun xiangcun guanxi" [Dominance, conflicts, and cooperation: an analysis of township village relationships], in *Zhongguio nongcun yanjiu* [*China Rural Studies*], Beijing: China Social Science Publishers.

Xia, Linglan (2002) "Jiating baoli falü ganyu xiankuang diaocha jieguo fenxi" [Analysis of the results of an investigation into the current situation of legal intervention in domestic violence], in Rong Weiyi and Song Meiya (eds.) *Fandui zhendui funü de jiating baoli: Zhongguo de lilun yu shijian* [Opposing domestic violence against women: theory and practice in China], Beijing: Zhongguo Shehui Kexue Chubanshe.

Xian, Qi (1997) *Lianzheng zhongguo* [*China under a Clean Government*], Beijing: Shichu Chubanshe.

Xian-an District Government (2003) "A Progress Report on the Work of Sending off Cadres," unpublished document.

Xian-an District Party Committee Secretariat (ed.) (2003) *Compendium of Materials on Xian-an's Reform*, internal document.

Xiao, Fei (2004) "*Yindao dubai* shi women geng tanran de miandui ziji de shenti" [*The Vagina Monologues* enables us to be even more comfortable with our bodies], *Zhongshan daxue xingbie jiaoyu luntan*. Online. Available at: http://school.gd.sina. com.cn/news/2004-11-20/831933.html (accessed July 6, 2006).

Xiao, Gongqin (2001) "Shi xi Zhong Mei zhengzhi wenhua zhangli" [A preliminary analysis of the tension between Chinese and American political cultures], *Zhanlue yu guanli* [Strategy and management], 2: 39–46.

Xiao, Yan (2004) "*Yindao dubai* rang hen duo nüxing renshi daole ziji de shenti jiegou" [*The Vagina Monologues* lets lots of women understand the composition of their bodies], *Zhongshan daxue xingbie jiaoyu luntan*. Online. Available at: http:// school.gd.sina.com.cn/news/2004-11-20/831934.html (accessed July 6, 2006).

Xie, Jajing (2006) "Housing Consumption of Chinese Residents Have Reached 14,200 Billion Yuan," speech by Xie Jajing, Chief Economist, Ministry of Construction, at the International Conference on Housing Finance, Beijing, April 25, 2006. Online. Available at: http://www.realestate.gov.cn/news.asp?recordno=54487&teamno=3&line =111 (accessed August 26, 2006).

Xie, Shan (2005) "Zhiming guoqi shi zhenyang beizhukongde?" [How was a state factory eaten up?], *Fanfubai daokan* [Anti-corruption journal], 3: 33–6.

Xie, Wei, Ailing, Liau, and Yenjun, Xie (2004) "Beijing tupo tudi guanlifa xianzhi jiansheyundi shidian liuzhuan" [Beijing breaks away from Land Management Law, experiments with circulation of (rural) construction land], *Xingjing Bao* [*New Beijing Daily*], October 21.

Xin, Sun (2004) "*Yindao dubai* jiqi muhou gushi de ganxiang" [Reflections on the backstage stories of *The Vagina Monologues*], *Zhongshan daxue xingbie jiaoyu luntan*. Online. Available at: http://school.gd.sina.com.cn/news/2004-11-20/831936. html (accessed July 6, 2006).

Xinhua News Agency (2003) "Women look for ways to defeat domestic violence," Xinhua New Agency, November 26. Available at: http://www.china.org.cn/english/ 2003/Nov/80939.htm (accessed July 8, 2006).

—— (2006) "Foreign-Funded Enterprises Gained 200bn Profit in China," Xinhua News Agency, May 21. Available at: http://news.xinhuanet.com/english/2006–05/21/content_4578429.htm.

Xu, Hanming (2004) *Zhongguo nongmin tudi chiyou chanquan zhidu yanjiu* [Study on Chinese farmers' property rights of land], Beijing: Social Sciences Documentation Publishing House.

Xu, Jianguo (2004) "A Win–Win Deal: China and the World Share the Wealth," *Beijing Review* 47(52): 25–7.

Yan, Da and Gao, Song (2002a) "Tunpu: Dinggu Mingdai Hanzu de Fengsu," [Tunpu: Frozen Customs of the Ming Dynasty Han] *Zhongguo Guojia Dili* [Chinese National Geography], 5: 36–49.

—— (2002b) *Liubainian Tunpu – Ming Wangchao Yimin Jishi*, Guiyang: Guizhou Renmin Chubansh.

Yang, Dali L. (2001) "Rationalizing the Chinese State: The Political Economy of Government Reform," in Bruce J. Dickson and Chien-Min Chao (eds.) *Remaking the Chinese State*, London: Routledge.

Yang, Guangfei (2004) "Difang hezuo zhuyi zhong de quanli yuewei" [Power abuse in local corporatism], *The 21st Century*, June 27. Online. Available at: http://www.cuhk.edu.hk/ics/21c/index2.htm (accessed March 12, 2005).

Yang, L. and Wang, Y. K. (1992) *Housing Reform: Thoughts in Theory and Choices in Reality*, Tianjian: Renmin Chubanshe.

Yang, Liping and Xu, Guangrong (2005) "Shangwubu qidong shangye dichan xuncha" [Ministry of Commerce started investigation of commercial real estate projects], *21st Century Business Herald*, July 14.

Yang, Youren, Wang, Hongkai, and Guo, Jianlun (2004) "Kuaisu gongyehua xiade zhongguo dalu quyu zhili: Yi Suzhou diqu tudi chanquan tizhi zhuanhua weili" [Regional governance under rapid industrialization in mainland China: a case of land rights transformation in Suzhou region], *Zhongguo dalu yanjiu* [Mainland China studies], 47(3): 111–41.

Yep, Ray (2004) "Can 'Tax-for-Fee" Reform Reduce Rural Tension in China? The Process, Progress and Limitations," *China Quarterly*, 177 (March): 43–70.

Yüdice, George (2003) *The Expediency of Culture: Uses of Culture in the Global Era*, Durham, N.C. and London: Duke University Press.

Zha, Daojiong (2005) "Comment: Can China Rise?," *Review of International Studies*, 31(4): 775–85.

Zhang, Fanghua (2002) "Zhuanxing shiqi defang zhenfu feizhengdang xingwei de youxiao kongzhi" [The effective control over irregular behavior of local governments in the transitional period], *Shanghai Social Science Academy Academic Quarterly*, 1: 67–74.

Zhang, Forrest Qian, Ma, Qingguo, and Xu, Xu (2004) "Development of Land Rental Market in Tural Zhejiang: Growth of Off-Farm Jobs and Institution Building," *China Quarterly*, 180: 1,050–72.

Zhang, Leying (1999) "Chinese Central–Provincial Fiscal Relationships, Budgetary Decline and the Impact of 1994 Fiscal Reform: An Evaluation," *China Quarterly*, 157(1): 123–6.

Zhang, Li and Zhao, Simon X. B. (1998) "Re-examining China's 'Urban' Concept and the Level of Urbanization," *China Quarterly*, 154: 330–81.

Zhang, Naihua (2001) "Searching for 'Authentic' NGOs: The NGO Discourse and Women's Organizations in China," in Hsiung Ping-chen, Maria Jaschok, Cecelia

Milwertz, and Red Chan (eds.) *Chinese Women Organizing: Cadres, Feminists, Muslims, Queers*, Oxford: Berg.

Zhang, Qi (2005) "*Yindao dubai* Guangxi yanchu renwu gushi" [The story of the characters in the Guangxi performance of *The Vagina Monologues*]. Online. Available at: http://stopdv.org.cn/article.asp?id=2089 (accessed July 8, 2006).

Zhang, Shan (2005) "Guozi liushi de 19 tiao qudao" [The nineteen ways of draining away the state assets], *Fanfubai daokan* [Anti-corruption journal], 3: 14–20.

Zhang, Yanjin (2004) "Jinyan *Yindao dubai*" [*The Vagina Monologues* performance banned]. Online. Available at: http://www.sina.com.cn/s/2004-02-16/08232869960. shtml (accessed July 6, 2006).

Zhang, Yongjin (2003) "The 'English School' in China: A Travelogue of Ideas and Their Diffusion," *European Journal of International Relations*, 9(1): 87–114.

—— (2005a) *China Goes Global*, London: Foreign Policy Centre.

—— (2005b) "Zhongguo Gongchandang zai 21 shiji de zuoxiang" [The trajectory of the Chinese Communist Party in the twenty-first century], *People's Daily*, November 22.

Zhang, Z. (1998) "Jia kuai zhu fang huo bi fen pei ji zhi zhu huan, pei yu zhu fang jian she xin de jing ji zeng zhang dian 1" [Speed up the transformation of the mechanism of monetary distribution and build up a new economic growth pole of housing construction (part one)], in *Zhong guo fang di chan* [China real estate], 209(5): 4–10.

Zhang, Zhengming (1998) *Jinshang yu Jingying Wenhua* [Shanxi merchant and management culture], Shanghai: Xingjietu Chubanshe.

Zhang, Zhongyou (1997) *Baoli dui xinfu de huimie: Hunyin jiating zhong de baoli wenti toushi* [Violence destroying happiness: perspectives on the problem of violence in marriage and the household], Beijing: Zhongguo Jiancha Chubanshe.

Zhao, Bingzhi (2004) *Zhu ke guan xiang tongyi: Xingfa xiandaihua de zuobiao – yi jianyin younü xing qiangjian zui wei shijiao* [Integrating the subjective and objective: coordinating the modernisation of the criminal code – taking the perspective of sexual assault of girls and rape], Beijing: Zhongguo Renmin Gongan Daxue Chubanshe.

Zhao, Ling (2004) "Significant Shift in Focus of Peasants' Right Activism," *Southern Weekend*, September 3. Online. Available at: http://www.chinaelections.org/en/read-news.asp?newsid=%7BA0B4FFF9-1F57-460D-BBB3-824B59420C2F%7D (accessed June 2, 2005).

Zhao, Y. and Bourassa, S. C. (2003) "China's Urban Housing Reform: Recent Achievements and New Inequities," *Housing Studies*, 18(5): 721–44.

Zheng, Bijian (2003) "A New Path for China's Peaceful Rise and the Future of Asia," Bo'ao Forum, November 3. Online. Available at: http://history.boaoforum. org/English/E2003nh/dhwj/t20031103_184101.btk.

Zheng, Yongnian and Tok, Sow Keat (2005) "*China's Peaceful Rise: Concept and Practice*," China Policy Institute Discussion Paper No. 1, University of Nottingham, November.

Zheng, Zhengqiang (2002) *Dashan Shenchu de Tunpu* [Tunpu deep in the mountains], Shijiazhuang: Hebei Jiaoyu Chubanshe.

Zhou, M. and Logan, J. R. (1996) "Market Transition and the Commodification of Housing in Urban China," *International Journal of Urban and Regional Research*, 20(3): 400–21.

Zhou, Shangyi and Kong, Xiang (2000) *Wenhua yu Difang Fazhan* [*Culture and Local Development*], Beijing: Kexue Chubanshe.

Zhou, Weiwen (2001) *Chenmo de nüxing: Xingbie toujing zhong de jiating baoli* [The lonely woman: the lens of sexual difference in domestic violence], Shijiazhuang: Hebei Renmin Chubanshe.

Zhou, Xiaoguang and Li, Linqi (1998) *Huishang yu Jingying Wenhua* [Hui merchant and management culture], Shanghai: Xingjietu Chubanshe.

Zhou, Yixing and Ma, Laurence J. C. (2003) "China's Urbanization Levels: Reconstructing a Baseline from the Fifth Population Census," *China Quarterly*, 173: 176–96.

Zhou, Yunqing (2005) *Xing yu shehui* [Sex and society], Wuhan: Wuhan Daxue Chubanshe.

Zhu, Dongliang (2003) *Shehui bianqian zhongde cunji tudi zhidu* [*Village Land System in the Changing Society*], Xiamen: Xiamen University Press.

Zhu, Mingshan (2004) *Qiangjian zui* [The crime of rape], Beijing: Zhongguo Fazhi Chubanshe.

Zhu, Y. and Lee, J. (2004) "Redistributive Justice and Housing Benefits in China: The Guiyang Model," *Journal of Societal and Social Policy*, 3: 47–62.

Zoellick, Robert (2005) "Whither China? From Membership to Responsibility," remarks to National Committee on U.S.–China Relations, New York City, September 21. Online. Available at: http://www.state.gov/s/d/rem/53682.htm.

Zukin, Sharon (1991) *Landscapes of Power: From Detroit to Disney World*, Berkeley, CA: University of California Press.

—— (1995) *The Cultures of Cities*, Oxford: Blackwell.

Zweig, David (1992) "Urbanizing Rural China: Bureaucratic Authority and Local Autonomy," in K. Lieberthal and D. Lampton (eds.) *Bureaucracy, Politics and Decision Making in Post-Mao China*, Berkeley, CA: University of California Press.

Index